BY HER OWN ADMISSION

BY HER OWN ADMISSION

A Lesbian Mother's Fight to Keep Her Son

Gifford Guy Gibson

with the collaboration of

Mary Jo Risher

Doubleday & Company, Inc., Garden City, New York
1977

Grateful acknowledgment is made for permission to include excerpts from the following copyrighted publications:

Portions of "Homosexuality on Trial," by Gifford Guy Gibson, first appeared in January 2–9, 1976, issues of *Iconoclast*, news magazine of Dallas. Reprinted by permission of *Iconoclast*.

"Hidden Things," in *Collected Poems*, C. P. Cavafy. Translation © 1975 by Edmund Keeley and Philip Sherrard, ed. by George Savidis, p. 361. Reprinted by permission of Princeton University Press and The Hogarth Press.

ISBN: 0-385-12445-7
Library of Congress Catalog Card Number 76-50767
Copyright © 1977 by Gifford Guy Gibson

CONTENTS

INTRODUCTION

On December 23, 1975, a Dallas Domestic Relations Court jury of ten men and two women found that a "material and substantial change" had occurred in the home of thirty-eight-year-old Mary Jo Risher, and awarded custody of nine-year-old Richard Calvin Risher to his father.

The "material and substantial change" in question was a life style—homosexuality. Mary Jo and Douglas Risher were divorced in 1971, with Mary Jo getting custody of the two children, Richard and teen-age Jimmy.

In 1973, Mary Jo established a loving relationship with Ann Foreman. Ann was divorced and the mother of an eight-year-old girl, Judie Ann.

Mary Jo, Ann, Jimmy, Richard and Judie Ann formed a family unit and lived quietly in Garland, Texas, a suburb of Dallas.

In October 1974, Douglas Risher, who had since remarried, learned of his former wife's lesbianism and filed suit to secure custody of the two minor children. A temporary custody hearing was held in October 1974, where Mary Jo's attorneys introduced a motion barring the issue of homosexuality as a cause for *immediate* removal of the children. Domestic Relations Court Judge Oswin Chrisman upheld the motion and the two children remained with Mary Jo.

At a Motion in Limine hearing in September 1975, Judge Chrisman heard expert witnesses testify as to the relevance of homosexuality in child rearing. Judge Chrisman reversed his previous decision and ruled that any act, event or situation dealing with the environment of the children or any life style that may affect the children could be made part of the court record.

This set the stage for the trial that began on December 16. This was the first known *jury* trial involving the custody rights of a homosexual parent.

My involvement with the Mary Jo Risher story began as a fluke of timing. I had spent the year doing investigative reporting under the sponsorship of The Fund for Investigative Journalism in Washington, D.C. The stories I developed were carried by dozens of newspapers through the Pacific News Service, based in San Francisco. I had just received substantial funding for a series of articles on county governments in Texas when the editor of the *Iconoclast,* a weekly newspaper of Dallas, asked if I would guest edit an issue during the Christmas holiday. Since I wasn't geared to begin the government investigations during the holidays, I agreed.

The most appealing story lead he left on his desk was a custody trial involving a lesbian couple. I did a pretrial interview with Mary Jo Risher and Ann Foreman and decided that rather than assign a reporter to the actual trial I would cover it myself.

The trial was absorbing, with all the elements of a major story. It involved homosexual rights and the abundant pathos of a bitter struggle for child custody. Still, something was lacking. The rules of evidence, the narrow logic of the law and the carefully rehearsed dialogue of witnesses are illuminating but leave deep shadows that hinder true perception. Life just doesn't proceed as court testimony. Truth, as legally defined, is too narrow, too vapid. The structure, flow and reality of people's lives can't be condensed and molded by questions and answers in a courtroom. Human sensibilities are erased in the legal arena leaving us with hallucinations—a by-product of this unnatural distillation of reality.

Working with the full collaboration of Mary Jo Risher on this book, I have sought to restore human sensibility, lighten the shadows, and tell the real story of a lesbian mother who lost her children.

The material here presented is taken entirely from hundreds of hours of personally tape-recorded interviews and the trial transcript for complete authenticity. And, of course, I personally observed the trial and the aftermath.

The quotes in the book and the dialogue are constructed from memories of the participants. Thoughts of the persons are printed in italics to facilitate easy understanding.

The lesbian friends of Mary Jo and Ann are given fictitious names to protect their privacy. They are, however, real people. All other names and events are actual.

Perhaps the easiest part of writing any book is the dedication. Rather than naming a person who helped me, for there were many, I wish to borrow from the work of one of this century's most gifted poets, C. P. Cavafy. His poem "Hidden Things" can speak both for Mary Jo Risher and ultimately for the millions like her who will never be the subject of any book.

> From all I did and all I said
> let no one try to find out who I was.
> An obstacle was there distorting
> the actions and the manner of my life.
> An obstacle was often there
> to stop me when I'd begin to speak.
> From my most unnoticed actions,
> my most veiled writings—
> from these alone will I be understood.
> But maybe it isn't worth so much concern,
> so much effort to discover who I really am.
> Later, in a more perfect society,
> someone else made ust like me
> is certain to appear and act freely.

GIFFORD GUY GIBSON, *Dallas, 1976*

BY HER OWN ADMISSION

PART I

COMING OUT

Mary Jo Risher received few telephone calls at work. Gaston Episcopal Hospital, like most regimented and precision institutions, was a labyrinth of unyielding traditions and regulations. Nurses were discouraged from leaving the duty floor to accept personal calls unless they were family emergencies.

In theory, Mary Jo approved of this rule. After five years of nursing the professional code of conduct was deeply ingrained. She was careful to limit herself to legitimate crises, and this usually meant calls from her two sons or Ann.

It was the final Sunday of September 1974. Mary Jo was surprised when a hospital volunteer entered the room where she was working. "Mrs. Risher, there's a phone call for you from a lady named Mrs. Davidson." Mary Jo felt a trace of uneasiness as she walked to the nurses' station.

"Mary Jo," her mother began, "I want you to drop by here on your way home from the hospital. There's something serious we got to talk about."

The nurses' station was busy and lacked any element of privacy. "Serious, in what way, Mamma?" Mary Jo whispered.

"Just come on by on your way home; we'll talk then."

Her mother's cool urgency irritated Mary Jo. In recent weeks an unsettling formality had crept into their relationship, and this summons, disguised as conversation, left her puzzled.

Characteristically, Mary Jo was absorbed in her work the remainder of the day. Sunday was just another twenty-four hours of medical demarcation inside the hospital. Traditional work and rest cycles of the outside world were ignored. Seconds, minutes and hours were gauges for pulses, dosages or injections, not sequences of calendar time.

Mary Jo's day shift ended at 3:15. She considered telephoning Ann to inform her of the pending delay in getting home, but remembered that Ann was taking the children to a new shopping mall and they would likely wander around all afternoon.

During the drive from the hospital in east Dallas to her mother's home in suburban Mesquite, Mary Jo reviewed the terse conversation with her mother and concluded that something new had developed concerning Jimmy. Her sixteen-year-old son had been the center of a family dilemma for several months. He started living full-time at her mother's some two weeks ago and refused to return home.

Mary Jo was perpetually tardy in grasping the radical shifts in moods associated with that rare state of human development lumped under the title of "adolescence." The seriousness of Jimmy's move-out had slipped up on Mary Jo. Jimmy was in the habit of spending several nights a week at his grandmother's, dating back to the first of the year, when Mary Jo moved into Ann Foreman's household in neighboring Garland.

Jimmy attended North Mesquite High School and rather than transfer during his junior year and lose his friends and school activities a minor deception was instituted. The school wasn't notified when Mary Jo moved the family out of the district. The school records still listed Jimmy's address as Mesquite, his grandmother's house. In order to uncomplicate the transportation burden, Mary Jo allowed her son to sleep at her mother's when he wished.

When school started in August, however, Jimmy stayed permanently at his grandmother's. For Mary Jo, it was one thing for Jimmy to be away a few nights a week, but to totally abandon her home was a disaster.

She regarded her son's flight as an ultimate pressure tactic to force her to buy him a car. The issue of an automobile was a maddening point of contention since Jimmy's sixteenth birthday in May. He hounded her daily, with the nerve-fraying persistence that most teen-agers perfected to an art form.

It wasn't that Mary Jo disapproved of her son driving; she had bought him a motorcycle two years ago, over the strident objections of her family. Jimmy needed a car, and not just for ego gratification. The matter was simply one of economics. The family income was comfortable, if modest. She had just been given a cost of living raise at the hospital, and Ann was assistant to the auditor of Lakewood Bank. The bills were paid, but the margin was nickels and dimes.

On top of that, Richard, her seven-year-old son, had a reading problem, discovered during his first year of school. A private tutor was hired for the summer, and this expense absolutely foreclosed financing a car for Jimmy.

The ruckus over buying Jimmy a car ended in mid-September, when Doug, Mary Jo's ex-husband, purchased a used Ford for Jimmy. Normally, Mary Jo bristled when Doug interjected himself into her affairs, but this time, with all the furor and alienation over Jimmy's obsession with a car, she acquiesced.

The hard feelings didn't subside once Jimmy was driving. Ann had loaned Jimmy several gasoline credit cards to help him maneuver around his meager paydays as a busboy at a restaurant. Jimmy signed the credit slips at a somewhat faster pace than he reimbursed Ann. After repeated reminders and nudges, Ann had a heated argument with Jimmy, lost her temper and blurted out, "Oh fuck." Jimmy seized upon the incident as the final excuse he needed; he wasn't going back home, ever.

Although she regretted the flare-up, Mary Jo had a suspicion, validated by recent family history, that Jimmy was drawn to her mother's more for creature comforts than because he was experiencing the angst of hearing vulgar language. Naturally, his grandmother was more lenient. There were later curfew hours, meals virtually on demand, someone to clean his bedroom for him, and all the spoiling little amenities offered by a doting grandmother as opposed to the primary parent whose chief lessons at this point were self-help and responsibilities.

Mary Jo's mother came out of the kitchen when she heard her daughter's car drive up. Mary Davidson was sixty-one. Family members insisted that all three of her daughters and her son favored her in looks. Perhaps . . . when she was young. Age had blurred any strong resemblances. Mary was five feet of feisty energy. She was slightly stooped, with a small pouch of a stomach that kept her from being truly petite. Her brown and gray hair was tightly curled and always neat, but it had lost its natural luster. Her facial wrinkles curved into a mischievous expression that was accentuated by shrewd, darting eyes that often glimmered with ironic humor, a humor that was broad and occasionally bawdy. When punctuating a point in conversation or delivering the punch line of a story she peered over the top rim of her glasses to get an unobstructed view of your reaction. Her ready smile and pleasant demeanor were absent that Sunday as she greeted her daughter.

"Mary Jo, I've been meaning to talk with you and I couldn't wait no longer." Mrs. Davidson's accent was a mixture of Arkansas nasal and Texas drawl. "I don't think you did right over Jimmy's car. You knew how that boy lived for a car. You should have been proud of it and made a fuss."

Mary Jo accepted this parental tutelage calmly. At thirty-six, she was part of a generation that believed showing deference to one's parents was beyond duty; it was a virtue.

She explained to her mother that she was relieved, even happy, that Doug was able to buy the car for Jimmy. Mary Jo knew she was wasting words; the car wasn't the reason she had been summoned. Her discretion, aroused by her mother's recent remoteness, caused her to play along. She knew that eventually her mother would bend the conversation toward what was really on her mind. She was content to wait.

Mrs. Davidson expressed her displeasure at the way Ann was "pressuring" Jimmy over the money he owed her. She was especially upset over Ann's "Oh fuck" exclamation. No one in her family, not even one on the peripheral edge, talked to children that way.

Mary Jo agreed about not using gutter language around the children, but she was mildly amused at her mother's newly found self-righteousness. Surely, she didn't believe that Jimmy was shocked by it. His companions at the high school weren't that sheltered. Mary Jo withheld any comment on Ann's choice of words and settled for a lecture on Jimmy's financial obligations and the importance she attached to her son acquiring a sense of responsibility in money matters.

Mrs. Davidson seemed satisfied, or at least she wished to end that part of the conversation. It was a prelude to her real concerns. "Well, I just wondered what goes on over there at your place. I've been hearing some things from Jimmy."

Mary Jo was piqued; she now knew the direction her mother was headed. A prudent retreat normally would have stalled any argument, but Mary Jo guessed that her mother had reached an important decision that would drastically alter family relationships. Dreading the tempest, Mary Jo was compelled to listen.

Mrs. Davidson's tone was salacious. "I just don't see, Mary Jo, how you can think a relationship like you have going on over there can amount to anything." Mrs. Davidson paused, expecting a rebuttal. "It's nothing; it's not going to last or anything else. It's not good for the boys to be in it."

Mary Jo inhaled deeply to calm herself. Her mother's objections about her life style had been endlessly discussed over a year ago when she and Ann announced to Mrs. Davidson that they were lovers. But if her mother was agitated by Jimmy talking about the home situation, perhaps she needed reassuring. Mary Jo spent several minutes telling her mother how she and Ann loved each other, and how they provided a good home for the children. Nothing was lacking.

Mrs. Davidson wasn't pacified. Her voice chilled as she ridiculed the concept of a meaningful love between two women. All of her original doubts spewed forth. Finally, she managed to expel the singular new item of her argument: "I tell you what, Richard needs to be with his father."

Richard needs to be with his father, Mary Jo thought. She was terrified. Her mother was talking away, listing the reasons that Richard would be better off with Doug. Mary Jo caught only scattered syllables; her mind was reeling.

Mary Jo's hidden fear was materializing through her mother's words. The overpowering fear she had harbored since the day of her divorce. No matter how much she loved her sons; no matter how good a mother she was, endlessly watching out for their welfare; no matter how guarded her life style was; no matter what she did, it was down to one thing. She was gay, and someday Doug would find out. He would use it to try to take away the boys. Now, incredibly, her own mother was Doug's ally. Her mother was saying she should give up Richard.

"You've got to be out of your goddamn mind," Mary Jo screamed. She was striking out in her terror. Mrs. Davidson continued her harping; how sick Ann and Mary Jo were; how detrimental their relationship was for the children; how Mary Jo needed a psychiatrist. The longer Mary Jo rejected her mother's contentions, the louder the two women became.

They were in a fury, hurling insults and threats. Their voices cracked from the yelling, their faces flushed and distorted; their bodies jerked about as they gestured wildly.

Soon they reached an impasse; the adrenalin depletion dropped the decibel level from shrieks to snarls. Mary Jo lost the ability to concentrate; she was exhausted. Eight hours on her feet at the hospital and now this marathon, shrill fight with her mother. Her last defiant thrust was to tell her mother there was nothing, nothing she could do about her life style; either accept it or leave her alone.

Mary Davidson's stamina wasn't waning. She sputtered something about "queers" and was about to continue when Mary Jo interrupted. "I'll show you how little you can do," Mary Jo challenged. "I'm going to make out my will and leave every last penny to the gay church."

That threat had the desired effect on Mrs. Davidson. She sat for a minute or two mulling it over. The scathing condemnations were set aside; Mrs. Davidson mercifully eased up and appealed to Mary Jo's devotion to the family. "Mary Jo, hon, we've got your best interest at heart. And you'll never know what all this business has done to the family, your brother and sisters. It's torn them up. I think it's killed my soul, what's happened to you."

Mrs. Davidson elaborated on the damage already suffered by the family, emphasizing the pain that was to come if Mary Jo didn't recognize the best interest of Richard and turn him over to his father.

Mary Jo was drained, whipped into a stupor by the incessant droning of her mother. The door was a dozen feet away; she had to do something, anything to reach it and escape. "Maybe I will give him up." She shuddered, not knowing if she had thought the words or spoken them. She looked at her mother's open mouth. Mary Jo rose to her feet and edged toward the door. "Maybe I will give him up . . . maybe I will." She slammed the door savagely.

Mary Jo became conscious of time again when she arrived home and found no one there. She had been at her mother's for only two and a half hours, but each minute had been elongated so that it seemed like days since she left home. Ann and the kids were late; they should have been home and eating by now. Perhaps it was best. She went into the bedroom, turned off all the lights and fell into bed. *Where in the hell was Ann?* she thought. *Why wasn't she here?* Mary Jo wanted time to compose herself, to be able to face the children as if nothing had happened. Their absence made it worse. The more she thought of Richard the more she focused on her mother's demands. They, meaning her mother and Doug, they were going to take Richard away. She pounded the pillows into squatty lumps, then fiercely clung to them.

Ann, Judie Ann and Richard drove into the carport at the rear of the town house. The kids, exuberant from the shopping adventure, raced through the backyard, in through the patio door, anxious to show Mary Jo the coloring books and huge boxes of crayons that Ann had bought them at the mall. Richard went skipping into his mother's bedroom. "Mommy, look what I've got." He stood with his arms extended holding the coloring book and crayons. Mary Jo raised her shoulders and head, turned toward her son, but couldn't speak. Richard ran back to the patio door to meet Ann. "Ann, Mamma's in the dark and she's crying." Ann had no idea of what was wrong, but read the panic on Richard's face. She hurried the kids upstairs to play in their rooms.

By the time she had entered the downstairs bedroom the joy from the afternoon outing had vanished. She had seen Mary Jo upset before, but she wasn't prepared for the abject sight that awaited her in the bedroom. Mary Jo's uniform was bunched and wrinkled, twisted around her body. Her black and gray hair, usually smoothed in a gentle natural wave, was matted in moisture, shapeless and limp. Her skin was blotched, there were puffy, tear-streaked bags under her eyes. The normally clear gray-blue eyes, intense and captivating, were glazed, horribly bloodshot and wounded-looking. Her whole form was obsequious, the dignity and strength were ripped away.

Ann stood transfixed for a full minute, then drew a deep breath. "My God, what is wrong with you?"

Mary Jo lifted her head off the pillows, her body didn't move, the torso was locked. "They're going to take him away from me, they're going to take him away."

"Who?"

"They got me. He knows."

"Who knows? What?"

"Doug knows. They're going to take him away from me. Mother told me today."

Ann became agitated. "Your mother? Is that where you've been?"

Mary Jo raised up on her elbow. She recounted the highlights of the afternoon with her mother. Her voice, the timbre shredded by hours of shouting, rose in volume as she re-created her desperate exit from her mother's house. When she finished, Ann didn't say a word. After a long, ruminating silence, Mary Jo suddenly collapsed as if her muscle tendons had snapped. "I've got to give him up, I might as well, they've got me whipped. I'll never win in a courtroom, Ann. I'm gay . . . we're homosexuals. Jimmy knows it. I've lost, I've lost. Doug's going to take Richard away, there's no way we can keep him from it."

Mary Jo was moving back and forth on the edge of the bed, rocking from side to side in an age-old rhythm that ritualized her grief. The fury that couldn't be flushed from her tear duct membrane was slowly being rocked away, replaced by a sobbing fatalism. Everything was lost, there was no need to fight, no way to fight. The rocking went on.

Ann reached out, touched Mary Jo's shoulder, to reaffirm that she was there. Mary Jo rocked. Ann was overcome, she needed time, time to put this in some sort of perspective, to find the right words to bring Mary Jo back, to prove to her that everything wasn't lost, Richard wouldn't be taken away. She couldn't think while standing there watching her lover rock back and forth and moan as if some deep inner decay was eating away her body. She went to the kitchen and called two neighbors, Neila and Joline. "Help me, Mary Jo is hysterical." Ann spent several minutes on the phone briefing the women on the essence of what had happened and Mary Jo's present condition. They said they would be right over and bring a tranquilizer.

Neila and Joline knew that if Ann had been wrought up enough to call them something was seriously wrong, but they stood at the foot of the bed in muddled silence while Mary Jo rocked and moaned. They felt embarrassed. It was like when a close friend showed you the scar from a severe accident. You tried not to indicate surprise and glibly assured her it was not so bad looking when all the time you were repelled and horrified at its grotesqueness.

Plans were formulated in front of Mary Jo, as if she was too occupied with her agony to hear or care. Neila would take the kids to her house, where they could play with Joline's three children. Ann and Joline would try to get Mary Jo to take the tranquilizer and then call Mrs. Davidson to ascertain how much she really knew.

Ann girded for the ordeal of getting Mary Jo to take the pill. The combination of Mary Jo's conservative background and experiences as a nurse had created a disdain for all medication. Almost as soon as Ann offered the pill and a glass of water, Mary Jo took them, swallowed the pill, gulped the entire glass of water and reminded them, "Richard and Judie Ann haven't eaten yet." Recharged by the presence of a new person, she started telling Joline what had occurred with her mother. Ann left the room and went to the kitchen to call Mrs. Davidson, glad that Mary Jo had recovered enough to take an interest in her plight.

"Mrs. Davidson, this is Ann. Mary Jo came home crying and saying that Doug was planning to take Richard away from her."

"I tried to reason with her," Mrs. Davidson explained, "she's got to give up that boy. She told me . . ."

"She's not going to give up custody of Richard," Ann interrupted.

"She said she would. She told me right here that . . ."

"Mrs. Davidson, I don't care what she may have told you during an argument, she's not going to give up Richard. Now what is it that Doug knows?"

"He knows everything. Jimmy told him everything and he's got the papers drawn up and all she has to do is sign Richard over."

"Mrs. Davidson, what is it that Doug knows?"

"He knows that you're living in a homosexual relationship as man and wife."

"As man and wife?" Ann detested that phrase. To her, it epitomized all the ignorance and bigotry against gay people. Why, when two people of the same sex look to one another for emotional and physical needs, must there be role playing? Even in the gay world itself there were still archaic remnants of "butch" and "femme" roles. This paradox was present, she thought, to keep gays from realizing their final liberation. Eventually, her gay friends and straight friends alike would get around to talking about it. No matter how subtle, the common denominator was always, "Who plays what role? Who's the man?"

Ann laid aside her thoughts and questioned Mrs. Davidson: "How in the hell did Doug find out? What were you doing telling him?"

"Now listen, Ann, I didn't tell him anything. I said Jimmy told him. But I agreed with Jimmy doing it. You're just sick. Sick, that's all I can say."

"You've said too much already. You know, I'm sorry my own mother is dead, but I'm glad my mother was the woman she was. I'm glad I never had a mother like you."

"Well . . . we're going to win and you're going to lose that boy."

Ann slammed down the phone and trembled. She rummaged through the refrigerator and located a bottle of wine. She poured a hefty drink into a water glass and rapidly sucked away two cigarettes. *We're going to win,* she thought. *Why, that woman is engineering this crap with Doug. She wants to get her own daughter. Christ, what if the whole family is in on it. Mary Jo won't stand a chance.* Ann knew that she had to find out what everyone else knew, where they stood.

She called Carol Jean, Mary Jo's youngest sister. Ann had no illusions about Carol Jean, who had been against their union from the start. She displayed a polite sister-like front to Mary Jo, but her hostility toward Ann was never far below the surface. Ann thought Carol Jean would be a good family barometer indicating how far this collaboration with Doug had progressed. Her answer was quick in coming.

Carol Jean told Ann what a terrible relationship it was. Although she had never been in their house, she'd heard Jimmy speak of it, how the kids were forced to clean house; how Ann and Mary Jo made the kids fix their own lunches. Carol Jean insisted on talking with her sister.

Ann was caught off guard. *Surely, Carol Jean wouldn't have the guts to tell Mary Jo all this. When she heard how depressed Mary Jo was she would respond kindly. When she learned how real Mary Jo's fear of losing Richard was she would be compassionate.* Ann went and got Mary Jo on the extension phone in the bedroom.

"Carol Jean," Mary Jo cried, "you'll never know what it's like to be faced with losing your children. Remember how I had to fight five years ago to keep the boys. Remember the divorce. Well, I'm going to be faced with that again, only worse this time. Worse."

Carol Jean's response was brutally to the point. "Mary Jo, maybe you should give up Richard, the way you are living is no good."

Mary Jo was startled. "You sorry son-of-a-bitch, Carol, you'll never know what it's like to . . . No, no, maybe you . . . I don't know about that, you might know one of these days what it's like to lose yours."

Carol Jean apparently misunderstood. "Is that a threat?"

"That's not a threat, Carol, but it can happen to you."

Mary Jo hung up the phone. "She's in with them. She hates me. She's working with Doug; you heard her. She doesn't care if

I lose Richard, she wants me to give him up. My whole family is against me."

Ann and Joline held onto Mary Jo and began to reason with her, although at first it was more a matter of shouting her down. Joline stated the case. "Mary Jo, they can't take Richard away from you unless they prove you're an unfit mother. They can't do that. We're behind you. We could testify that you're a fit mother and take care of your boys."

The phone rang. Ann saw that Mary Jo was being assuaged by Joline's reasoning. Mary Jo had a lot of respect for Joline and knew she was completely sympathetic because she had three children. It was all right to leave them and answer the phone in the kitchen.

"Oh, hello, Doug. Mary Jo is in the bathroom now. Can I have her call you back in a minute?" As soon as Ann hung up the phone, Neila walked in. They went into the bedroom together. "Mary Jo, that was Doug and he wants to talk with you." Ann half smiled at the irony of the timing. "We've got to plan this out," she said. "Neila, you get the tape recorder, it's upstairs. Joline, you dial the phone and keep your hand on the button. If Mary Jo says anything wild, click her off. Understand? Now, Mary Jo, play it calm. Don't say anything but yes and no. Let him do all the talking. We've got to know what he plans to do, how far he plans to go. Just let him talk. Don't cry or raise your voice, don't give him any satisfaction. Be careful or you'll blow everything. The more we get out of these people the more we'll be prepared."

By this time, Neila had checked the tape recorder's batteries and set up at the phone in the kitchen. Ann joined her to listen in. Joline dialed Doug's number and kept a strong grip on the receiver with her finger poised on the disconnect button.

Mary Jo was subdued. Her voice was emotionless, weak and monotone. For a minute she and Doug discussed some of the boys' possessions and whether they were on the inventory sheet prepared by the court during the divorce five years ago.

Doug spoke slowly, almost a word at a time. He had a heavy Texas drawl with its measured cadence.

"Jo, I'm going to take those boys away from you. Why don't you make it easy and just sign them over to me?"

"No," Mary Jo whispered.

"Listen, Jo, you know I have the information and can take those children away from you."

"No."

"I've got all the papers. All you have to do is sign them over."

"No."

"How come you told your mother you were going to let me have them?"

"I didn't tell her that."

"You know in a court action I can get him."

"No, I don't know."

"You'll find out what it's like to pay child support . . . some of the hurt . . . you're going to know what it's like to have your own testify against you."

"We'll see."

"You're not going to change your mind?"

"No."

The low-keyed dialogue with Doug had an extraordinary effect on Mary Jo. She was stretched out on her back, serenely examining the ceiling. It was Ann who was bellicose, stomping through the house, bellowing obscenities and threats. What triggered her outburst wasn't the cynical, quiet assuredness of Doug, although it sickened her. It was Mary Jo's faltering answers. She was following the advice Ann gave her, but over the phone it sounded so cowed and pitiful.

Why hadn't she screamed at him, threatened him, told him to kiss her ass? Anything but that barely audible "no," that was the whimpering of a crushed spirit. If only she had thundered one unequivocal, magnificent NO.

Ann was still fuming in the living room when Mary Jo listlessly asked Joline to call her sister Pat in Galveston. Fearing a repetition of the earlier calls, Joline balked until Mary Jo explained, "If your family ties are as strong as mine have been over the years, all it takes is one family member, especially one I rely on, to give me backing." That was good enough for Joline, the call was placed.

Mary Jo dutifully recited the day's events. Pat's response was all she had hoped for. "Fight like hell for that baby."

A measure of rejuvenation swept over Mary Jo, but she couldn't totally dispel the bitterness. "Pat, I never want to see Mother or Carol Jean again. They betrayed me. Mother plotted against me and Carol went along with everything."

Pat suggested that it would be best if she kept quiet about her contact with Mary Jo. Pat's reassurances were getting home to Mary Jo. By the time the conversation ended, Mary Jo was sitting on the edge of the bed, actually able to talk with some lucidity.

Ann and Joline sat on either side of Mary Jo and Neila stood in the door, sipping from a watery glass of Coke. "You all don't realize what we are facing," Mary Jo said.

"It doesn't matter, Mary Jo," Ann interjected, "we all know you're a good mother."

Joline, by now looking as ragged as Mary Jo, held her friend's arm and looked her directly in the eye. "Please, whatever your thoughts now and no matter what anyone says to you, fight for that boy. If you don't, Mary Jo, you'll regret it for the rest of your life." There was a collective sigh in the bedroom, everyone nodded agreement. Mary Jo hugged Joline and patted her back. Both cried gently.

* * *

The next few weeks were a curious mixture of emotional dread and philosophical reflection for Mary Jo. She was fully confident that Doug was moving against her, and that it was only the slow machinations of the legal system that kept a full-blown custody suit from materializing. It was coming. In a way, it had always been coming. Her belief in predestination was absolute, when it came to her sexuality. Not that she always thought about exposure. It was more on the preconscious level. One day Doug would find out she was a lesbian and he would seize upon it and try to get the children. It was this awareness, more than anything else, that dictated her caution.

Mary Jo had an uncanny facility for remembering dates. Not only the usual mélange of birthdays, anniversaries or graduations that we all struggle with and eventually master through embarrassing lapses, but the little obscure dates—a lover's first kiss, strawberries Romanoff at an outdoor cafe, a child's skinned knee, the circa of a Civil War statue on a Mississippi battleground, a radical new haircut. She gathered date-event minutiae, not as a minor thread that runs through the tapestry of memory; for her, it was the epoxy that bound together all her personal history and gave it meaning.

*　*　*

February 6, 1973.

Mary Jo was in her sophomore year of the business-administration degree program at Abilene Christian College's Metro Center in Mesquite. The family was most supportive of her starting college after her divorce. Jimmy was especially proud that he had a mother who was in college. "Let's see who can get the best grades," he challenged her.

On her way to an English literature class that evening she was stopped by Don, a Dallas policeman who was taking advantage of the continuing education program offered by the city of Dallas. They had become casual friends during the past semester. "Say, Mary Jo, we have a new student. Have you seen her? No? Take a look down the hall. If you see her from the back, I swear, she looks just like a man. Come on, I'll introduce you."

Don couldn't resist any opportunity to play jester. In a pseudo-courtly manner, gesturing with either hand, he made the introductions. "Miss Newman, this is Mary Jo Risher. Miss Risher, this is Lisa Newman." Everyone smiled.

"Hi," Mary Jo said as a faint blush swept her face. She took a quick glance at Lisa's face, then averted her eyes. *I was very fearful of this woman, because there was this draw. Lisa was of average height with red hair, green eyes and a good figure.*

"Hello, Miss Risher," Lisa answered playfully. She didn't hesitate to boldly look Mary Jo over from head to toe. She liked what she saw: *Shoulder length black hair, a finely chiseled face with a great smile and a trim body.* Lisa kept smiling.

Don, almost forgotten by the women the instant after the introductions, chimed in, "Lisa likes to dance. Maybe we can make it a trio some night after class." He rambled on about some new club he had discovered, not knowing he was speaking only to himself.

Mary Jo, oblivious to Don's prattle, nodded her head. She thought, *I know you're a lesbian, Lisa, I can feel it. There is something there that is meant to be, but how it is going to develop is another thing.* They walked into the classroom, Mary Jo and Lisa, trailed by Don, who was still making plans. Mary Jo was careful not to look Lisa directly in the face as she muttered, "See you."

The English literature class met again in two days. Mary Jo was jumpy. *She looked like the Don Juan type,* she fantasized, *she really thought a lot of herself. Why was I so afraid? I was going to see this woman again, several more times, since she was auditing the class. She was possibly in the homosexual life, no, she was definitely in the life. This was what I was waiting for, someone to communicate with and be around. But I was still checking myself. If I turned to her and looked squarely in her eyes she would be able to detect that I was going to be easy to get.*

Mary Jo was stooped at the water fountain when a woman's figure entered her peripheral vision. "Mary Jo, how you been doing?" It was Lisa. "Don tells me you're converting your mother's garage into a bedroom."

"Why yes, I am."

"That's what I do. I like to build things."

Several other students were lingering at the fountain, waiting for Mary Jo to finish. "Well, I'll get you to help me sometime."

"I'll do that. When would you like me to come over?" Lisa laughed.

This was the first time Mary Jo had a chance to talk to a

woman she felt was a lesbian. It was exhilarating. "How about this weekend, Saturday."

"It's a date." Lisa smiled smugly and walked to the classroom.

*　*　*

Mary Davidson's home was in a perpetual state of open house. Years after her children left home and married it was a gathering spot for reunions, housing between husbands, haven for visitors, entertainment center and general nexus for family transitions. Mary Jo and her two boys had lived there since the separation from Doug in July 1970. Also since that time every one of her sisters and brother had moved in for varying periods of time. This home-port atmosphere even extended to Mary Jo's father, James Joseph Davidson. Mary and James Joseph had divorced in 1970 after thirty-four years of marriage. He remarried.

Mary Jo's stepmother, Jean, was well liked by everyone in the family, including Mary Davidson. Wthout recriminations or awkwardness normally present in such arrangements, Mr. Davidson, along with his new wife, gradually re-entered the family orbit. They were an integral part of holidays and festivities.

Mary prided herself on her traditional Southern civility. Everyone who entered her house, by her invitation or that of one of her daughters, was treated with hospitality and deference. Mary Jo's newest friend, Lisa, was not an exception.

Mary had reservations about Lisa, based on her appearance rather than personality. Lisa was independent and vibrant, charming and fun. Likeable in every way, but Mary was bothered by her physical appearance: "She was mannish. Her hair was cut real short. She told us she had been in Arkansas building houses. I've worked around so many of them, I can spot them pretty good. There was nothin' I could say, nothin' I could do. I was worried for Mary Jo, but Lisa was our guest and seemed like a nice person."

Mary Jo and Lisa spent most of the day working on the garage, converting it into a bedroom. That evening steaks were cooked and the three women sat around for several hours talking about the project, life in Arkansas and their families. Lisa brought her guitar from the car and played it for her hostesses.

After the initial visit, Lisa would stop by periodically, usually to help on the garage renovation. Mary Jo was deeply attached to her companion. "She always stopped me from lifting heavy things by myself . . . which was nice. It gave me a secure feeling. I was putting up acoustical ceiling once and stretching on the ladder. Lisa came up and took my waist and said, 'I'm just helping you up.' I felt a real draw power there. I knew that if Lisa and I didn't stop seeing one another that something was bound to happen."

On March 17, 1973, Mary Jo's sister Pat, and her husband Jack, arrived in Mesquite for a long weekend visit. This naturally signaled a gathering of the Davidson clan. Mary, James Joseph, Jean, Mary Jo, Carol Jean, and Carol Jean's husband Dwight. Mrs. Davidson invited Lisa.

After the dinner, a celebration of Southern kitchen splendor, everyone moved into the den. Lisa, as the one outsider, was carefully scanned by the family. The way she looked, the way she walked, the way she carried herself, the way she showered attention on Mary Jo, none of this was lost on the family. No one said anything, of course. After all, she was Mary Jo's friend. If she wanted to sit next to her, get her drinks, fawn over her the way lovers do, it was none of their immediate concern. Tonight was a reunion, the collective enjoyment of a family was the occasion, not to be marred by the "questionable" companion of one member.

Lisa, either oblivious to the subtle stares or unconcerned, quickly assumed a leadership role in the evening's fun. "We were all sitting there and Lisa was the star attraction of the whole thing," Mary Jo recalled. "She was a fantastic singer, with a beautiful voice. She played the guitar, the piano, organ, drums, a very talented person. She had her guitar and amplifier with her. We all were singing folk songs. Everyone treated Lisa real nice."

There was no question about it, everyone enjoyed the sing-a-long. Next, there was dancing. With not enough men to go around, some of the women paired off. This wasn't unusual, since Mary Jo often danced with her sisters at such gatherings. To her thinking, it was okay for Lisa to dance with her too, and it did go unobserved.

It was late when energies dwindled. Everyone said good night. Pat and Jack retired to one of the bedrooms as Mary Jo and Lisa helped Mrs. Davidson in a hasty cleanup of the den.

It was Mrs. Davidson who suggested it. "There's no need in your going home, Lisa, it's so late. Why don't you spend the night here?" The only place for Lisa to sleep, with Pat and Jack visiting, was Mary Jo's room.

They were alone. Mary Jo knew that Lisa wouldn't push the encounter if she was unwilling.

"You have to know how I feel about you," Lisa began. "I've felt this way ever since I laid eyes on you. But I don't want to do anything to you that you don't want." Lisa was giving Mary Jo a choice. "I feel love for you . . . it like to broke my heart, when the first time we met, you ignored me."

"Oh, that. I remember." Mary Jo explained her fears experienced at the meeting. "I thought you might see that I was a homosexual."

"I've really always known, Mary Jo." They laughed, then kissed.

*　*　*

Everyone slept late on Sunday. After lunch, Pat suggested they visit a dance club in Dallas. Why waste an afternoon sitting still? Four years younger than Mary Jo, Pat fed on motion. Her looks exuded energy. Short, casual black hair (no time to roll, pin or tease, just wash, blow-dry and go), large gray eyes, full lips, perfect teeth, a hint of chunkiness in her chin, a lively, broad face that would hold its youthfulness well into middle age.

Pat, her husband Jack, Mary Jo and Lisa spent the afternoon talking and dancing. Mary Jo and Lisa danced with several men at the club, but not with each other; this wasn't the safe haven of a family den. When they returned to Mrs. Davidson's, just before dinner, Lisa left.

A few hours later she returned to an agitated Mary Jo. They

went into the garage-room. "Look, we've been together Friday night and Saturday night you spent the night and we spent this afternoon together. They're going to get suspicious if you keep coming over here." Mary Jo was feeling threatened. Something had changed in her mind. Lisa's past visits were one thing; now they were sexual partners and this worried her. She thought about discovery. "I still had not made the decision that I would live openly in a homosexual life style."

Lisa understood Mary Jo's momentary panic and went home. Mary Jo went to bed early, unaware of how much her family really knew.

Monday morning, Mary Jo slept until nine. This was the final day of her three-day weekend. She showered, dressed and entered the kitchen, where Jack and Pat were having coffee. Through the window she saw her mother working among the tomato rows in her garden.

Pat poured her some coffee and sat down. Jack looked gruff. *Maybe he drank too much last night,* Mary Jo thought, *and he's got a hangover.* Jack lit a Kool and grimaced.

Jack was burly, with a craggy, blunt face, hazel eyes and a thick gray-brown mustache. When he was relaxed or smiled he looked warm, a friendly, big bear. When he was uncomfortable or tense his demeanor was menacing. Perhaps a useful tool for a police sergeant, but unsettling to Mary Jo.

After some shifting in his chair and fingering of his cigarette pack, Jack began his reluctant "duty." "Mary Jo, look, you shouldn't be messing around with this Lisa character." Jack's voice was heavy.

"What do you mean? I go to school with her."

"I understand that, Mary Jo," Jack rumbled, "but she's a homosexual, a lesbian."

"Yes, I know." Mary Jo was mad. She loved Lisa and didn't want anyone to insinuate that there was something wrong with her. *And what the hell business was it of theirs anyway?*

"Well, if you know, then you ought to be aware . . . or watch out or she'll get you into a relationship."

"Jack, look, I've already had sex relations with Lisa."

"When?"

"Saturday night." *You were crazy to tell them,* she thought.

Jack inhaled the last whiff of smoke from his cigarette. He had smoked it so short there wasn't anything to stump out. Small bits of tobacco and ash rolled off his fingers into the ashtray. This distraction gave Pat her opportunity.

"I want to tell you now, we discussed this last night, Mother and the rest of us. The rest of them think you should be committed or see a psychiatrist. But Jack and I don't feel that way."

"No," Jack confirmed, "I don't feel you need to see a psychiatrist. I told them you should see a minister."

She knew it was serious, deadly serious, but Mary Jo laughed out loud. She had worked in churches since she was twenty years old, either as a Sunday-school teacher for children and adults or as a choir director. This had put her in a close working relationship with ministers. She had yet to find a minister she felt could sit down, listen to all her problems and weigh them out, as a psychiatrist could do. Except for counseling about the Bible, Mary Jo surmised that ministers were ill equipped to deal with her homosexuality and they would be critical.

Her laughing wasn't doing much to placate Jack and Pat. She wasn't crazy. *They needed the help for thinking gays were nuts.* This, however, wasn't the approach needed to satisfy their inquiries.

"I feel a strong love for Lisa, but there's a good possibility that I'll never see her again. Heck, right now she's in the midst of getting back together with a woman she's had a long-term relationship with." Mary Jo was playing with the truth. Lisa did live with a woman called Fran. They had been together in Arkansas for eight years. Lisa moved to Texas, ostensibly to end the union. Fran had followed, but no reconciliation was imminent. Mary Jo's convenient reordering of the truth was calculated to reassure Pat and Jack that she wasn't going to run off the next day and abandon her sons for a furtive life with Lisa. That was never a real danger anyway. Going to college full time and working as a nurse five days a week severely curtailed *any* social life and virtually eliminated the possibility for an involved affair with Lisa.

While savoring the fulfillment of her first lesbian love affair, Mary Jo had already analyzed its implications. "Even though the relationship with Lisa was a very warm, loving relationship and one that I will always remember, always remember, I had major commitments, to graduate from college and two boys to raise and I had to consider what was best for them. I wasn't the type to run off."

Mary Jo later realized it was a dubious judgment to tell Pat and Jack so much about her sexuality, or, indeed, admit to it at all. "I didn't want to have any more trouble from them because I knew they would be going back to the rest of the family with what I was telling them. I wanted to keep it low-keyed."

"Jack, I will still see Lisa at college, but the chance of us getting back together is remote." While she was mouthing the words Mary Jo was planning to see Lisa that night. She had no illusions that the relationship would be permanent, but she knew, from Saturday night, that she wasn't going to cut herself off from Lisa. She would be available when they could get together.

Jack lit another cigarette and leaned forward on the table. "I've observed a number of homosexual situations in Galveston, Mary Jo. From what I've seen, if you went into that life, you would be completely controlled by the other person. Your life would be ruined. You're too good-looking a woman, Mary Jo, to waste yourself on another woman. You wouldn't have any freedom. There's nothing worse than a jealous woman, a jealous lesbian woman."

All enmity toward Jack disintegrated with his naïve pronouncements on lesbians. "I think Jack had my best interest at heart, but he, like most people, was uninformed about homosexual life styles per se. He knew nothing of a working homosexual family unit. I think they were pretty content that I was not going to continue the relationship, so I didn't say anything else."

It didn't escape Mary Jo's attention that Jack's little talk was a family ultimatum. "I wasn't going to put myself in a situation to go against them. Should I have stood up and said, 'You sons-of-bitches, you're not going to tell me how to live my life'? Then they all could have come down on me full force. I just wasn't prepared, at that time, to take it." Nothing more was said by any family member during the remainder of Pat's and Jack's visit.

* * *

Several days after Pat and Jack returned to Galveston, Mary Jo rode to the airport with her sister Carol Jean. Carol's mother-in-law was flying in from St. Paul, Minnesota. During the ride, the topic of Lisa arose, verifying for Mary Jo that Pat and Jack had reported back to the family what transpired at their confab.

"I understand Pat and Jack talked with you," Carol Jean said.

"Yes, there was no need to worry. Nothing is going to happen. What you all don't realize . . . this is pretty much the way I have always thought."

Carol Jean looked at Mary Jo in genuine surprise. "I didn't know that. I thought it was sort of a sudden thing."

"No, I have often thought that way."

This unremarkable exchange between sisters apparently prompted more family discord. The next night Lisa telephoned Mary Jo.

"Your sister Carol Jean called me and said she and your mother are convinced that we are still seeing each other. She implied she didn't want me to see you or call you. I told her we went to the same college and it was impossible for us not to see each other. You know what her reaction to that was, Mary Jo? She said I'd better lay off or I would have the family to contend with. I told her it was none of her damn business and if she persisted in harassing me I would consider a lawsuit. I think that took care of her problem, but what in the hell is going on over there, Mary Jo?"

She hadn't wanted Lisa to know about the Monday-morning confrontation with Pat and Jack and how hard her family was pushing her. Now, there wasn't any choice. Mary Jo relayed all the germane points.

Lisa was incredulous. "You were a fool to tell them you had a homosexual relationship. There is one thing you're going to have to remember. They have to prove it beyond a shadow of a doubt. And if you admit it, you have incriminated yourself."

Incriminate yourself? Mary Jo was flabbergasted. Surely it was a foible to have told anybody she had a sexual experience with a woman. And it was compounded by telling Carol Jean she had always felt that way, not that anything had happened beyond the one night, but the feeling was there. *Yes, she had fouled up. Quite a few people were carrying around her secret. They all were family, but still they knew. But "incriminate yourself." Beyond a shadow of a doubt. What was Lisa trying to tell her?*

* * *

Mary Jo and Lisa saw each other constantly during April. The rendezvous was always brief—a few minutes at school, a restaurant, or a drive—but convivial and emotionally sustaining. Once, when Lisa's parents were away, they stayed at the house and made love.

The latter part of April, Mrs. Davidson quit her job at a downtown Dallas restaurant. She needed a change. Pat asked her to come down to Galveston and live during the summer. She accepted.

On May 1, Mary Jo and her mother drove south. When they arrived, there was a new intrigue arranged by Jack. He had no more than said "hello" when he announced that Charlie, a fellow cop, would be over when his shift ended at eleven.

Mary Jo had dated Charlie during her periodic trips to Galveston. He was a pleasant, amicable guy. Given the family concern over her relationship with Lisa, she didn't think it too politic to refuse to see Charlie. She was miffed at the implications of Jack's matchmaking, but agreed to a late night dinner when Charlie arrived.

Dinner and drinks with Charlie were agreeable and Mary Jo accepted his invitation to cap the evening at his apartment. She spent the night.

It was just like they thought. She spent the night with Charlie, that's it now, she was all fixed up, she'd be right back with men.

~ 26 ~

Mary Jo had four hours, during the drive back home, to mull over the incident. *It was a put-up deal. They had arranged everything and possibly even told him of my homosexuality and that it was his job, his duty, to be the male that was going to get me back on the right road, to save me. It made me mad. Even though I knew the man, I had put myself into a trap. I was really dumb. I didn't know what people would try to do to get you out of the homosexual life. They tried to get a stud to get me out of the life. It was in a way sort of funny. I thought, How stupid.*

There was another side to the Galveston incident that Mary Jo didn't consider at the time. Lisa had told her, just before she left, that Fran and she were seriously thinking about getting back together. Mary Jo understood, but her limited knowledge of the gay world hobbled her perspective. She simply didn't know that other lesbians existed in any great number. "I knew I wanted to continue in the homosexual life style, but just like when I was married, I didn't know if that option even existed for me. I was at a point where I might have to continue in the old heterosexual life if I wanted any social life at all. I might have to go back to men. It was possible. I needed another adult to relate to."

Jimmy was fifteen on May 9, and Mary Jo was determined to make it his best birthday ever. She bought him a motorcycle, a machine that sparkled with status among his peers. Mary Jo's finances were depleted, but she managed a loan of forty-five dollars a month over a year. Jimmy was thrilled. He was the only one in the family so affected. When Mrs. Davidson learned of the motorcycle she was adamant. "When I get away from that house for a week, it falls apart. I don't know why in the world you bought that boy a motorcycle."

"He wanted one so much, Mamma."

"I know that, but you have just killed your son. Those things are deathtraps. He'll get out and kill himself, just wait."

Even Lisa, who studiously avoided meddling in family matters, was critical of the gift. "You really shouldn't have, Mary Jo. I've watched you since I've known you, and you just give your oldest boy too much. You can't give him everything he wants."

Mary Jo was seeing Lisa infrequently. Fran had definitely re-entered the picture and rekindled Lisa's interest. This troubled Mary Jo much less than she originally imagined. She loved Lisa, and Lisa had special feelings for Mary Jo. From the first, however, both accepted that someday they would part, but not with any rancor. It would taper off; a quiet, warm ending for a cherished interlude.

One of the final times they went out was May 19. Lisa had told Mary Jo about the gay life centered around clubs and bars. Women would meet, dance and socialize without the stares or harassment of the "straight" establishments. Until now in their relationship, Lisa carefully avoided taking Mary Jo to any lesbian bars, as if exposure to a wider world of lesbians would jeopardize the relationship. Now there was an understanding, a tacit recognition that each would eventually go her own way. Now, it was safe for Mary Jo to be introduced to the gay scene in Dallas.

Mary Jo's apprehension at visiting her first lesbian bar was comic. "I was scared, just like everybody else. They think that when you walk into a gay club, everyone is after you. I told Lisa, 'Don't leave me under any circumstances.' She laughed and said, 'Nothing is going to happen.'

"We got in there and it looked like any other dance club I had been in. Dimly lit, a long bar at one end, tables surrounding the dance floor, candles, a large crowd. The only difference was women dancing with women, men with men, and even a few mixed couples. I found out I could go to the bathroom without anyone following me. It was very nice. I enjoyed it. Even while we were still there I realized I had a feeling of comfort, I had found some valuable thing I only dreamed existed. It was here, and it was real. I knew that I was going to build my life in the gay community, and that there was, in fact, a gay community."

* * *

Mary Jo was well aware that the gay bar subculture could hardly be classed as a community in the traditional sense. A community had schools, churches, businesses, courts, hospitals, governments, a myriad of components and places. She also understood that all of that still didn't make a community. People made a community. Individuals, with beliefs, goals and purposes, made a community. It was a collective of individuals, a mutuality of essences, a devotion to the best interest of the whole, however loosely organized and diverse, that made a community. This was what she had in mind when she spoke of the gay community.

Sexuality, one small facet of their lives, which was denied by law, spurned by convention, abhorred by the ignorant, was the uniting bond that imposed a sense of belonging, of community.

How pluralistic the gay community really was she didn't know. Its history and future were unknown to her. Maybe it wasn't organized or even a conscious entity. She didn't know. Didn't care.

It was still a community, as real as any place, as viable as any set of buildings, as lasting as any political dogma could ever be. It was a feeling, an idea. Whenever any gay person confronted his sexuality, fought for acceptance, struggled for recognition of his value and worth as a person, there was a community in spirit, where millions of other beings existed. No gay would ultimately be alone.

That this community had eluded her for so many years saddened Mary Jo. If only she had sensed it, visualized it in reverie when she was young. How liberating it would have been. . . .

                    *   *   *

By the time she was a high school senior in Little Rock, Arkansas, Mary Jo was a deeply frustrated young woman. Her grades were good, she was well liked by most of her classmates and her performance in sports, basketball and football had won her the unique admiration reserved for athletes in our educational system. Besides, she was beautiful. Lustrous black hair, large gray-blue eyes, a classic, dazzling smile and the firm, shapely figure of a well-toned female athlete.

The source of her discontent was sexual. She traced it back to when she was six years old and would engage in childish fondling of her body. "It was a sexual feeling of sorts . . . inspired by the sight of other little girls." Ever since that time her sexual fantasies involved only girls. "Along with other girls I would go down to the creek in the summertime. Grandmother would always say, 'Take the soap with you and the washrag.' We would all bathe in the creek. There was never any touching, any involvement, of course. The involvement was within me. I felt attracted to some of these girls."

Athletics had always been the main avocation of the Davidson family. Mary Jo's father, James Joseph Davidson, was an all-state football player in high school and college. Most of his leisure time away from his railroad job was spent in conditioning his son James to follow in his footsteps. Mary Jo's role was one of coach. She trained right along with James and in many ways surpassed him. By her senior year she had mastered football. "I could throw a football anywhere I wanted to. I could run and jump and throw from mid-air. If I picked a target, I could hit it. I could throw it through an inner tube from fifty feet." What started as an aid to her brother's athletic development gradually turned to the touchstone of Mary Jo's popularity. "I always wanted to excel in sports. I guess I wanted to be a hero to the girls, just like the star of our school team was. I couldn't have cared less if the boys admired my abilities. I wanted to please the person, the girl, that I had an infatuation for at the time."

Mary Jo dated boys in high school: "If you wanted to go to any of the school's social functions, it had to be with a boy or you sat at home. I enjoyed myself, but would often see a girl I liked and would long to be with her, dance with her, hold her. It was always painful, the distance between us."

With her popularity it was never hard for Mary Jo to work her way into any clique of girls at the school. "There were a few girls that I really did like and as a group we all ran around. I never tried to put myself into a situation where I was completely alone with her. I was afraid of myself. Should an opportunity come about where there might be a touch, a gesture or something, I would give myself away. I was always very careful. That was uppermost in my mind, that I might be discovered."

This paralyzing fear of discovery thwarted Mary Jo's every opportunity for sexual expression. "Sometimes in school friends would spend the night with one another. There was always an aroused feeling for me, being in the bed with another girl. But it was never the person I was infatuated with. I made it a point never to put myself into so intimate a situation with a person I was focusing on. I was a strong willed person . . . I had to be in order to combat a lot of situations that could have happened if I wasn't able to check myself. I always held back."

Mary Jo had fully identified her sexual preference; she even memorized dictionary definitions of homosexual and lesbian.

This knowledge, in the abstract, did nothing to alleviate the alienation and the desperate fear that she would never be able to be herself, openly express love for another woman. Lesbians might exist on the pages of a book, but that was a comfortless thought to a young woman about to enter nurse's training.

Mary Jo did find a close friend at Arkansas Baptist School of Nursing. "I was very much drawn to this woman. We studied together, went to movies, lived in the same dormitory." As the relationship deepened, complications set in. "I literally became paranoid over this woman. I needed her kindness, her attention, we were very close. Yet, it was incomplete. I could have easily had sex with her. If anything was ever started, she would have gone through with it, she liked me so well. But in the end, we would have probably broken up as friends. It wasn't worth the risk."

While still at the point of indecision about her roommate, an incident occurred that shocked Mary Jo back into her sexual shell. She was coming in from duty around eleven one night when one of the instructors approached her and asked her to help out. Someone had seen a student nurse and another woman together in bed. The other woman was not a lesbian. "At eleven at night the instructors were packing her bag, she was thrown out. Her parents were called to come and get her. They were out of town, but had to drive over that very night. Again this showed me what society would do to you should you be yourself. Every time I saw anything like this, it was me. It could have been me they were kicking out. This was a girl that was exactly the way I wanted to be. The same fate was waiting for me, if I went on. It even frustrated me more." On her way to her room, the instructor walked past Mary Jo and smirked. "You get one lesbian in a dorm full of girls and she'll ruin half of them before she gets out of school."

Arkansas Baptist had a school basketball team that played in the city league, and naturally Mary Jo signed on. Sports, which had given her so much pleasure and status in high school, would become an ironic torment in nurse's training. Among the teams in the league was a squad comprised entirely of lesbians. "They were a rough team," Mary Jo remembered, "they never hesitated to foul you. This was very frustrating, especially to members of my team. It was to the point where we hated to play them. Some of the women on my team would say, 'I don't want to play that team, they foul too much, they hit you when you're going up for a shot.' The lesbian team seemed to take pride in the terror they caused. They knew how their rough approach to the game rattled us. You see, I saw this team in a different way than the others did. They reminded me of myself in a different way than the others did. They reminded me of myself in that they were pleasing a person of the same sex. Whenever this team played, all along the sidelines sat the women they were going with and they cheered and cheered when they scored or did something fantastic. I was more fearful of this team than the other women were, because this is what I was, or at least what I wanted to be. I wanted to be myself, the way these women could. They were happy the way they were. They celebrated it. They were not ashamed about what they were. They were able to have a member of the same sex, who they loved very much, be there with them and share their skills on the court. One member of my team got disgusted during one game and called them 'those damn homosexuals.' Of course I was one of those 'damn homosexuals.' It was a conflict. I had, in a way, a very frustrating life."

Mary Jo's family was Southern, conservative and traditional. With three female children much of the family talk centered around homes, the potentiality of grandchildren and above all getting married while you could still "trap" the right man. Women's working for a living was acceptable, but it was never thought of as a career. The family, meaning a house full of children, was the primary goal, or should be, of every well-bred girl. The pressure for marriage was unceasing.

During her nurse's training Mary Jo dated several men; again, as in high school, the options were narrow. Men, a social life, or nothing. The proximity of a curious and prodding family stymied any alternative.

"The guy I was dating asked me if I could get a date for his friend Doug. I did. We all four went swimming at a lake. Doug and I were the only two that could swim, so we spent the evening in the water and had fun. I broke up with the guy I was dating and five months later Doug called me up. We went together seven or eight months."

In 1956, at Arkansas Baptist, nurses weren't allowed to marry while in training and this posed a dilemma for Mary Jo. She was quite serious about Doug and had thought through the merits of marriage versus finishing her training, several months before he actually asked her to be his wife. What to do about her nursing career wasn't the only problem she had to resolve. "At that time I was still occasionally aroused by women. Not all women, but I still had a basic drive that was homosexual."

Doug, who was entering the Air Force, told Mary Jo that he might have to go overseas. "I felt I would miss him terribly. Then I began to think, He may be going and I may never see him again, and of course when he asked me to marry him, well, I loved him." Mary Jo had one final pang of hesitation. "When I was standing in front of the justice of the peace, it went through my mind, 'Am I doing the right thing?' It passed and I said to myself, 'Yes, I'm doing the right thing.'

"I was always faithful to him. I guess he never really had to worry about another guy. I never felt that I was cheating him, I gave all that I could. There were only a few times during the marriage that I would notice a woman at a party who would arouse me, but then I thought, I can never be myself and do what I want to do. Then, the feeling would pass."

* * *

All this reminiscing about her high school years, nurse's training and marriage had been prompted by her first visit to a lesbian bar on May 19, 1973. She spent the entire next morning reliving these experiences. Mary Jo wondered what had become of her friend from Arkansas Baptist. She had known the family for twenty years. In fact, an older sister now lived in Dallas. Why not give her a call, renew a childhood friendship and learn how her nurse's training companion was doing?

Rose Bell wasn't listed in the directory, but there was an R. Bell. A woman's voice answered the phone. Mary Jo inquired, "Is Rose there?"

"No, she's out now. Could I take a message?"

"This is Mary Jo Risher. I went to high school with Rose in Arkansas. Her sister and I went to nurse's training together. Could you have her give me a call when she returns?"

Mary Jo was pleased. She should have done this before. Rose was a marvelous person; they always enjoyed each other's company. Good memories from the past.

In less than an hour the phone rang. "Mary Jo, it's so good to hear from you. Yes, I'm fine. I saw your mother about six months ago, but I couldn't stop to talk. Yes, Sis is married, with three kids. No, I don't visit since my divorce. You might say I was the black sheep of the family. Look, hon, why don't you drop over this evening. We'll cook some steaks on the grill and talk. Yeah, about the old days. Around seven. It's really good to hear from you, Mary Jo."

The reunion was delightful. Nonstop talk. The span of years was covered in hours. High school. Sports. The big dance. Vacations. Romances. Careers. Children. Divorces.

"So you don't have much to do with your family these days?" Mary Jo's question was innocent enough. Rose looked at her roommate Barbara. There was a pause. "No, Mary Jo. But I guess you'd say it's my family that doesn't have much to do with me. It's their choice, not mine."

Rose's wistful answer stirred Mary Jo. She seemed able to share fully in the isolation. She might be known as the black sheep of her family. What could she say now? Could she pry further?

"Barb, in case she didn't tell you, Mary Jo is quite a dancer. Do you still dance much?"

Rose's question had come just in time, the awkwardness was over. "As a matter of fact I do. Only the slow dances. I never mastered the wilder stuff."

"Barb and I get out now and then. We both like to dance. What clubs do you go to, Mary Jo?"

Almost without thinking Mary Jo blurted out, "The Entre Nuit. I was there with a friend last night."

"A friend?" Rose cautiously asked.

"Yes, she had promised to take me there for some time."

"Barb and I go there a lot, Mary Jo. It's sort of a special place, if you know what I mean."

Of course she knew. Nothing had been said about whether you were, or I was. Just the name of the club they all frequented. That was enough. It was out. They laughed and relaxed.

*   *   *

During subsequent weeks Mary Jo and Rose were inseparable. Though only a few years apart in age, Rose gracefully mothered Mary Jo. She talked with her of the gay life, its styles and ramifications. She schooled her novice charge in the subtleties of meeting and approaching other lesbian women for dates. She and Barbara would take Mary Jo to various clubs, each different in clientele and atmosphere. They told her of the gay movement, the organizations, leaders, literature. There was even a gay church, with congregations all over the country.

An eager pupil, Mary Jo was astounded. The infrastructure of the gay community was broader and more complex than she had ever imagined. It was more than a spiritual bond, it was real, a tangible, organized community. She was out, a lesbian woman with limited practical experience but giddy with anticipation.

One of the first obstacles Mary Jo encountered was getting women to dance with her at a bar. "It's pretty hard for a woman to go up to another woman, believe me it is. In 1973 the gay community hadn't progressed too far. Stereotypical feminine women, with long hair, lipstick, make-up, just didn't show any aggressiveness in social situations. It was role playing in a sense. Rose told me as long as I looked like a 'Barbie' doll I would have trouble.

"I was at a point where I really couldn't afford to keep my hair in a long flip at fifteen dollars a week. Besides I couldn't do anything with the boys, like swimming. So the idea of getting my hair cut was appealing.

"Here was really a change. My hair had always been long, in a bubble type effect, ratted. During the haircut on June twentieth I was sitting in the chair for ninety minutes while they whacked off my hair. I almost died in the chair. Before my very eyes I was becoming a different type person. In a way, my whole looks changed. It was a transformation. Going from one hair style extreme to another, it does have some psychological effect.

"I called Lisa when she got home from work. We still saw each other at college and I didn't want her to see my hair in front of everyone else, where she couldn't comment or say what she thought."

"I got my hair cut today."

"You did?"

"Yes, it's quite short."

"I was wondering when it was going to happen."

"What do you mean?"

"Never mind."

"No, tell me."

"Well, Mary Jo, I knew from the start that you were going to end up an aggressive lesbian woman. You wouldn't be content in a submissive role. You're just out. You want to see something of life."

Mary Jo accepted the accuracy of Lisa's remarks. She had long talks with Rose about what she wanted in life. She could no longer be smothered by another person. She didn't know, not with any exactness, who she was. Always subservient to another person, *Mary Jo* was lost. As a lesbian and a person, she was embryonic.

The next day Mary Jo learned that her ex-husband's father, Douglas Risher, Sr., had been admitted to Gaston Hospital, seriously ill. She had not seen Mr. Risher since the divorce, though they had been close during the years when she was married.

"I asked one of the nurses if she would go into his room with me. If anything happened, I was worried that I would be blamed. The minute I walked in . . . it was like I had just seen him the day before. He looked exactly the same. I said, 'Hello, Dad.' He said, 'Jo.' I walked over and kissed him. He said, 'Jo, I will always love you.'

"The man in the bed next to Mr. Risher's asked me if I was Mary Jo. I said yes. He said, 'Mr. Risher called for you all night long.'"

That night Mr. Risher suffered a coronary and was placed in intensive care. Mary Jo went to see him every break she had. Normally a person in intensive care was limited to a few visitors a day and then only for five minutes. Mr. Risher was too ill to talk, so Mary Jo just held his hand and spoke, often about the good times they had together with the boys, whom he idolized. The time they spent together, under such taxing circumstances, meant very much to both of them. "To me it was God's will that Mr. Risher came to Gaston Hospital where he and I could make amends over what the divorce brought."

On June 22, one of the nurses found Mary Jo changing a patient's bandage. She said Mary Jo was needed in intensive care. Quickly, she finished and started down the hall. A second nurse, off another floor, met her and said, "You better get down there now."

Mary Jo rushed to the IC unit and was several steps from the door when Mr. Risher's attending physician came out. "It was too late. I was terribly upset. The rest of the family hadn't arrived yet. The chaplain of the hospital asked me if I wanted to go home. I said no. I called Mamma. She told Jimmy about his granddad."

The funeral was on Monday. Jimmy was a pallbearer. "Mamma said Mr. Risher had carried Jimmy so much during his life, it was only fitting that Jimmy should carry him his last time. That was hard for me to take, watching that boy carry his grandfather's casket. Jimmy and I went back to the grave, later, to see the flowers."

*　*　*

By July, Mary Jo was venturing out, alone, to the gay clubs. Her clothing had changed but was appropriate for Dallas' night life environment. Casual, hip huggers and a Western shirt. Her circle of friends had slowly expanded to a dozen or so women.

Early one evening she spotted Johnnie and Maria. She walked over. "Hi there." Both women looked puzzled as if to register, We know you from somewhere, but can't quite place you.

"I'm Mary Jo."

"My God, Lisa's Mary Jo?"

"Well, Mary Jo."

Johnnie and Maria caught the drift of Mary Jo's conversation. They had not heard about the "breakup," although that is hardly an accurate description of what transpired between Lisa and Mary Jo. It was a common term, meaning simply that two people who used to be together had called it off, split.

Mary Jo was to learn an inescapable fact of life about her newly found friends. First, they were almost exclusively paired off; it was rather rare to find a single woman who remained that way for any length of time. Secondly, they were incorrigible matchmakers, almost as if it were some unspoken duty that came with the territory. It wasn't even subtle. This obviousness took the sting out of being constantly enveloped in a "fix-up." Aboveboard and well intentioned. Nevertheless, a fix-up. Yes, Johnnie and Maria happened to know a woman who was in the midst of a breakup and yes, they wanted Mary Jo to meet her. It was all set, they would meet at a restaurant and then go to a club on Cedar Springs.

Ann and Darla came together. Darla was a close friend who was staying at Ann's town house for a few months.

Ann had a habit when she was entering an unfamiliar situation of sauntering when she walked. She placed both hands into her pockets and swayed her body from side to side as her feet covered the distance. It was a walk like you see on a big awkward kid who is new in the neighborhood and must walk up to the kids at the ball diamond for the first time and sheepishly greet them with "Hi, guys."

Before her guard was up and she assumed the posture of a worldly woman, Ann conveyed the jauntiness of an oversized child. A member of the "Our Gang" comedy team who had grown tall but retained all the childhood mannerisms that made you want to tweak a cheek and say, "How cute."

At their first meeting, however, Mary Jo wasn't moved. Ann was attractive, a tall broad-shouldered woman with a full figure. Long straight blond hair. A round, fleshy face that usually had a wry smile. Uneven dimples when she smiled. Her voice was edged with gentle sarcasm, often self-directed. No doubt about it, here was a woman who had been around, knew a little something about the world, in fact was weary about it. "I'm Ann Foreman." Direct, without conceit.

Just the way she introduced herself told Mary Jo something. She had used her last name, something no one else was doing at that time. Still, there was no real attraction there.

Ann sat between Johnnie and Maria and immediately plunged into an involved conversation. Mary Jo listened. After an hour of chatter Mary Jo and Maria went to the restroom. On the way back one of the show dancers stopped Mary Jo in the hall and suggestively offered her one of her pasties. Flattered, she took it and went back to the table.

Maria couldn't wait to tell the group about the gift. "You'll never guess what Mary Jo got hold of." There was general laughter, a few snide remarks: "Oh well . . . superstud." With this enlivened atmosphere, Mary Jo asked Ann to dance.

The dance clinched it for Mary Jo. Ann and she just wouldn't hit it off. All during the dance Ann kept complaining that she couldn't dance well, that Mary Jo was unfortunate to have to put up with her. Mary Jo assured her she was doing well and not to worry about it. "The whole time she was apologizing about not being a good dancer and I kept building her up by saying she was fine."

What troubled Mary Jo was the fluctuating mood of Ann. One minute a radical lesbian, using her full name and where she worked with no reservation. Now, a meek, stumbling, insecure girl. Later, she would learn that Ann was seriously miffed at Johnnie and Maria for playing cupid. She felt it was distasteful and humiliating.

As soon as the dance ended and they returned to the table, Ann quickly engaged in three-way chatter with Johnnie and Maria. Mary Jo was excluded. *What goes on here?* Mary Jo thought. *They want me to meet this person and now they monopolize her and we don't have a chance to talk. The hell with this.*

"I began to look around. I saw this beautiful, striking woman at the bar, all by herself. She looked over my way. I asked her to dance. She had curly blond hair, about shoulder length. Five foot or so. One hundred eighteen pounds. Dressed in jeans and a pale blue shirt. She asked me if I was with anybody. I said, 'Well, not really.' The second dance she told me she was a schoolteacher, on vacation, staying with her sister and brother-in-law. She would be leaving for California in a few days. She asked again if I was with anyone. I asked her if she would like to sit at our table. She said yes. And we talked. I didn't direct any more of my attention to Ann that evening."

When Mary Jo left her house earlier in the evening, she had made up her mind to return at a reasonable hour. When the schoolteacher asked if she had to be home at any certain hour she said, "No, but I am going home early."

"Well, I'll just come right out with it. I want to be with you, in fact, I'll rent the hotel."

"I just can't do it. For one thing, I have to be at work at 6:45 in the morning."

"It'll only take a few hours."

"Yes, I know, but I can't."

When the bar closed, around midnight, the group decided to

drive to an all-night restaurant on Oak Lawn and have an early breakfast. Mary Jo walked the schoolteacher to the car, said good night, and went home. She felt bad about not meeting her friends at the restaurant, but no one else had to get up as early as she did.

*　*　*

Mary Jo's mother and Richard were in Arkansas for the week, and Jimmy was staying over at a friend's. The house was empty and immediately after work she called the number Darla had given her. She liked Darla and thought they might pal around together, since neither one had any romantic involvement at the time.

Darla didn't answer the phone, although Mary Jo thought she knew the voice. "Hold on, I'll get her." Mary Jo asked Darla who answered the phone. "Oh, that's Ann. I stay at her house." Ann? Maybe she could make up for running off last night. "Let me speak to Ann."

"We chitchatted and I asked if she would like to go out for a drink or something." Ann agreed. "I'd like that. The only thing is I have to go pick up my daughter in Wilmer. She's been staying with her father."

At the club Mary Jo and Ann had their first real chance for a talk without other people being present. They talked about their children, families and occupations.

Ann explained her discomfort of the previous night. "I felt like I'd been fixed up and I didn't like it. I just don't like blind dates and I don't like people trying to put somebody off on me. I don't like surprise attacks, so to speak. Everyone does it, but I'll never accept it, get used to it."

About a half hour before they were scheduled to pick up Ann's daughter, Judie Ann, they talked about the situation between Ann's former lover for five years, Neila, her ex-husband, Mike, and her.

Ann and Neila were putting on a charade for Mike's benefit, so he would feel comfortable in returning Judie Ann. "Neila and I brought each other out," Ann explained to Mary Jo. "We experienced a lot of traumatic things. She still had her old boy friend in the way half the time, and I still had my ex-husband Mike interfering. And there were other women that would fly through Neila's life every once in a while. We were not ready to settle down. It was our first gay relationship. Neila had this big guilt thing about her mother and being gay. Over the years this all caught up with us and we just couldn't stay together. The fighting, bickering began to wear us down and finally I thought it might affect Judie Ann. I asked Mike if he could keep her for a while, like a long visitation, and he said yes. But now that Neila and I have decided to split up, I can handle Judie again, I want her back. Mike thinks we are back together and things are settled down. It's really best he go on thinking that way."

Mary Jo could certainly identify with what Ann was saying. She felt drawn to her; they had a lot more in common than she first supposed. They were mothers and the welfare of their children always came first, all the rest of life's chaos might go unordered, but the children had to have stability and love.

Mary Jo was curious about Judie Ann. How had living with a lesbian couple affected her? What did she know?

Ann wasn't the least hesitant: "When Mike and his new wife, Jan, were dating, that's during the hell of our divorce and custody battle, the word 'queer' was shouted around quite a few times. Judie Ann picked it up and questioned me about it. I tried to explain to her that it meant nothing, just that Mike and Jan were upset that Neila and I were living together. I don't know if that satisfied her or not. You sometimes can't tell with kids that young. At least she didn't bring it up again, not to me.

"About a year later, after they were married, Jan calmed down quite a bit and had a long talk with Judie. She told her that some people don't understand or accept people doing what they want to do. But sometimes people have loves that are different. 'Just because your mother and Neila love each other in a different way there's nothing wrong with it.' By the way, Mary Jo, I didn't know about this talk between Jan and Judie until a few months ago. Neila and I were splitting up and Judie found me in my bedroom crying. She said, 'Look, Mommy, if you don't think about it, it won't hurt so much.' I said, 'What do you mean?' 'Well, I know you love Neila, but if you wouldn't think about her being gone, it wouldn't hurt so bad.' I said, 'Judie Ann, do you know how much I love Neila?' She said, 'You love Neila like Daddy and Jan love each other and I understand that.'

"Oh . . . another time, just before that she told me she didn't know why it was wrong for us to sleep together, why we had to hide the fact that Neila and I slept together. She knows to keep quiet about this all the time. Somehow during the years Neila and I lived together it all gradually sank in. She understood the situation."

Mary Jo didn't know what to say. The best she could muster was an offhand remark about how precocious Judie Ann was. How advanced for her age. The remark didn't affect Ann.

Mary Jo was enthralled by Ann's frankness and trust. "I was sitting across from her and there was a young, radical almost, type of person. You could just see it, hear it in the way she talked about life and her daughter. Her daughter knew about her lesbianism. And she was a woman who was proud of what she was and she didn't give a damn who knew it. I saw in her a woman who had been in the lesbian life for over five years. She knew who she was and was even able to tell people at her office that she was gay. Now this was radical to me. I didn't want anybody to know. Ann didn't know my last name; she didn't have my phone number or know where I lived. You can't get much more conservative than that."

Darla and Neila arrived. Ann acted calm around Neila, amazingly so, considering the agony they had put each other through. It was time to go and pick up Judie Ann. The plan was to introduce Mary Jo as a friend. Judie Ann, who knew that her mother and Neila were no longer living together, would be discreet and say nothing. She wasn't deceitful; it was more of an acquired wisdom that silence, in certain situations, was mandatory. Survival between warring parents, whether they were of the same or opposite sex, created an adult-like caution in Judie Ann. She was virtually unflappable in the world of grown-up games.

Judie Ann was an adorable child. A fifty-pound, stick-figured

waif, with a yard of blond hair, oval green eyes, several prominent freckles and an enchanting grin. Judie didn't walk. No, she
glided as if the air space surrounding her body was subject to
lunar gravity, where even full-grown men come and go as
sprites.

Mary Jo, like almost everyone who met her, teased Judie Ann
at their first introduction. Judie tilted her head, flashed an indignant pout of disbelief, and then crinkled her face into a jubilant
smile.

Before they left, Judie Ann made one last attempt at getting a
dollar from her father. Her piggy bank was stuffed, but she
didn't want to touch the principal for a new skate board. The ne-
gotiations called for some serious charming.

Without the slightest knowledge of any sexual connotations,
Judie tossed her blond hair, batted her spidery eye lashes and
dangled her delicate hand off her protruding hip. She didn't
know why this body language got her smiles and concessions,
but she was always prepared to use it. It worked. One dollar
from dad.

The next day Mary Jo called Ann and made a date for Friday
night. Already they were entering a pattern where it was acceptable to give little or no notice when asking for a date. They assumed, without directly discussing it, a mutual availability.
What Mary Jo hadn't assumed was that Neila still had all her
possessions at Ann's town house and came and went as if she still
lived there. They weren't physically intimate, but Neila was
there.

That Friday, July 13, was a special date for Mary Jo. Her
friends in the gay community had multiplied, and she was having as full a social life as her job and college would permit. She
had met a splendid woman, and yet she wasn't absorbed by another person; she was beginning to be a whole being, herself. She
could be true to herself, know that she had the responsibility for
her actions. She was, at last, making her own way.

The club was packed and many of them were familiar faces to
Mary Jo. They all greeted her, welcomed her. Even Lisa was
there with Fran. They were back together. Mary Jo was glad,

~ 44 ~

she didn't harbor any resentment. That page had been carefully turned in her personal history, its significance never diminished. She was simply writing on another page, the next one over.

Lisa came over and began a conversation. Finally, quietly, their faces inches apart, Lisa said, "I'll always love you, but you're ready now. Go out and . . . do your thing."

* * *

The club closed at 1:30. Some of the group wanted to get some food, but Ann and Mary Jo bowed out and drove to Ann's home. They sat in the car for a few minutes, talking about the evening. It had been fun. Lisa's farewell only heightened Mary Jo's growing fondness for Ann. Even while her first lover, the woman who had brought her out, was letting her go completely, she was longing for Ann. "Something told me I wasn't going to let her go. I kissed her and then got out of the car and went around and opened the door for her."

Ann said good night. Mary Jo suggested that she walk her through the backyard to the patio door. When they got to the patio door, Ann turned and said, "It was a great evening, Mary Jo, thank you."

"Aren't you going to ask me in for a Coke or a drink?" Mary Jo already knew the answer. Ann smiled a bit nervously.

While Ann rummaged in the freezer for some ice cubes, Mary Jo made a quick tour of the downstairs of the town house. She may have been en route to being a liberated woman, but at times remnants of her obsessive housekeeper days returned. Mary Jo liked what she saw. The house was finely ordered, freshly cleaned and comfortable. The style of the furniture was similar to her own taste, what was known as "Mediterranean." There was wall-to-wall carpeting, a deep green shag. The drapes were textured satin in a light green. There was a large sofa against the far wall. Gold with orange and brown stripes. A matching chair was placed under built-in bookshelves on the wall adjacent to the bar. The bar had a counter that opened into the kitchen. There were four orange-colored stools. The most striking thing in the living room was a large mahogany player piano. It had been in Ann's family for a number of years.

Mary Jo sat down on the couch as Ann brought in the Cokes. She noticed the ceiling had two large, dark-stained wooden beams running across it, and commented to Ann about them. She complimented Ann on her house.

For ten or fifteen minutes they discussed furniture, decorating and mortgages. Mary Jo's family had numerous houses over the years, and she was well acquainted with the ebb and flow of the real estate market. Ann, working for a bank, brought an accountant's expertise to the discussion.

Finally, the house talk wound down. Mary Jo put her arm around Ann and held her face with her other hand. They kissed. Mary Jo asked Ann to turn out the lights over the bar. While she was up, Ann turned on the stereo receiver to a "soft rock" station. The volume was low, just a presence for mood. Ann returned to her seat next to Mary Jo. "Ann laid her head on my shoulder. We talked about each other. We began to pet a little. I told Ann she looked very nice, always appeared very attractive to me. She wore a very sexy cologne, 'White Shoulders.' At a certain point in the petting I began to unbutton her slacks. She protested, in a gentle way. 'No, don't do that.' She didn't seem to be resisting too much, so I took that to mean continue on."

Mary Jo and Ann made love the rest of the night. Near dawn they were cradled in each other's arms, about to drift off to sleep, when Ann whispered to Mary Jo: "I think I love you." Mary Jo's eyes widened and blinked as if to shake off sleep.

Oh, no, no, I'm not hearing what I think I'm hearing. I'm not ready to get real serious about someone. What can I say? This is frightening to me. I'm not ready for such a commitment.

Mary Jo moaned slightly, pretending she was asleep. In the dark Ann couldn't tell. Her words went unanswered.

When Mary Jo awakened it was fully light outside. She was lying on her stomach, her arm was hanging off the couch. Ann was sitting on the floor, holding her hand. "What are you doing?" Ann placed her other hand over Mary Jo's. "Oh, nothing. I was just looking at your hand."

Late that Saturday morning Darla came bounding in and enlivened the day by serenading Ann and Mary Jo on her guitar. After ample doses of coffee and "Puff the Magic Dragon," Mary Jo was ready to leave. Ann talked her into staying for a while and they prepared an elaborate breakfast of omelets, fried tomatoes, sausage and toast. The three women eagerly devoured the food while lightheartedly talking.

Ann and Mary Jo cleared the table, rinsed off the plates, and placed them in the dishwasher. They moved to the sofa to talk and let the food do its work to rejuvenate them.

Without a knock or a ring of the doorbell Neila entered. Mary Jo assumed she still had a key. Neila and Ann were the same age. Neila was a businesswoman with a keen mind that she labored to hide behind a matter-of-fact personality and carefree chatter. She had medium-short, straight brown hair, worn in a severe blunt cut. Her face was pleasant, the features firm and attractive. Her skin was lightly pockmarked from teen-age acne.

Neila was genuinely shy and often would wait for what seemed an endless time before speaking. After a minute or two of scrutinizing the situation, she innocently greeted everyone, "Hi, how y'all doing?"

Mary Jo was uneasy. *I don't know what to say to the woman. Fine? Hell, I've been here all night.*

Ann asked Neila, "How have you been doing?" but she didn't expect any answer. "Want something to eat? Coffee?" Neila shook her head "no," then started for the center of the room. "I guess it's about time we divided up some of the stuff," she said, and sat down next to a stack of a hundred or so record albums.

Ann shifted to the edge of the sofa and leaned toward the floor with arms folded across her knees. Darla slouched down in the armchair, anticipating a boring ordeal. Mary Jo crossed her legs and stared at the two women in disbelief.

Recounting the scene several years later, Mary Jo still vividly remembered the surrealistic feelings: "Oh, I tell you, I hope I never have to go through anything like that again. It was very distressing, very emotional . . . bad. A very sad thing to watch. Here were two people, that didn't have any type of bond, no marriage, nothing else. They were dividing up record albums. 'This one's yours. This is mine. Here's one we bought together. You keep it. No, you keep it.' Ann said, 'No, that's one I bought for your birthday.' And then things like: 'That's the record Judie Ann and I got you, so you take it.' Neila argued, 'No, Judie Ann likes it so well you go ahead and keep it.'

"I tell you the honest truth, I hated to be there. I was stuck right there on the couch. I couldn't say goodbye to Ann, halfway decent. I couldn't just get up, climb over a floor full of records, say so long, and walk out the patio door."

Ann and Neila sorted and stacked their respective records. Ann helped Neila pack her share into several cardboard boxes. Ann asked, "Where are you going to live?" Neila didn't stop packing the records or look at Ann. "I've got an apartment. Ann, why don't you keep the sofa and chair? I don't need them for now. I've rented some furniture. I'll come by and get the stereo next week." Ann helped Neila carry out the boxes of records. When she returned, Mary Jo said goodbye and arranged to see her that night.

* * *

Mary Jo thought it would be nice for her friend Rose to meet Ann. Perhaps she wanted approval; after all Rose had been her adviser and close friend. The situation with Ann was getting crucial. Ann had told her that she loved her. Mary Jo resisted that encompassing a feeling, but she was undeniably attached to Ann and was actively pursuing the relationship. From what she had observed that afternoon, Neila wasn't exactly out of the picture either. That certainly complicated things. No matter what they said, Ann and Neila obviously still had strong feelings for one another. You just don't live with someone for five and a half years without something between you. She might be facing another situation like Lisa's. At one time Lisa and Fran were supposedly separated. And she knew that Lisa loved her. Yet, several months later Lisa was back with Fran and Mary Jo was abandoned, or at least out of that triangle. Of course she didn't object to Lisa reuniting with Fran. She hadn't encouraged it, though. Things were getting more complicated, in any event, and the very last thing she needed was to get embroiled in a messy liaison. That had to be avoided.

Once Rose met Ann, got to know her, she might be able to offer some objective advice. Not that Mary Jo couldn't make up her own mind. She was quite capable of that; only, the opinion of someone who understood her and what she was going through must surely be useful. She called Rose and arranged the meeting.

Mary Jo was to pick up Ann at seven and they would go over to Rose and Barb's, have a few drinks, talk and later go to a drive-in movie. Ann seemed agreeable, even excited, when Mary Jo talked with her on the phone at midafternoon.

No plans had been made about dinner. Mary Jo made a sandwich just before she left home. That, plus the obligatory popcorn and candy at the movie, should hold her nicely. It was precisely seven when she knocked on Ann's door.

Ann answered the door, held it open, but stood in the doorway with her arm against the doorframe. "I hate to tell you this . . . I just can't go out with you tonight." What Ann was saying was bad enough without her standing in the doorway blocking the way. Mary Jo shifted her weight onto her left foot. "Why not?" Ann looked contrite and down at her feet. "I just can't." Mary Jo shifted to her right foot. "Look, I've got these friends of mine waiting to meet you. They're very important to me." Ann's arm dropped from the doorframe. "Mary Jo, I'm really sorry, I am. I can't explain right now." Mary Jo stared at Ann in a bewildered fury. "All right, then, good night."

What in the hell was going on? she thought. *We'd been dating, we stayed up all night making love, she told me she loved me, I spent all my free time with her and now she wouldn't go out with me. Won't even tell me why. She didn't even ask me in, I had to stand in the yard like some goddamn door-to-door salesman and discuss our life. I'll bet that Neila was behind this.*

Rose was irked when Mary Jo called. She had canceled other plans at the last minute to accommodate Mary Jo. After hearing

~ 49 ~

what transpired at Ann's door she dismissed the whole affair with a snap judgment, "Forget her."

Interlinked with Mary Jo's ire was a seriously confused ego. One day an irresistible lover, the next a snubbed victim of some female treachery. She wavered between wanting to return and force her way into Ann's house and have it out or just chucking the whole thing, writing it off. She needed a drink.

It was early and the sparse gathering at the club off Live Oak contained only one face Mary Jo was familiar with, Darla's. She was at the end of the bar, near the dance floor, jovially sipping a beer. "Wanna brew, Mary Jo? I thought you had a date with Ann tonight."

"So did I," Mary Jo allowed. She toyed with the beer bottle and told Darla about the strange brush-off from Ann. Darla suggested that Ann must have a good reason or she would never have acted like that. "Why don't you give her a call later, Mary Jo, and maybe she'll explain?"

Mary Jo scanned the club. At the far corner was a table against the wall. There were several glasses on the table, but only one person was sitting there. A gorgeous blond-haired woman in a low-cut black dress.

Mary Jo took a long, full drink of her beer, peering over the top of the bottle at the woman. She waited another moment, to make sure the woman was alone, then walked over and asked her to dance. The woman, whose baby face made her look years younger than she was, smiled at Mary Jo. "You'll have to ask my butch."

This caught Mary Jo off guard. She had never been confronted with anything like this before. "Okay . . . I . . . will. Ah, where do I find her?" She hadn't finished the question when she saw the answer approaching from the area where the pool tables were kept.

Up walked this, I really mean, a truck-driving butch. She was unreal, like all the stereotypes you saw in bad movies. Keys hanging from the belt loop, cowboy boots, a man's shirt and real short hair combed like they did in the fifties. For the first time I was seeing something I heard about, suspected went on, to a minor degree, in the gay world, but had never observed firsthand before.

The woman, known around the clubs as L.C., stood unsmiling. Mary Jo managed a half smirk and calmly laid it out. "I would like to dance with your femme."

L.C. didn't smile or frown. Blankly she said, "Sure."

The prize was hers. She wasn't too sure she wanted it now. Mary Jo was stuck. After that exercise in axiomatic sexism she had to dance with "Blondie." The woman turned out to be a mild and pleasant person and, oh, so lovely. She told Mary Jo she had three children. She hinted that she'd like to dance again. Mary Jo wasn't tickled with that bit of gabble. As she walked the woman back to her table the blonde said, "Sometimes you get into things before you realize what they are all about."

Mary Jo went to the telephone booth and dialed Ann's number. She let it ring a dozen times. No answer.

Another woman was sitting at the blonde's table now. Her heft wasn't in the same class as L.C.'s. Mary Jo walked over. "How would you like to dance?" she asked the blonde. "You'll have to ask me first," responded the other woman.

Mary Jo was in a quandary. *What was this? Really. What had I got myself into? Before I had to ask her butch.*

Mary Jo was relieved when the song ended. She was getting worried. She cornered Darla and demanded, "What the hell is going on here?"

"It's rather simple, Mary Jo," Darla teased. "Actually, the blonde is the property of L.C. and when L.C. is playing pool or is not around there are other women who are watching her."

Mary Jo exclaimed, "Ohhhhhhooo." She took a serious drink of her beer and pondered the mess she had stepped into. *I began to realize that in the gay world, like any other existence, there was such a domineering type of person that they could control your very existence . . . your every move.* Mary Jo's learning experiences had not been complete, she had not really ventured out alone where she would come across such arrangements. She felt threatened. *I believed that one more move to that table could be my last. I hated the idea that a woman could control another woman to that extent. This woman was a trapped animal.*

Mary Jo had absorbed about all she could handle for one night. A prudent withdrawal was in order. First, a final attempt to reach Ann. This time she let the phone ring for two minutes; if she was anywhere in the house she had plenty of time to answer. Ann wasn't home.

Mary Jo started toward the door. She hesitated, deathly sick. She almost fell down. Darla saw Mary Jo's wavering and rushed over. "What's the matter, Mary Jo?" Mary Jo was trembling all over. Her stomach was swelling. "I don't know. I'm sick. Get me outside." Darla grabbed Mary Jo across the back and under the arm. She was almost carrying dead weight. They got to a wooden sawhorse at the side of the building. Mary Jo's head was bobbing up and down, her mouth was open. She stumbled against the sawhorse and began retching. Darla dabbed at Mary Jo's face with a handkerchief. In a moment the nauseous surge subsided. "Darla, help me to the car. Walk out to the parking lot with me." Mary Jo's legs were numb. She scraped her shoes along the sidewalk. Sweat beaded on her forehead. Her body was twitching. More vomit, this time in a splattering force that covered her clothes. Water was running off her forehead. Her body was wringing with perspiration. She stumbled, propelling Darla and her against the side of the car. Mary Jo was drooped across the trunk. Her face was pressed against the chilled metal, where her own sweat formed a suction lock. She was panting for air.

Darla, in a state of panicked helplessness, kept asking Mary Jo if she wanted an ambulance. She hesitated between leaving Mary Jo to get to a phone back in the club and staying with her in case she strangled on her own vomit.

The mercury vapor street light made Mary Jo's pale skin look orange. Gradually she stopped heaving and was breathing in short shallow gasps. "I don't know what's wrong with me. I only had one beer, not even all of that."

"Let me take you home, Mary Jo."

~ 52 ~

"No, look . . . I'm better now, at least I'm able to drive. Don't wreck any more of your evening. You go ahead."

Darla didn't want to leave Mary Jo. She had never seen anyone that convulsively sick. Mary Jo had slipped in behind the wheel and slumped far down in the seat. She fumbled with the ignition key. "Look, Rose and Barb live a few minutes away, if I don't feel like I can make it home, I'll go there."

"I don't know, Mary Jo. You look awfully sick. Better give me your telephone number so I can call and see if you make it home all right."

Knowing that her mother and Richard were still in Arkansas and Jimmy wouldn't return from his visit until Monday, she gave Darla her number.

She angled the car out of the parking lot and headed toward the Thornton expressway. Her actions were deliberate and slow, and she maintained the car on a relatively straight course that at least wasn't a danger to oncoming traffic.

By the time Mary Jo entered the freeway her stomach cramps were radiating throughout her body—gurgling bursts of pain that shot across her torso. Saline beads of sweat stung her eyes. Her vision was blurred, she had difficulty focusing on anything that wasn't directly in front of her. She navigated by following the red maze of taillights, as if they would lead her safely home. She had little conscious control over where she was going. Progress along the expressway was instinctual. Finally, she made the exit near her mother's home. Entering the driveway, she put on the brakes so clumsily she was thrown forward and bumped her head on the windshield.

She sat in the driveway for a moment in utter exhaustion and in thankfulness that she had made it. Barely erect, she walked to the door, fumbled for the keyhole, flung open the door, lumbered to the back bedroom, sprawled across the bed and was instantly out.

Sixteen hours later, at four in the afternoon, the raucous ringing of the telephone awakened Mary Jo. Her body was sore, like she had spent the night in tumbling exercises. Her head was pulsating, with an oppressive weight from her eyes over the top, to the back of her neck. Her mouth was foul, her tongue was swollen and sore. When she answered the phone with "hello" she noticed a thickness in her speech.

"Mary Jo? Darla. How do you feel?"

"I'm too numb to tell. Like I was stinking drunk last night."

"You said you only had one beer."

"I know. That's all I had. I think it poisoned me."

"I didn't know where you were. Rose said you never got there and I've been calling your number all day. Where were you?"

"I've been here, asleep. I didn't hear the phone, I guess."

"Well, are you going to be all right?"

"Sure. If I haven't died yet, I'll make it. Do you suppose someone slipped something into my beer?"

"You're kidding . . . well, it's possible. You were involved in some trouble with L.C.'s crowd. Remember?"

"Uh-huh."

"Maybe you should call Rose to let her know you're okay. I might have scared her. She probably tried to call you too."

"Okay, Darla, I will. Thank you for taking care of me. I'll talk to you later."

Mary Jo decided the best course of treatment would be liquids only, for the rest of the day. Two aspirin and a quart of ice-cold tomato juice. Before she showered she called Rose. She had quite a tale to tell, but it would wait until she got over there.

She spent the rest of the afternoon and early evening with Rose and Barb. There wasn't enough distance, yet, between her nightmare experience and now that she could laugh about it, but she did tell about it with gusto. Later that evening she telephoned Ann.

Ann said she had been waiting all day to hear from Mary Jo. She was disturbed when Darla told her how sick Mary Jo was at the club, but she didn't know where she lived and didn't even have her telephone number. Darla must have called her from work. They agreed to go out the next night and Ann would explain why she couldn't see Mary Jo Saturday night.

Before she left for Ann's Monday evening, Mary Jo told Jimmy she might be late getting home and to be sure to have his clothes ready for the trip to Arkansas the next morning. They were going to pick up her mother and Richard.

After dinner on Monday, Mary Jo picked up Ann and they went to dance for a short time and then returned to Ann's. Mary Jo was still hurt by Ann's Saturday-night spurning, but she waited for Ann to broach the subject.

"Neila and I had planned to go out to dinner that night, even before I met you, Mary Jo. I know it sounds kind of foolish, but this was our farewell dinner, so to speak. I had forgotten about it until she called me that morning. I had promised and I couldn't back down. She was in the bathroom, when you came to the door. If you came in and saw her there, it might have been hard to explain. Especially since I was going out with her that evening. Nothing has changed. We are still going our separate ways, only that dinner and talk just marked the official end. I couldn't hurt her by saying no, not that final time. Do you understand what it meant?"

"Sure, Ann. I understand. I just wish you could have told me before I got there and all." Mary Jo had more reservations about the incident than she let on. It didn't sit well with her, this hold that Neila seemed to have over Ann. How many more times would Neila be around? Had she truly given up Ann? Mary Jo wasn't used to any competition, especially the sort Neila represented. She and Ann had lived together, loved one another for years. And they were high-school friends. They had entered the gay world together. It was a lasting bond. Mary Jo wasn't positive they could remain the kind of close friends they were, without sexual involvement. She was jealous of this woman's lingering place in Ann's affections. Of course she would cope with it and not show Ann how she felt, but it was a nagging sensation.

Mary Jo spent the night at Ann's. They remained downstairs on the sofa instead of going to the bedroom. She suspected that Ann was having difficulty adjusting to the breakup with Neila and wasn't ready to welcome someone else into the bed they had shared for five years. Mary Jo surmised this was a natural phase that would soon pass. Also, it showed that Ann had a deep respect for the person she lived with and couldn't lightly fling away the years of built-up memories.

At 6:15 the next morning, Mary Jo dragged herself off to pick up Jimmy and drove to Arkansas.

* * *

Mary Jo was in the midst of a new existence. "I couldn't leave the name and number of a club where I would be, because it was in my mind, always, that someone would find out. For three and a half months I was living two different existences. I was living with my mother and two sons and going to college, full time. That was one life. When I left the house to meet Ann, I lived another life that my family and friends at work knew nothing about. The other nurses knew me as a mother, a nurse, a daughter living at home and a college student. Whenever my social life came up I would give the names of men I had gone with when I was first divorced. When some nurse would question me about my dating I would say, 'In fact, I just went out with So-and-So last night.' Yet, it was not with any of these men I was going with; it was Ann. At this point 'she' became 'he' and names of clubs were not identified. In the heterosexual world you could give names of clubs freely. In the realm of the homosexual life you couldn't give names of places for fear that someone would pick up on it and know that they were gay clubs. It was hard to live that way, very hard. I never had to lie before and this was what I was forced to do. It was a world, and until you were there, you didn't know how hard it was to live in. I became a different person. I was much more quiet in the dual life. In the period of a month I went from an outgoing, lively, talkative person to someone who put up barricades to almost everyone at work, for fear they would find out.

"The one out I had was college. I was midway through my degree program and I could say the college severely hampered my social life. Most everyone understood this and they wouldn't press me so much about who I was going with or whether or not I was serious, or would remarry. At home, Rose and Barbara were my out, my alibi. The only stipulation was that whenever I used them as an excuse to be away from home, I would have to let them know in advance. And I would never use them unless, indeed, they would be at home so my family could reach me in an emergency. I did spend time with my family; the boys got to see me and talk with me every day. Jimmy, of course, as a teenager, was always on the go and didn't rely on me for emotional support and love the way Richard did. When I got home from work, at around 3:45 I would spend time with the boys. Mother would prepare dinner and we would be together until shortly before seven when I would go to school. After class I would go to Ann's for thirty to forty-five minutes and then return home, except on the weekends. Richard was always in bed by nine, so he didn't miss any of my time in the evening, and Jimmy was occupied with TV or his stereo by then anyway. At this point I think Mother was beginning to suspect, but she didn't want a firm answer. Didn't want to know the truth. At one point during these three months she did come right out and ask me if I was seeing Lisa. I was truthfully able to say no. I saw her at class but never went out with her or spent any time with her after or before class. That seemed to hold Mother's questions. She couldn't quite figure out what else to ask."

* * *

During the three months of her dual life, there were times when Mary Jo would plan weekend activities with Ann and some mutual friends. Usually this occurred when the boys were spending the weekend with their father.

Mary Jo's brother, James David, had a camper that would sleep four people. The weekend of August 8, she borrowed it and after a minor hassle getting it hitched to her car, she, Ann, Rose and Barb headed for sprawling Lake Dallas for an overnight camp-out.

That evening, they built a fire and held a cookout. Darla dropped by and they sat around the campfire and sang songs and talked until late in the morning. "It was nice and peaceful," Mary Jo remembered, "very relaxing to be on the water, with the outdoor smells and sounds. It was a wonderful trip. Ann and

I got to know each other better, away from all the pressures, in a free environment."

It was during this period that the range of their dates broadened. Ann, in particular, loved unusual food. Mary Jo, until then, wasn't very adventurous with her palate. They dined at some of Dallas' specialty restaurants: Brennan's, Ports o' Call, Royal Tokyo, Chablis, Mario's, Peking Palace. Ann and Mary Jo went to musicals, live theater, parks, museums, antique shops, curio shops. More than amusement, these dates involved a sharing and exploration of tastes and interests, a foundation for a deepening interest in each other.

The last of August, Ann held a big fete at her house and invited some thirty people. One of her friends prepared an authentic Mexican dinner. This was the time Mary Jo would make her debut with all of Ann's friends. The party was a tremendous success. Mary Jo was quickly accepted and she enjoyed meeting the diverse ethnic, racial and social-economic people that Ann counted among her friends. Mary Jo was from a culturally sheltered background and had never mixed socially with anyone that wasn't a traditional WASP.

After the last guests left, Darla, Ann and Mary Jo straightened up minimally and went upstairs. Someone knocked at the door and Darla went down. In a moment she was at Ann's bedroom door. "It's Neila. She wants Ann to come downstairs." Mary Jo gestured toward herself—meaning I'll go down.

Neila was leaning against the wall in the foyer, "skunk" drunk. Mary Jo told her that Ann was ready for bed and if she wanted to see her she could return tomorrow. Neila looked annoyed but grunted a good night and left. Mary Jo knew that Neila still had a key, but at least she had felt enough of an outsider to knock on the door. She went back upstairs. Darla greeted her on the landing and said she was going out. Ann asked her why; it was late. Darla didn't answer.

"Neila will be back," Mary Jo explained.

"No, she won't, she'll go home," Ann countered.

Mary Jo knew otherwise. She didn't undress for bed, but sat on the edge and talked with Ann. In about twenty minutes music started playing from the stereo downstairs. "You Lay So Easy on My Mind."

"What's that?" Ann asked.

"It's Neila. I told you she would be back." This time she had used her key. In less than thirty seconds the door to the bedroom was flung open, the knob pinged against the wall. Neila stepped in, leaned against the doorframe and said, "Hi there, what are y'all doing?"

Mary Jo thought to herself, *What should I do? How am I going to reason with this girl?*

Neila was just staring.

"Well, we were sort of thinking about going to bed. What are you doing?"

"Oh, nothing, Mary Jo. I just thought I would come over."

Mary Jo got off the bed and moved to the foot of the bed between Ann's side and Neila. Neila watched her with a cold, appraising look. Then she took a step sideways, restoring eye contact with Ann. "I want you to come with me."

Mary Jo didn't know what to do. She didn't want to cause a worse scene. Neila was overstepping her bounds. She was living with someone else and knew that Ann and Mary Jo were seriously going together. Yet, there she stood . . . making demands on Ann. Mary Jo looked at Ann's face for a clue. Seeing what she thought was an indication in Ann's eyes that she would do what Neila wanted, Mary Jo stepped directly in front of Neila. "Ann is not going anywhere tonight with anyone."

"Who says?" Neila was belligerent.

"I say." Mary Jo raised her voice. "Tomorrow, if you want to talk with Ann, that's between you and Ann. But it's late and no one is in any condition to do any talking. So, I'm going to ask you to leave."

"What? Who says?" Neila was weaving.

"I do. In fact, step out into the hall." Mary Jo walked toward Neila, forcing her to back into the hall. Mary Jo closed the bedroom door as she went out. "Neila, I don't want any trouble with you, but if you are here for trouble, I'll oblige you." Mary Jo hesitated, fully expecting to be pushed down the steps. Neila didn't tense. She glanced at Mary Jo with a sour pout on her lips.

"I don't know what has happened between you and Ann," Mary Jo said. "You seem like an awful nice person, Neila. But I'm with Ann now. If you want to talk with her tomorrow, that's between you two. You're not going to do any talking tonight and I'm going to ask you to leave this house, now."

"I don't want any trouble with you, Mary Jo. I like you."

"That's fine, Neila. I like you too."

"Okay, I'll leave." They walked down the stairs. Neila went out the back door.

* * *

The next day, Mary Jo called her mother and asked her to get Richard ready, she was taking him on a picnic with some friends. Ann fixed a basket full of food. Mary Jo picked up Richard and they met Ann, Judie Ann, Rose, Barbara and Darla at White Rock Lake.

Richard and Judie Ann hit it off at once, despite two years' difference in age. Richard was as gregarious a little boy as you could meet. He had a warm, affectionate nature, an unquenchable curiosity and a natural politeness that endeared him to every adult he met. The most compelling thing about him was a deep, husky voice, out of place in his boyish frame. His light brown hair was in a "Prince Valiant" cut and he wore wire-framed glasses. Richard was still at the giggly age. He laughed as readily as he talked. If he liked someone, he would catch him off guard, and give him a spontaneous hug. A free and loving child.

About the same time of the picnic, Jimmy met Ann. Ann was twelve years older than Jimmy, but near enough to his generation to relate quite well. They both loved sports and rock music. Ann was more than just a friend of his mother's. He could talk to her, "kid to kid," if you will, about the unique world of a teenager. Ann's ideas about raising children were aeons away from Mary Jo's. Her liberalism didn't escape Jimmy's notice. Ann was attractive for another, slightly more material reason; she had an authentic, official-size billiard table in her game room. That skyrocketed her charm to a teen-ager.

~ 60 ~

Ann, Judie Ann, Mary Jo, Richard and Jimmy were doing things together for several weeks before Ann was introduced to Mrs. Davidson. Their meeting was uneventful. Ann was ostensibly helping Mary Jo in one of her courses, accounting. She would invite Ann over, they would work on accounting problems, and then Ann would retire to the living room, where she talked with Mrs. Davidson.

Mary Jo was happy to note the evenings when Ann tutored her had become mini-social occasions at Mrs. Davidson's. "Mamma would offer tea, beer, Coke, what have you, but she soon learned what a Coke fiend Ann was. Mamma obviously liked Ann. She would always be sure there were plenty of Cokes on hand. I was glad that Ann would at least be able to get to talk with Mamma, and Mamma would know something about her."

On August 28, Mary Jo arrived at Ann's immediately after dinner. They were planning an evening of cards with Ann's great-aunt Kizzie. Mary Jo told Ann she had something to give her. They went up to the bedroom. "I guess it was some sort of bond, presenting her with the ring." The ring was yellow gold. Two interlocking hearts, with a diamond in the center of each heart.

Mary Jo was pleased that Ann accepted the ring; the meaning of the gift was clear. Commitment. "I'll never take it off, it's beautiful." Ann always wore the ring.

As rhapsodic as the giving of the ring had been, it was September 25 when Mary Jo and Ann made what they refer to as the "final commitment." They had been out with friends and returned to Ann's early in the evening.

At a very tender moment Ann said, "I wish that we were married."

Mary Jo held her. "Today we are."

"Do you mean it?"

"I do."

Mary Jo and Ann cried a little. A happy cry, a sentimental cry. It was a complete union, forever. It was the same as if they had a legal right to marry and make a life for themselves and their kids.

The placidity of the days following the "final commitment" ended brusquely the first Wednesday of October. Mary Jo was entangled with her textbooks and notes, hedging against an anticipated surprise exam at college. Jimmy haltingly entered the study. He walked over to his mother's desk and stood, waiting for her to recognize his presence. Mary Jo looked up.

"I have a question to ask you," Jimmy began.

"That's fine with me." Mary Jo smiled. "What's the question?"

"Are you a lesbian?"

Mary Jo looked straight at her son. "Do you want me to answer that question?"

"I want you to answer."

"Yes, I am a lesbian." Mary Jo sensed her son was relieved he got a straight, truthful answer. "Do you want to talk about it?"

"I would like to, yes."

"What made you ask me about it, Jimmy?"

"Well, I sorta overheard a few things between you and Grandma. Also, I found a book over at Ann's house. It was a book on homosexual people."

Mary Jo knew that, in order for Jimmy to have found the book he was referring to, he had to go through the shelves in Ann's study. She also realized if that had been the sole basis for his inquiry, she could have avoided telling him. Obviously he had heard discussions, on more than one occasion, between herself and her mother. He knew Ann and was perceptive enough to tune in on the emotional flow. He had put it all together, mulled it over, and couldn't keep it locked away any longer.

It wasn't within Mary Jo's frame of reference to weigh the potential danger of admitting her lesbianism to her fifteen-year-old son. She never lied to the boys. There wasn't an iota of distrust between them. She had done all she could, asking him if he really wanted to know the answer. That gave him an out. He could have walked away. But Jimmy had come this far, obtained his mother's admission; it was out, a topic for detailed discussion.

"How could you love Ann, her being a woman?"

"It's like loving anybody. I can love you. I can love Richard. I can love your grandma. I can love Ann. I can love Ann like I loved your father, but for me the love I have for Ann is much more meaningful. I'm happier with Ann."

The conversation was elaborate, rambling along for over three hours. During the talk, what used to be called a "heart-to-heart," Mary Jo broached the possibility of her moving in with Ann at some future time. She assured Jimmy that, if and when the move would transpire, it would be after a long get-acquainted period. She wanted her sons to get to know Ann and Judie Ann and be happy with the idea. By the way he acted and talked, Mary Jo felt Jimmy looked forward to the venture. She cautioned him about the need to keep it a secret until the planning was complete and an opportune time could be found to tell her mother.

At the end of the talk Mary Jo and Jimmy stood up. "Well, what do you think?" she asked.

"It makes no difference. You're my mamma and I love you anyway." Mary Jo thought she saw moisture in the corners of Jimmy's eyes. They stood there for a moment, hugging one another.

Mary Jo wondered if she had done the correct thing, explained it the best way, so that Jimmy would understand, accept it. "It wasn't like I had knocked him over with news he didn't know. It was like I had relieved the tension that had developed between us because he could not cross over until he knew this one thing about me. In other words, Jimmy and I had always been open. I relied a lot on Jimmy. We discussed things before I ever made any real decisions on buying things or making important changes. We talked things over, like the car I bought or my attending college.

"I was surprised at the fact that Jimmy was real enthusiastic about moving. In the beginning, especially when I was going out with men and would show any kind of interest, Jimmy was always jealous. He didn't want anybody to take his mother away from him, I don't know whether or not he considered another woman a threat or not. Also, we had been living with Grandma

~ 63 ~

for a length of time and perhaps he saw the move as something new, something exciting. In any event, I was pleased at the way he took the whole thing."

Whatever Jimmy's feelings about his mother's homosexuality, he internalized it and gingerly adopted his mother's friends. Ann proposed to Jimmy that if he would do some yard work at her house she would take him shopping for some new clothes as payment. Mary Jo had always bought the boys fine quality clothing, but her tastes were too bland for her teen-age son. He had been hankering after "mod" fashions for some time. Ann was the vehicle for his getting silky, brightly patterned shirts with large collars, tight pants with bell-bottomed, flared legs.

Jimmy played in the high-school band and after one football game Mary Jo and Ann picked him up, along with his date, and took them to a pizza restaurant in Mesquite, where a gathering was scheduled. Several hours later Ann and Mary Jo returned and drove several couples home from the party.

After the annual Texas-Oklahoma University football game in the Cotton Bowl, Jimmy and his girl friend met Mary Jo and Ann and another lesbian couple and they spent the day at the Texas State Fair. "It wasn't because we invited them or encouraged them in any way," Mary Jo insisted. "It wasn't because of money, he had asked me for more money and I gave it to him. Jimmy knew Ann and I were homosexuals and the couple with us were friends of his, also. He wasn't embarrassed to have his girl friend around us."

* * *

November 1, Mary Jo's mother met her daughter at the door when she came home from classes. After a brief hello, Mrs. Davidson followed her daughter into the bedroom. "I think it's about time you and I had a talk." Mrs. Davidson's mouth was firm, her eyes flat and serious.

Mary Jo laid her books and jacket across the bed and sat down. Her manner was matter-of-fact. "If you want to."

"Well, I think we ought to get this out in the open now. You're a lesbian, aren't you?"

Mary Jo remained nonchalant. "Why do you ask that?"

"Well, I know you are. I found a book that you hid in your room."

"A book? What are you talking about?" Mary Jo had forgotten about the book, *Lesbian-Woman*, by Del Martin and Phyllis Lyon. She had borrowed it from Ann several months ago, but with the extra reading material required that semester at college, she hadn't progressed beyond the title page. To avoid anyone seeing the book, she had slid it under her mattress. Mrs. Davidson had chosen that morning to turn the mattress while changing the linen.

"And you underlined things in the book."

"I haven't ever read the book. The person who owns the book is probably the one who underlined everything. By the way, since you've gone to so much trouble and read it, how is it?"

"Now, Mary Jo, don't get smart with me. I'm serious. It's time we talked about this. I mean it."

Mary Jo reluctantly agreed. She and her mother had been moving inexorably toward this conversation for some months. It was a petty embarrassment that it was prompted by some book, secreted away under her mattress. There were hardly ideal circumstances in such matters. It could have been worse. One woman she knew was caught flagrante delicto by her parents. That wasn't conducive to rational discussion; not that her situation was going to be any less traumatizing. With some thought to symbolism, Mary Jo suggested they move out of the bedroom and into the living room.

Mrs. Davidson was already up-tight. "I just cannot see . . . I just cannot see how you think that you love another woman like you would a man."

"Mamma, it's not for you to really see, it's for me to know. And I know."

"It's impossible. I think I know who it is. I think I know."

Mary Jo flashed a tolerant half smile at her mother. *She must still be hung up on Lisa. That's who she thinks it is—Lisa.*

Mrs. Davidson ignored Mary Jo's amusement. "I just don't think . . . I just don't . . . how could you actually love a woman?"

"I do, Mother. I love another woman very much, very much. In fact to the point that I would want to live the rest of my life with this person."

"It's impossible, Mary Jo. You've got to be out of your mind."

"I'm not out of my mind. I know exactly what I am doing. I'm thirty-seven years old and I know what I'm doing."

"You don't know what you're doing. You don't." Mrs. Davidson was flushed and desperate-looking. Mary Jo didn't want to frustrate her mother needlessly. Perhaps if she had to meet Ann face to face with the knowledge that they were lovers, she would more readily understand. At least she couldn't deny it was true. Two women, sitting before her proclaiming their love for each other. A dose of rational emotive therapy.

"Mother, the person that I go with . . . I could call her right now and she would come right over and we could talk."

"I think that's a good idea." Mrs. Davidson's response was a little too combative for Mary Jo. As she got up to go to the phone, her mother added an afterthought, "I think all three of us should sit down and talk this out."

Did her mother really entertain the idea that she could talk her daughter out of lesbianism, the way an itinerant faith healer and his shills part people from their money? Or would she revert to threats about the children's welfare? That wouldn't work either. Mary Jo was comfortable with the way Jimmy was responding to her sexuality. There wasn't any weapon her mother could use to divert her now.

"Ann, Mother has found that book on lesbianism that you loaned me and she knows that I'm gay. She wants to talk about it, with the person I go with, and I told her you would be willing to come right over here."

"Mary Jo . . . you know I'll come over if you really think I should."

"Probably this is the time, yes. Hurry."

It was thirty minutes before Ann arrived. During the wait, Mary Jo and Mrs. Davidson observed a verbal truce. Ann knocked at the door. Mary Jo got up and let her in. She was dressed in pastel slacks, newly pressed, a flowered blouse, earrings and carefully made up. Mary Jo was surprised that Ann would take the time, that late at night, to get fixed up. They smiled and walked into the living room.

Mrs. Davidson looked mildly surprised. "Hi, Ann."

"Mamma . . . Ann is the person I go with, the person I love."

Mrs. Davidson began her spiel all over again, this time with more restraint. "I just don't know how you two claim you love each other, you both being women." The way she stressed certain words, the change in inflection, suggested that Mrs. Davidson was less condemning. She didn't approve of homosexuality in any manifestation; it hurt her deeply that her daughter was a lesbian. She would try her best to convince Mary Jo to reject her sexuality for the sake of everyone involved. Something, however, had been modified the instant she saw Ann walk into her house. Mrs. Davidson had difficulty ostracizing Mary Jo and Ann. Their chosen life style was repugnant to her, in the abstract, but an attempt at understanding was blossoming. She loved her daughter and could never be made to reject her as a person. Experience had taught her the pitfalls of ignoring reality. Ann's arrival and identification as Mary Jo's lover certainly constituted a reality.

Ann was never more sincere and eloquent in explaining the day-to-day life of a lesbian couple. Most of Mrs. Davidson's questions centered around social activities, the home, roles and responsibilities. She didn't ask details about sex, except to observe she didn't understand how two women could make love.

At one point, some forty-five minutes after Ann arrived, she excused herself and went to the bathroom. Mrs. Davidson leaned over toward Mary Jo. "You didn't tell me it was Ann you were going with."

"Mamma, you never asked me for a name. Well, what do you think of Ann?"

"She's nice, she seems like a good person."

Nothing was said about Mary Jo moving in with Ann. Mary Jo knew that would have to evolve gradually. To spring that on her mother the same night she admitted her lesbianism to her mother would cause an emotional overload.

Soon after that evening, Ann and Judie Ann stayed over at

Mrs. Davidson's two nights a week. They would be there waiting when Mary Jo got in from school. "Judie Ann would sleep on the sofa in the living room. The boys and Mamma had their own rooms. In a way it began to be a better relationship for us. That way, Ann would be there and she and Jimmy could talk.

"Richard loved Ann. I swear, when she would come over, Richard would be spoiled rotten. They would play catch in the yard, hour after hour. They would be in there watching TV and Ann would hold Richard and stroke his hair. He had found a new friend. One night when Ann left, Richard wouldn't go to bed. He cried and cried, calling for Ann . . . Ann . . . Ann."

✿　✿　✿

Thanksgiving ranked higher than just a holiday at the Davidsons'. Every member of the family returned to home base to renew family citizenship. Preparations were extensive and involved all the women.

Mary Jo was working with her mother one afternoon, a few days before the big day, when Carol Jean called. The family communications system had been superb, as usual, and everyone was fully aware of Mary Jo's new lover and how far the situation had progressed. Carol Jean had taken it the hardest. She loved Mary Jo dearly and would do anything for her, but she didn't understand. In time, Carol Jean would accept Mary Jo and Ann living together simply because she respected Mary Jo's right to live as she wished.

Carol Jean wanted to know about the final arrangements for the Thanksgiving dinner and who would be there. Mrs. Davidson obliged with the list. ". . . there will be Ann and Judie Ann . . ."

Mary Jo was delighted: "I was standing there in the dining room and I couldn't believe it. Mother had not even indicated to me that she was going to invite Ann to the family gathering. My father and his wife (my stepmother), my sister and her husband and my brother and his family were all going to be there. I just didn't think that Mother would want Ann over there with all the family. I was surprised. I didn't know what to say, really, but I was very happy that Mother had included Ann in a family gathering."

Thanksgiving Day, Ann spent midday with her father, Moughon Davis, and her great-aunt Kizzie. She took them to dinner at a restaurant. It was around three when Ann and Judie Ann arrived at the Davidson home. Mary Jo introduced them to everyone, getting some predictable reactions from the males. "Ann was blond, very attractive. She was thin and shapely, big breasted and all. Nobody had to tell me what was going through the minds of the men. How in the hell can all of that go to waste on ol' Mary Jo? I knew these men. I knew their values. Shapely women really get them. And here, right in front of them, was a nice young woman. I don't think they could really believe it. Judie Ann looked very cute. I think they both made a good impression on my family.

"We watched some football games on TV and during the half times we got out and passed the football to the kids.

"My stepmother, Jean, wanted to know what school Judie Ann attended. Since she goes to a special private school, they discussed that at some length. They wanted to know where Ann worked and what her position was. Where she lived, what type of a house it was. They all talked about her family. Ann told them about her dad and his service station.

"Everyone was sorry to hear that Ann's mother had died less than two years ago.

"Carol Jean had little to say to Ann for the longest time, there was a barrier between them. Later, they discovered they had gone to the same high school, at the same time, but didn't know each other. Ann had once watched a terrible fight between ten Mexican girls and three Anglo girls that took place behind the Dallas Lighthouse for the Blind. By the oddest coincidence, Carol Jean was one of the girls that got beaten up that day. My God, they talked about that fight like it was the highlight of their lives. At least this opened the door for conversation between them. In no time they were recalling different classmates and commenting on where they were and what they were doing today.

~ 69 ~

"The family left one by one and Ann and I stayed to help Mother clean up. The day had gone well. Everyone was fully aware that Ann and I were homosexuals, and while I won't say it didn't matter, they could at least relax around us and enjoy themselves."

The Thanksgiving festival elevated Mary Jo's spirits. She had never been an overly spontaneous or adventurous person, but suddenly she suggested to Ann they pack some clothes and take off for a few days. Where? Did that matter? East. A different city, just a few hours away. "We threw some things together and drove to Shreveport, Louisiana, and checked into the Sheraton Hotel in the far east part of town. I called Mamma to let her know where I was staying. I talked with my sister Pat, who was visiting for the weekend. She couldn't get up for Thanksgiving Day, so she was visiting then. I talked with Jimmy, who had met a girl that summer while on a camping trip. She lived in Shreveport and he wanted me to call her and say hello and tell her he would write."

Saturday, Mary Jo and Ann decided to visit the Civil War battlegrounds at Vicksburg, Mississippi. This proved a comedy of errors. They overslept and were further delayed by Ann insisting on a gargantuan breakfast. Mary Jo misjudged the travel time to Vicksburg, it wasn't just "down the road," as she had told Ann. By the time they reached the historic sites, it was dark.

Perseverance, bordering on pigheadedness, was a hallmark of Mary Jo's personality. Ann may have been suffering from her periodic stomach trouble; it may have been as dark as pitch, but they were going to see the landmarks and statues of the battleground. At every site, Mary Jo maneuvered the car so the headlights gave maximum illumination to the scene. Then, she took a flashlight, climbed guardrails, tripped over wire cordons, and read inscriptions. She had to yell them back to Ann, who was almost doubled over with stomach cramps and was ensconced in the car. "Over here, we have a figure of a fighting man from the Ohio volunteers." Mary Jo didn't abbreviate any of the inscriptions, she read them fully, savoring the dry facts.

Ann humored her madness. When they finally got back to

Shreveport, they checked into another hotel, at the west end of town. After a recuperative dinner they went to a gay club. The trip, spur of the moment though it was, proved vital for Mary Jo. She and Ann were alone without phones, family obligations or stress. It was then Mary Jo decided to make the move to Ann's house the week after Christmas.

* * *

Ann and Mary Jo did their Christmas shopping together. Ann was irrepressible and bought as much for Mary Jo's children as she did for Judie Ann.

Christmas Eve, Mary Jo, Jimmy, Richard and Mrs. Davidson went over to Ann's. Presents were opened. Mary Jo knew that Ann loved leather; the leather fad was at its height that winter. Ann had found a beautiful leather and suede jacket and put a few dollars down for the store to hold it on layaway. She had planned to finish paying for it when she got her income tax refund in the spring.

Mary Jo paid off the jacket for Ann's gift. When they exchanged packages Christmas Eve, the boxes were quite similar in size. When Ann opened hers she was thrilled, but laughed silently, waiting for Mary Jo to unfasten the wrapping on her gift. There was the same leather and suede jacket.

The boys got a bountiful wardrobe of new clothes, coats, shirts, pants, socks, shoes.

As the evening wore on, Mrs. Davidson and the kids went upstairs to sleep. Mary Jo decided she couldn't make it any longer and joined them. Jimmy and Ann stayed in the living room and talked, mostly about the move, which was set for the day after Christmas.

Ann tried to awaken Mary Jo several hours later. They had to go over to Mrs. Davidson's and put up the toys that Santa Claus had brought Richard. Mary Jo wouldn't budge from the bed. Ann had already learned that once Mary Jo got to sleep nothing short of catastrophe, and a noisy one at that, could rouse her. While she was awake, Mary Jo was energy personified. At a certain point, however, she crumpled, like nickel-cadmium batteries that run down in an instant, without warning. If she happened to be sitting up talking, she closed her eyes and nodded her head. Instantaneous sleep in the middle of a sentence.

Ann and Jimmy had to play Santa, setting the toys around the tree at Mrs. Davidson's.

Mary Jo worked Christmas Day, but Ann drove Mrs. Davidson and the boys down to the hospital for lunch. The hospital furnished turkey dinner for all employees and their families during the holidays.

Later in the day, Doug picked up Richard for the week visitation allowed at Christmas time.

The move to Ann's was more than a logistic headache. Mary Jo knew it was a trying time for her mother. "I could see the hurt in Mother's eyes, because she had had the two boys with her for over three and a half years. She had been used to a full house and doing things for the boys and me. Here, all of a sudden, she was going to be alone."

Figuring out the bedroom situation wasn't difficult. Darla had moved a few months ago. Jimmy got the largest upstairs bedroom. Richard moved into Judie Ann's old bedroom, and the study was easily converted into a bedroom for Judie Ann. Ann and Mary Jo had their bedroom downstairs in what was once the recreation room. There was an adjoining bathroom.

The problem was what to do with the massive billiard table. The kids loved it, especially Jimmy. If they wanted to keep it, there was only one place to put it, in the living room. The billiard table and the player piano covered the entire living room except for a few side chairs at the bar. This made for an unorthodox arrangement, but the children lobbied so hard Mary Jo and Ann agreed. Mary Jo left her living-room furniture at Mrs. Davidson's. The entire move took about ten days.

Mary Jo and Ann anticipated some adjustment problems. They weren't quite prepared for the conflicts that arose the week they merged their households. Every one of the children had a room, a preserve of privacy. Everyone had a television, radio and individual toys. There was an eight-by-five-foot storage room upstairs that harbored the overflow from the rooms.

The first point of contention was the upstairs bath. Judie Ann wasn't used to having people around, especially two active boys. Mary Jo's boys didn't meet her standards of fastidiousness. "When Richard first went to the toilet and left urine drops on the toilet seat I thought she was going to come unglued," Mary Jo recalled. "She came running down the stairs yelling, 'I can't use that bathroom with the boys.' From that point on, Judie shared our bathroom. I guess the boys were a little careless."

Mary Jo knew that Ann was an immaculate housekeeper and wasn't accustomed to having active boys in the house. "Here you had two boys who had a mother and grandmother to pick up behind them, do everything for them." Mary Jo didn't fabricate excuses for her sons, but she did accept the blame for fostering their slovenly attitude. "Even when they went to school they were used to someone laying out their clothes for them. They didn't have any sense of responsibility for taking care of themselves. They left their beds unmade, left clothes and toys where they dropped them. Judie Ann had duties around the house. She cleaned up her own room, folded up her clothes, fixed her lunch for school, helped with the backyard, dusted, and helped wash windows. One of the hardest things for the boys to discover was that they had to have similar responsibilities, if the house was going to stay straight, sanitary and livable. When I lived with Doug, I didn't work or attend college, so all my time was spent as a housekeeper. Now things were different. Even at Mother's the boys did as they pleased, with no consequences. Mother cleaned after them. Now, there was no one to act as their maid. I got home by 3:45, but four nights a week I attended classes at college. Ann, as a supervisor at the bank, often didn't get through until six. We had quite a struggle to do the shopping and cook dinner. One of the most irritating aspects of trying to get the boys into a measure of helping around the house was the simple act of having them rinse off their plates from the dinner table and put them in the dishwasher. They just refused to do it, saying it was girl's work.

"There were a few times we all sat down at the dining-room table for a family conference. I said, 'Look, this is going to cease.

I go to school at night after working eight hours a day. Ann works a minimum of ten hours a day. Ann and I are going to see that everyone carries his own load around here. We will see that food is on the table. We'll do the washing. But it's your responsibilities to pick up your clothes off the floor and make sure all dirty clothes are put into the wash. You'll have to fold up your own clothes and put them away in your chest of drawers. When we eat, no one leaves the table without rinsing his own plate and putting it in the dishwasher. Ann and I will do the pots and pans. You're completely responsible for your own rooms. I'll check the rooms, giving you one day's notice.'

"I think it went pretty well for a while. There were times when they made mistakes, like getting up late and leaving the beds unmade. Then they would make them when they got home from school.

"Ann and I handled our bedroom and the downstairs bathroom. The boys were the only ones who used the upstairs bathroom, so they had to clean it. Ann and I rotated with the vacuuming. We taught them to make their own lunches. Jimmy just had a fit when he had to prepare his own lunch. He just couldn't understand why he had to fix his own lunch. He was fifteen and for fifteen years his mother had done everything for him, and when I couldn't there was another woman, his grandmother, who waited on him."

Children, by their very nature, have a propensity for pressing, probing parameters established by adults. Mary Jo and Ann learned early in the game that the children would test them endlessly about the household duties. Ann, an emerging parental figure for the boys, had the most trouble maintaining discipline the nights when Mary Jo was away at college. "Ann came to me and said, 'I love you and I love those boys more than anything, but it's getting to me. Nobody wants to do anything. It's all right when you're around, they know you're in control but when you're gone I could just pull my hair out. They ignore me and that constant bickering back and forth. "Jimmy's not doing this or that, so I'm not going to . . . how come we have to do everything? . . . I'm not going to do it unless she has to do it. Richard didn't do this, why should I have to? He has an excuse," etc.'"

Mary Jo continued, "I was midway through college; a B-plus grade average, on the dean's honor list, twice. I was spending all my spare time correcting the mess. The minute I walked into the house Ann confronted me. They just wouldn't mind her. She forced me to go after them. So we had another sit-down at the dining-room table.

"I told them as firmly as I could without yelling that I was going to school and there were certain things I had to do to finish my degree. Ann was in the midst of a department reorganization at her job and we just couldn't be there every minute of the day. They had to shape up. 'Oh yes, Mother, we understand,' Richard said. 'Oh yes, Mary Jo, we will do better,' Judie promised. Then Ann smiled and she was happy for about fifteen minutes until I walked out the door."

What type of foods to buy and in what quantity were the next major obstacles. Ann and Judie Ann were used to natural foods; fresh vegetables grown organically, large quantities of fruits, nuts, little or no bleached flour and a minimum of processed sugar. They took natural vitamin supplements and liquid protein.

Mary Jo and the boys were meat and potato people. Fried foods were their favorites. They ate candy and the full spectrum of packaged junk foods like potato chips, Crinkles, corn chips, pies and cakes. They were used to formal meals—a lunch and dinner—but in between those specific times they ate a copious selection of canned meatballs, spaghetti, miniature pizzas, dips, blends and candy.

A trip to the grocery store was a royal battle for Mary Jo and Ann. Mary Jo was adamant: "I told Ann, 'Look, you buy your food the way you want it and I'll buy what my boys will eat. Now, they are used to these things and I'm going to buy it for them.'

"As time went on, we compromised. Actually, we couldn't afford to keep up separate grocery shopping. We cut down on the kids being allowed two or three big packages of potato chips and cans of bean dip. The meals were starting to be well balanced. If anyone wanted to snack, they ate leftovers from dinner. Eventually we even ate fruit, something that was nearly alien to the boys. Vegetables were a daily fight, but soon even Richard was eating things he'd refused for years. Jimmy still made a bowl of popcorn every night to finish up his day. And later, when he worked after school he would buy the same old junk food and store it up in his room. It was just too late to reform his eating habits to any degree. But we did eliminate something my mother had started. Sometimes she would cook a second meal for Jimmy around 9:30 in the evening. Hamburgers and french fries or what have you. Or if Richard didn't like something at dinner, she would start over and cook something else. We never did that."

The Risher-Foreman household had a strict rule about privacy. No one was to enter any bedroom without first knocking and being asked in. Unlike the household duties rift, the privacy rule was upheld.

Richard's exuberance led him to violate the privacy rule at first, especially when he wanted to see Judie Ann and couldn't wait for the formalities of knocking. Judie's protestations didn't reform him, he needed an object lesson. One day she turned the tables and charged into Richard's room while he was still in his underwear. "See, Richard, that's what it's like when you run into my room." Little Rich got hung up on Judie's intrusion. He talked about it for a month. After that, he didn't breach the privacy rule again.

Judie Ann was an only child and had never lived around other children before. "Even though she had lots of friends," Mary Jo stated. "She was kind of sheltered. When two kids get to playing and things don't go right, one or the other might start swinging. Richard being the boy he was . . . one day things got out of hand and he started swinging. By the time we got to them they were on the floor trying to beat each other to a pulp. This was Judie Ann's first big fight. Ann was really upset and said she was going to take Judie to a boxing instructor. Ann had always taught Judie to walk away from fights. It irritated her that Judie was getting the raw end of the deal. Finally Judie Ann learned to defend herself. Threaten, if not punch. This calmed Richard down a lot. In fact, Judie would take up for Richard when he got involved in scraps outside. Judie Ann was fearless, she would take on kids twice her size. This impressed Richard. They got very protective of each other."

An expense bank account was opened at Lakewood Bank. Mary Jo and Ann deposited their checks in the Foreman-Risher account and paid all the bills from it. Mary Jo maintained a separate checking account to pay her personal debts. The house payment was split. With three children, there wasn't anything left to put in savings.

In February 1974, Jimmy was heading home from school on his motorcycle when he hit an oil slick on the wet pavement. The cycle slid out of control and tipped over. Jimmy's knee was badly skinned. Mary Jo walked in from work and found Jimmy talking on the phone to Ann. He thought he had broken his leg. Mary Jo drove him to Baylor Hospital's emergency room. "Jimmy's leg was X-rayed. He got the wound cleaned and bandaged. They gave him a shot for pain. The leg wasn't broken, but soon it stiffened. Jimmy was unable to do anything for a while. The kids had to wait on him hand and foot."

The motorcycle caused more problems later in the month. It wouldn't run, the engine compression was down. The repair shop demanded $175 to fix it. Mary Jo put up the money. When they picked up the cycle, Jimmy didn't get two blocks away from the shop when another malfunction struck. Mary Jo had a rousing argument with the repair shop. They wanted an additional $75 to cure the new trouble. By the time the cycle was operational again, almost half the purchase price had been invested in keeping it running.

On March 4, Ann's father, Moughon Davis, fell and fractured his arm. It was a multiple fracture and Mr. Davis's arm, brittle with age, was slow to heal. He was off his feet for over a month.

The two mechanics who rented garage space at Mr. Davis's service station in north Dallas tried to keep the station operating. The press of their mechanic business, however, left the gasoline sales to drift. When Mary Jo got off from work at the hospital, she would drive to the station and tend the pumps until the seven-o'clock closing time. Ann would help on the weekends. Jimmy, who was working part time, would help when he could arrange it. Somehow the station survived through the series of impromptu gas jockeys, and Mr. Davis returned to work without being bankrupt.

* * *

After school was out for the summer, at the end of May, Ann was offered a discount Colorado vacation through the credit union where she had borrowed money. Judie Ann was already off to spend three weeks with her father, and Richard had been asking to spend some time with his grandma. After a spring of disasters, Mr. Davis's accident, Jimmy's motorcycle mishap, and the time-consuming exams at college, Mary Jo and Ann were ready for some time together.

They drove to Denver, stayed two days, and then motored to Estes Park. Ann had never been to a mountain terrain and she made Mary Jo stop constantly so they could walk among the pines and toss pebbles in the streams. At Central City, they panned for gold. At every stop they collected an assortment of rocks. "Coming back home we had so many rocks that we had to put some of the larger ones up front under Ann's feet so the back of the car wouldn't drag bottom. The car was packed to capacity. Seven or eight suitcases, everything we owned, naturally. Clothes hung across a bar in the back seat. Rocks piled everywhere. If we had hit anything it would have been over. Killed by a rock slide, in our own car."

They visited Colorado Springs. "We stayed in a cabin, out and away from the town," Mary Jo recalled. "We went to the Garden of the Gods on horseback. The guide told us the story of some other Texans who had made the trip. When they saw the hill where there were three crosses, one of the Texans asked if that was really where the crucifixion happened. The Garden was extraordinarily peaceful. We watched an outdoor wedding at the site of the three crosses."

Late in the afternoon Mary Jo tried her hand at fishing in the lake. "It was quite mild weather, so Ann and I just had on some light windbreakers. I had caught two trout, both small. Then it started getting cold. It clouded up and the wind picked up. It started snowing. It was June, summertime, and it started snowing like hell. It was an inch thick in minutes. I didn't want to give up. I wanted to catch some decent-sized fish. Ann brought me hot coffee from the lodge and swore at me to give it up and come inside. 'Not until I catch some more,' I yelled. My luck was finished. After a few more minutes in that cold, I gave up. We went to our cabin and started a fire in the fireplace. I'll never get over the snowstorm in June."

The next day Mary Jo and Ann joined a tour group and took the ride up Pikes Peak. "Ann and I rode in the front seat with the limo driver. It was great. You don't realize until you're on your way up how scary it can be. We were just a foot or so from the edge. Ann was having stomach problems and the ride up made it worse. By the time we got to the top, she was sick and had to spend the entire time in the restroom. I took some pictures and walked around. It started to snow again, so we started back down the mountain."

The final agenda item on the Colorado trip was a visit to the Air Force Academy. Mary Jo and Ann were impressed with the sprawling architecture, especially with the church, where rehearsals were underway for the weddings that were scheduled for the next day, after graduation. A minor dispute marred the academy tour. Ann was petulant over the educational goals of the academy. "The thing that upset me was all the grand ceremony, religious and otherwise. Everything was clothed in religion, yet they were training these men to go out and kill. It made me sick. It was a beautiful place, but why didn't they have such a place to teach love, understanding, to create doctors and scientists? Where the graduates would go out to help and save people rather than go out and kill them. It was such a waste and it was deeply depressing."

Mary Jo and Ann drove back to Garland on Friday. Exhausted by the long drive and an hour of unloading the car, they decided to turn in early that night.

Neila called to ask them over to her new house. In the months after she and Ann had broken up, Neila had become close friends with Ann and Mary Jo. Neila was living with Joline Arthur, a divorced mother of three children. Joline was attending college, working toward her elementary education degree. She planned to teach school.

Ann and Mary Jo declined Neila's invitation, but Jimmy decided he would stop over and see their house. He took his girl friend with him. Later that night Jimmy awakened Mary Jo and Ann and asked if he could go on a vacation with Neila and Joline. They had told him they would pay for everything but his meals. Mary Jo didn't approve. "Jimmy was supposed to look for a job the following week. He was already getting rebellious, wouldn't sit still and wouldn't listen to his grandmother when she told him what to do. We felt like he was getting restless, this was one of his problems. We talked with Jimmy and we all agreed he should find a summer job. Now he wanted to back down. I knew he liked Neila and Joline very much. He visited them often and had dinner with them a number of times. Neila even loaned him her Charger [auto] for a big banquet he attended at school. Jimmy was enthusiastic about the vacation and I was sorry he couldn't go, but it was in his best interest to get the job, assume some responsibility and pay off some of his debts."

Within a few weeks Jimmy got a job.

At the end of the school year, Garland school officials held a conference with Mary Jo about Richard. They had discovered that Richard was a full semester behind in reading, he lacked the basic reading skills of a first grader. The Mesquite school had said nothing about any possible problem. Garland school officials didn't pinpoint the source of Richard's problem, but decided to place him in a resource class the following year.

Mary Jo had Richard's eyes tested. He needed glasses. Even with the glasses Mary Jo was not satisfied, so she arranged for her son to undergo testing and evaluation at the Dallas County Crippled Children's Society. On June 18 she accompanied Richard to the society for his testing. The results were to be ready in a week, but the psychologist promised a preliminary report by phone the next day. It turned out that Richard was just a slow reader. He didn't have any impairment.

The evening of June 18, however, Mary Jo had no knowledge of how serious Richard's problems might be. Ann, the boys and Judie Ann and she had dinner at a restaurant a few blocks from the house. "Jimmy had been after me for some time to buy him a car. While we were eating he got to harping on it again. I told him I had just been to see what the problem was with Richard and I didn't know if we would have to send him to a special school or what. We got home and Jimmy started up again. I told him I didn't know how much money I would have to spend. I had given him everything he had ever asked for and it was time I had to do something for Richard. To me Richard's special schooling needs seemed a lot more important than a damn car.

"Jimmy said he would just move in with his father, in that event. Jimmy had never used that type of threat before and it just hit me the wrong way. Without really thinking I told him to pack his bags and call his father. I said, 'You're going out there with him.' Jimmy looked at me sort of puzzled. I said, 'Go on.' He called his daddy. I talked with Doug and told him Jimmy was after me for an automobile and there was no way I could get it for him. I said at the present time I had Richard to think about. I told Doug that Jimmy could stay out there with him however long he wanted to. Maybe he could get his head together.

"Jimmy didn't pack his good stuff. He left his stereo and motorcycle. He left his best clothes. Anyway, Jimmy left. Oh, I'll tell you my heart went with him. I cried, I was so upset. It was just like part of me was leaving and I didn't know how long he would be gone. Just before he left I told him, 'There will always be a place for you. If you come back, you come back under my terms. This business about an automobile has got to stop.'

"Ann didn't go back to work that evening. I called my mother and sister Carol. Mamma said I shouldn't worry about it; if an automobile was that important to him let his daddy buy him the car. Carol Jean told me it was my fault. She said when Doug and

I were married we gave Jimmy everything he wanted and when we split up I continued to give him everything. That's all he thought about was give me, give me. I told Carol about what I said to Jimmy as he left. She said she hoped I would keep that promise. She warned me that I was going to ruin Jimmy, giving him everything. That's all he expected out of everybody.

"The next morning at seven the phone rang. The voice said, 'Happy birthday, Mamma.' Jimmy's voice was cracking. I had a bad night, but I thought to myself, He probably had a worse night.

"Doug picked up Richard for visitation Saturday. He dropped off Jimmy. On Sunday when he brought Richard back, he picked up Jimmy."

✳ ✳ ✳

By the end of June, Mary Jo had the final report on Richard. She was greatly relieved. Still, his reading problem had to be dealt with immediately. She and Ann contacted a reading tutor, Sandra Keyes. Ann would take Richard over to Miss Keyes before she went to work. Richard received the special tutoring for thirty minutes, three days a week.

A group of Mary Jo's friends, Johnnie, Maria, Rose and Barbara, organized a Fourth-of-July picnic at Lake Ray Hubbard. Mary Jo called Jimmy and invited him. He accepted.

At this juncture, Mary Jo believed it was just a matter of time before Jimmy would reconsider and return home. He was supersensitive and was probably more hurt at her attitude than the issue of the car. Both of them had lost their tempers and couldn't find the method of talking it out and resolving the tension. Mary Jo allowed Jimmy time to reflect and think it through. The picnic invitation, she hoped, would be an overture to a reconciliation.

Mary Jo picked up Jimmy at Doug's house in Lewisville. When he got in the car he told her that he wasn't going back to live with his father and stepmother, Delaine. Jimmy didn't elaborate on what prompted his sudden decision.

The picnic was a smash. "Lord, we spent a fortune on fireworks for the kids," Mary Jo recalled. "Thirty or forty dollars. I shot off the fireworks with the kids. It was crazy. They loved it."

* * *

In August, Jimmy secured a new job at the restaurant where Mrs. Davidson was a waitress. He primarily had to rely on his mechanically faulty motorcycle for transportation, although on weekends he would borrow Ann's car. School was about to open for the year and Jimmy would, as he did during the previous term, live at his grandmother's house three days a week.

Jimmy was intent on getting a car. Mary Jo knew her son was trying to save money for the down payment. "Jimmy wouldn't pay his credit card bills or his long-distance telephone calls. He was still paying back the money I loaned him for motorcycle repairs. He was screaming that he didn't have to pay the gasoline charges. He said we were draining him of his money that he was going to use for a down payment on a car. All we were doing was showing him the responsibility of paying his debts."

During this time Jimmy and Mrs. Davidson had discussions about the state of personal relations at Mary Jo's home. Mrs. Davidson was a sympathetic listener; after all, Jimmy was very dear to her. She reinforced his apprehensions, at one point telling him there was no way his mother and Ann would purchase him a car.

The more Jimmy articulated his alienation from his mother, the more negative Mrs. Davidson's attitudes became. Her dormant reservations about Mary Jo's lesbianism revived as she became increasingly disturbed at Jimmy's despair.

Mary Jo detected her mother's negativism and stayed away from her to escape the consequences.

On Sunday, September 15, Jimmy called Mary Jo and informed her that he had a car. His father had bought it for him. Mary Jo said she wanted to see the car and asked when Jimmy was coming home. He didn't answer.

Ann was aware that a car would take all of Jimmy's money to maintain. She wanted to know when and how he would pay her the money he owed. Jimmy said he didn't have the money and wasn't going to pay it back. It was at this point that Ann lost her temper and said, "Oh fuck."

Two weeks later, September 29, Mary Jo received a call at work. Her mother wanted to discuss something important with her when she got off. That was the night of the ghastly argument when Mrs. Davidson insisted that Mary Jo give up the children and sign them over to the custody of Doug. If she didn't, her mother warned, Doug was poised, ready with a court suit.

* * *

On October 16, 1974, it was late afternoon and Mary Jo was waiting for Ann to arrive home from work. She had been home for over an hour, changed into the clothes she planned to wear to class that night, and started a roast for dinner. The children were playing at a neighbor's house until dinnertime.

Mary Jo thought she heard Ann drive into the carport. She laid down some cooking utensils and started toward the patio door, when someone knocked vigorously on the front door.

She went to the door, glanced through the peephole. "There stood a nice-looking black-haired guy." Mary Jo opened the door.

"Sheriff's Department. Are you Mary Jo Risher?"

"Yes, I am."

"This is for you." He handed Mary Jo a seven-page document, folded over twice and loosely held together with a rubber band. She managed to see, "Citation. In the interest of James Douglas Risher, Richard Calvin Risher, Children," before the deputy spoke.

"Don't I know you from somewhere?" he asked.

Mary Jo was distracted. She gazed at the man as if he had suddenly materialized on her front step. He caught her blank stare.

"I mean, I have seen you a number of times."

"I don't know . . ." Mary Jo showed a glimmer of recognition. "A lot of police officers attend the college where I go. Abilene Christian, Metro Center."

"Sure, I go there myself."

~ 84 ~

Despite herself she was drawn into a conversation. She knew the citation was from Doug. *It was about the boys. How much did it contain? What did he want?* She wasn't about to stand there and read it in front of this deputy. Mary Jo heard Ann rummaging around the kitchen. In a moment she would be behind her at the door. Now was the time to wrap up the conversation with the deputy.

"Look, I've got a roast in, it might burn."

"Sure. Nice to see you again. Good luck."

He looked concerned, she thought. *He was bound to know what was in the citation.* She turned around. Before she could close the door, Ann was standing there, smiling. "What have you got there, Mary Jo?"

"A little ol' citation from Doug—delivered by a deputy sheriff."

That was it. They had been waiting seventeen days. Fantasizing. Now it was there. Real. Seven legal-sized pages of reality. Ann grabbed at the first page. Mary Jo read the second. Ann snatched that. Back and forth. Read. Grab. Read. They were in a race to absorb it.

The citation alleged that they would run away with the children.

"I may have threatened such a thing to Mother. I've never really considered it."

CITATION: ". . . living in a homosexual relationship as man and wife."

ANN: "I had heard that before, from Mrs. Davidson, and I expected it to be there."

MARY JO: "I was shocked, seeing it in black and white. They were accusing us of being homosexual. We knew both of us were women and so there could be no husband and wife relationship."

CITATION: "Children should be removed from immoral and undesirable environment."

ANN: "That was crazy."

MARY JO: "I didn't think a thing in the world about that, because I knew what kind of situation Jimmy and Richard both had lived in with me. They were being cared for and loved. I had no qualms about morality."

CITATION: "Jimmy became so incensed at the relationship, he ran away."

MARY JO: "Since Jimmy knew about it since October 1973, before I ever moved in with Ann, he hadn't been incensed and run away from home."

ANN: "And he lived with us for nine months. If he ran away when he found out, he was slow getting out the door."

CITATION: "Wild parties, on numerous occasions, in the presence of the children, inviting other homosexuals to these gatherings, for the purpose of openly engaging in homosexual activities."

MARY JO: ". . . Of the whole citation, this made me the maddest."

ANN: "We tried to figure out what in the hell they were talking about since we hadn't had more than four people in this house at any time. We didn't have any parties in this house since Mary Jo moved in, period. No one ever saw any homosexual activity, period."

CITATION: "Have left children unattended."

ANN: "Not true."

MARY JO: "Ann and I went out once a month, a few times. There were a few times when Jimmy would stay home with the kids."

CITATION: ". . . Young child left alone and unfed."

MARY JO: "No, that's not true. Doug came once to pick up Richard. We were both at work. Richard was left at a neighbor's, along with his clothes for the visit. Richard walked around front from the rear of the neighbor's house, where he had been playing with an older child. As for being unfed. He may have missed his lunch for some reason that one day."

CITATION: "House left unattended for weeks at a time. Children had to do work normally done by mother."

ANN: "I knew what that was. Jimmy was asked to wash dishes twice during the time he was here. He also had to clean up his room."

MARY JO: "To me that was stupid."

CITATION: ". . . Viciously beat the children for several years . . . Once bitten the children, requiring medical attention."

ANN: "We could never figure out where that came from."

MARY JO: "I have never beaten Richard or Jimmy. Bitten them? That was insane."

CITATION: ". . . Beats Richard for calling his father or expressing other interest in his father."

MARY JO: "I never limited Richard from calling his father. If anything I encouraged him to spend time with his father."

CITATION: "Customarily uses abusive and vulgar language in front of the children."

ANN: "We used damn and hell. The one time I blew up and used the word fuck around Jimmy it caused his mother and grandmother not to speak to me for days."

MARY JO: "Words, as Ann said, would slip at times. I really wasn't a cussing person until I learned that my family was siding with Doug to take away the boys."

Mary Jo and Ann reread the citation several times. Certain sections were laughable, others were vitiating hyperbole. "The thing that disturbed me most was to say we had wild parties and homosexual activities in front of the children." Mary Jo cringed, just recalling this. "That literally turned my stomach. To think that a person could stoop to such vulgarity. Me—a mother, who had always thought of her children first. It actually made me sick to think that Doug or his lawyer could suggest things like that."

* * *

The remainder of the evening was spent hashing out the potential problems in getting a lawyer to take the case. There weren't legions of liberal lawyers in Dallas waiting to joust with a homophobic society. Ann and Mary Jo pondered the cost, where they could raise the money to support competent attorneys. They studiously avoided one topic: "If Ann remained with me, there was a possibility that her ex-husband would join Doug and jointly they would seek custody of all the kids."

There was a second issue. A public trial would expose them to publicity. Everyone would know they were gay. The hospital staff, neighbors, the boys' schools—everyone. This ramification, though recognized, was skirted over. It couldn't be avoided. To keep Richard meant to fight. To fight meant the open courtroom. If the media picked up on it, so be it. Publicity was part of the equation, but not central to how they would proceed.

The next day, Mary Jo used her morning break to call a well-known Dallas attorney. She knew she would have to give him the general background of the case and what the citation contained. This prompted her to use a pay phone on another floor, to forestall any interruption.

The lawyer listened, interrupting occasionally with condescending comments. At the conclusion of Mary Jo's thorough briefing he paused a second, drew a deep breath, grunted it out, and dryly observed, "Well, it's going to be a pretty hard fight, but you have one thing in your favor."

"What's that?" Mary Jo asked enthusiastically.

"Your children are boys."

"Why should that make any difference?"

"Well . . . if your child had been a girl it would be a lot harder to fight in a courtroom and win."

"Why?" Mary Jo was slow in getting the drift.

"Well, Mrs. Risher," the lawyer's air was concupiscent, "you're a lesbian and the woman you live with is a lesbian. And a daughter grows up and gets to be a teen-ager and who knows, your daughter might look good to you or look good to the woman you are with."

That turned Mary Jo off completely. She didn't have the presence of mind to ask him if his teen-age daughter looked good to him, and he was projecting his own sexual phantasm onto her. She scratched him off the list. *He wouldn't be acceptable on any level. He wouldn't understand me, the person I'm with, the warm relationship we have with the children, if indeed, he thought at a later time my own daughter would have looked good to me. To me this was crazy thinking and shows how little he knew about gay people.*

As soon as Mary Jo hung up with the call, she reached Ann. Ann was incensed at the suggestive impertinence of the lawyer. She was still ranting, when she paused midsentence and said, "I think I've found a good lawyer, who is gay, attends meetings for gay rights. We talked, just before you called. This lawyer had handled a few child custody cases, involving homosexuals, was interested in our case, and told me to bring the checkbook when we come to the office. It's going to be expensive."

"What? Bring the checkbook?" Mary Jo was again struck by the crassness of some attorneys. *This one hadn't even seen us or heard about the details of the case. I wondered about the depth of understanding, even of a gay lawyer. Of course it was a difficult case, but money seemed to be the prime consideration.*

Again at noon she called Ann and told her to forget about the checkbook lawyer. They could do better. Mary Jo contacted Rose. Rose knew of a woman who had been involved in some controversial cases, while working for Dallas Legal Services. She would phone her, for Mary Jo, and see if she would be interested.

Before she left work, Mary Jo telephoned Rose. Yes, she had reached the lawyer. She was interested. Her name was Aglaia Mauzy. She was about to go into private practice with a fellow staff member at Legal Services, Frank Stenger. Mary Jo and Ann were to meet them at Frank's apartment that night.

Meeting at a stranger's apartment struck Mary Jo as a bit odd. All her dealings with attorneys had been during business hours, in their offices. Rose had said they were just preparing new offices; perhaps that was the reason. In any event, Rose had a great deal of confidence in Aglaia Mauzy's ability. And Rose's advice was always sound.

Mary Jo and Ann made a special effort that evening to be on time. They showered and dressed in their better clothes. It was part of our society's custom, a peculiar desire to win approval of those agents we hire to render us service. Both were nervous. This was the first time they would sit down with a total stranger and talk, in detail, about their life together.

Their tension was quickly allayed when they met Frank

Stenger. He was dressed informally and moved with a fluidity that reflected an inner tranquillity. Frank was just under six feet tall. Handsome. Curly black hair and flowing mustache. He spoke in a musical, gentle voice. He shook hands with both Mary Jo and Ann, looking them directly in the eye. His eyes were dusky, sagacious and kind.

Frank's apartment was an amalgam of functionalism and camp. Tent chairs, rock garden, a ten-speed bike propped against one wall.

It was obvious to Mary Jo that Frank Stenger lived as he pleased, to please himself. He wasn't overly concerned with convention and he wasn't defensive about how things appeared to other people. Mary Jo admired that quality, felt relaxed around it. She had spent most of her life in a tight, enclosing environment, where people were judged primarily on appearances. Her homes had been traditional, everything in its place, sterile and neutral. Her homes didn't reflect any originality, or even the inner personalities of the occupants. They were interchangeable with her friends'. Acceptable to everyone. Homogenized middle class.

Five years ago, Mary Jo was burdened with racial myopia. Blacks and browns were troublesome minorities, agitators, struggling for rights against her class, her race. Now, she not only knew ethnic minorities socially, she fully grasped the scope of the injustices and prejudices against them. She was a minority. A gay person. The shadow minority. Frank Stenger was of Mexican heritage. That pleased her. She assumed, and in Frank's case it was true, that he would be more sensitive to the plight of her minority group. Mary Jo and Ann were free in talking to Frank about lesbianism, their fears, what they thought was necessary to educate a court about their life style. Frank was the first male Mary Jo could talk with about her sexuality. That too was a good sign.

After forty-five minutes Aglaia Mauzy arrived. To be more precise, she slouched in, pulled down by a heavy attaché case and an expanding cardboard file. Aglaia habitually worked to the limits of exhaustion. Just when you expected her to fall out of her chair, she perked up with renewed zest. Her energy reserves were vast. Her movements and speech were measured, methodical, almost labored. When she talked it was as if each word had been pulled from her and was spoken because it was the last option left for communication. She could easily go through life without talking. Her energy was used for evaluation, synthesizing, reduction of chaos to logic and order. It was incidental that she must speak to communicate, a necessary afterthought, a by-product.

At thirty-eight she was an attractive woman, sensual. Long blond hair, liquid brown eyes, a patrician nose and a full mouth whose softness melted away any clear definition between her lips and the rest of her face. Her face was hard to focus on, the features flowed into the whole so subtly. She was pale. When you talked with her, she furrowed her forehead, calculating your choice of words. She listened so intently you found yourself stopping to make sure she hadn't drifted off into some reverie. She hadn't. When she finally was forced to answer you, it was done haltingly, with no adjectives or verbs to spare. She always controlled the conversation, its ebb and flow were at her tempo, the emotional level at her plateau. This projected amazing confidence and integrity. Aglaia would have made a gifted psychoanalyst.

Mary Jo and Ann were impressed with Aglaia and Frank. Their anticipated fees were reasonable. They wanted the case, viewed it as a challenge and planned to win. They were more than sympathetic, they understood.

* * *

A week before the temporary custody hearing Mary Jo decided it would be prudent to move her furniture out of her mother's house. "I didn't know what would happen at the temporary hearing. I might not be able to get my furniture later." She rented a truck. Joined by Ann, Rose, Barb, Neila and Joline, Mary Jo stripped her mother's house. A professional mover had to be employed to move the six-hundred-pound billiard table into storage. For the first time Mary Jo and Ann had a true living room in the town house.

The day before the temporary hearing Mary Jo and Ann met with Frank and Aglaia to go over strategy and determine if anyone else should be subpoenaed to testify, aside from Richard's tutor, the baby-sitter and two neighbors.

As the meeting ended, Aglaia, with dogged realism, advised Mary Jo and Ann to wear skirts or dresses and fluff up their hair. She wanted to nullify any possible stereotypical reaction to lesbians prompted by a certain mode of dress.

Mary Jo and Ann understood. They went out and bought some dresses, suitably frilly, for the court appearance.

On October 25, 1974, the temporary custody hearing was held in Domestic Relations Court Number 4. The matter to be resolved was whether or not Richard and Jimmy should be immediately removed from Mary Jo's care and placed in Doug's custody, pending the actual trial.

Frank and Aglaia prepared a motion to keep the issue of homosexuality out of the proceedings. The judge upheld the motion and limited questions and answers to all the other allegations contained within the citation. Without the homosexuality, the substance of the custody challenge was trifling.

Mary Jo was the only witness for her cause. The lawyers had decided they had sufficiently muted the other arguments against her during their cross-examination. Judge Oswin Chrisman apparently agreed. He ordered the car returned to Doug Risher. Jimmy was told to return to his mother's home. A court-appointed psychologist, Dr. Robert Gordon, was to evaluate the individuals involved and make a custody recommendation to the court. Also, a social worker was supposed to make an investigation.

The first round was a clear-cut win for Mary Jo. She was glad that Richard would remain with her, but concerned over the judge's order in regard to Jimmy. "How could I order Jimmy back into the house? I tried to call him at Mother's. He wouldn't discuss anything with me, saying he hated me because he lost his car. Within a few days Jimmy got his car back, claiming the judge had said it was all right. Frank asked me if I wanted to go back into court and force the car issue, since the judge hadn't modified his order in the slightest. Also, Frank said it was possible to get the Sheriff's Department to move Jimmy back to my house. But we agreed the best thing would be to let things cool down. I did ask Jimmy to come back, but he said no, not even the judge could tell him what to do. Both he and my mother made some reference to the fact that they would be able to 'get me' the next time. The homosexual issue wasn't allowed this time, but it would be at the trial.

"After the temporary hearing I took Jimmy's TV and stereo over to my mother's, as there wasn't any reason for him not to have them. Then, we just sort of started living our own life again. No trial date was set. It could be many months away."

❋   ❋   ❋

During the temporary custody hearing, Judie Ann was being evaluated by a child psychiatrist. Ann's ex-husband, Michael, was paying the costs and it was partially at his urging that the testing and interviews were taking place. Mike was following Mary Jo's lead. She was concerned that Judie wasn't living up to her potential in school.

Ann had placed Judie in a private school over a year ago. The school was considered one of the finest, most progressive in Dallas. Judie already had been tested by several psychologists. She was diagnosed dyslectic. Mary Jo hesitated in accepting this, especially after Richard was found only to be a "slow" reader. She thought that Judie Ann might just be in a similar situation and was using the private school as a crutch. Ann disagreed but was swayed when Mike offered to pay for the new round of tests.

As he said, Michael's motives were broader than his daughter's school problems. "She was having a lot of problems in school. I knew that she was in a special school and had been evaluated by several psychologists. She just didn't seem to be getting anywhere. I felt like her home situation was causing it. My offer to pay for a psychiatrist was a two-sided coin. One, to try and help

Judie Ann and two, to see if her home life was causing her problems.

"I was gearing up to pursue custody again. Through all this we revaluated ourselves. The doctor talked to all of us, myself, my wife Jan, Ann, Mary Jo and Judie Ann, over a long period of time. In the process Jan and I changed our feelings. I got a whole new insight into the situation. I hadn't realized before how dependent Judie was on her mother and how adjusted she was to her mother.

"Judie had certain basic learning disabilities. Basic dyslexia. It was through learning about this and her relationship with her mother that my whole outlook was changed. The doctor told us our acceptance of Ann was the most beneficial thing we could do for Judie."

Jan underwent a similar fundamental change. "I was prejudiced against Ann, purely because she was a homosexual. The psychiatrist started telling me about this. At first it made me angry. Judie and Ann had a good rapport and it would help Judie if we accepted Ann. It made me jealous because I wanted Judie for myself. I had to accept the jealousy and accept that Judie and her mother were good friends.

"What I had to do was say to Ann, in so many words: Cool it Ann, I don't dislike you anymore because of your life style. I want to be your friend. Don't be scared that we are going to try and take Judie Ann away from you. Ann was cool at first, apprehensive. It took time to prove we were on the level. After I broke the ice she told us about Mary Jo's custody fight."

When Ann visited the psychiatrist who was evaluating Judie Ann, she was determined to head off any trouble from her ex-husband. "I was worried that once Mike got wind of the custody case he might enter with Doug and we would have both fathers fighting us for their children. I told the doctor all about my relationship with Mary Jo and what we were going through, because I thought that Judie might be up-tight over the custody fight. She might be afraid that she too would be taken away. The doctor said it would destroy Judie to take her away from me. He said he already knew I was a lesbian, as he had learned it from

Mike. We discussed child raising and what we had done for the children. He told me that he had talked with Jan and Mike at length and informed them there was nothing harmful in Mary Jo's and my relationship. It was very important not to relate any of their doubts to Judie Ann or think about trying to take her away.

"It was a few days before Thanksgiving that we got enough guts to talk to Mike and Jan about the custody case, what Doug was trying to do. Mike was extremely upset. He said five years ago this might have been possible, but he couldn't believe it was going on today. We were greatly relieved at his attitude and obvious support. He and Jan had come a long way. We have been very close to them ever since that time."

Prior to Thanksgiving of 1974, appointments were made with the court-designated psychologist, Dr. Robert Gordon. Mary Jo was wary of this encounter. She was told by her attorneys that significant weight was usually attached to the opinions of court-appointed experts. Traditionally it was assumed that court-appointed experts were inherently neutral and impartial, where experts appearing for one side or the other in litigation were biased in favor of their clients. It occurred to Mary Jo that anyone could bring his particular bias and preconceptions to a psychological evaluation, no matter who paid the bill for services. She also wondered how long any judge would continue to utilize the services of an expert if his testimony were diametrically opposed to the values and opinions of the judge. Comfort in such relationships usually followed agreement. Her musings were rather immaterial, for she had no choice. She had been ordered by the court to see Dr. Gordon and she would have to take her chances that he would be able to render a fair decision on her fitness as a mother.

"After we were introduced he asked me to give him some idea of what he was supposed to do. I told him I understood that we would be talking with him and he was to make some kind of recommendation to the court. He wanted to know some idea of what it was all about. Why the judge had ordered us to visit him, what was the problem.

"I told him that since he was the court-appointed psychologist he would learn the details anyway. At that time I told him I was a lesbian and this was the reason my ex-husband was trying to take away the children. I asked him if he was prejudiced. He said he had only counseled with two homosexuals and they were women. He said their problems were just like everyone else's: money, friends, sex. He asked me the ages of the boys and how long I had been married.

"During this interview I found that his phone rang constantly and his secretary came into the room twice. I felt there was no form of privacy within this man's office.

"Dr. Gordon said he hoped at no time he would show any prejudice. And if he showed any, he would appreciate it if I would tell him.

"During our second visit we talked about my college, what Richard and I did together and the relationship that Jimmy and I had. He revealed to me that Jimmy didn't want to live with me or his father. He said it was all right for Jimmy to live with his grandmother. He felt like Jimmy and I would get back together at a later time."

Ann had one interview with Dr. Gordon. The questions he asked her were similar to the line of inquiry used with Mary Jo. Ann was disturbed by the close of the interview. "He asked me if it would destroy Mary Jo to have Richard removed from her. I said I felt like Mary Jo was a strong person, but it would be extremely detrimental, it would hurt her severely."

Ann shared Mary Jo's discomfort over the lack of privacy during the interview. "During the whole conversation he was writing notes on the manuscript of a book he was writing. His secretary was running in and out. He even showed me some of the book. He seemed real interested in letting me know about himself, too."

*   *   *

Thanksgiving of '74 was a sorrowful day for Mary Jo. This was the first time that a major holiday passed without any contact with her family. As a compensatory gesture Ann invited her father and great-aunt Kizzie to dinner and made sure Mary Jo was involved in the elaborate dinner preparations.

Everyone watched the Thanksgiving Day parades on television. After the meal, Judie Ann and Richard, irrepressible as usual, got out the paper rolls for the player piano. Sitting snugly together on the piano bench, they pumped the pedal, four tiny feet in unison. First, the theme from *Midnight Cowboy*, then "Strangers in the Night," a half-dozen other songs, several encores and mimicking bows from the duo, as if their artistry went beyond pedal power.

The excellence of the meal and the obvious pleasure that Ann's father and aunt got from the enthusiasm and glee of the children mellowed Mary Jo and she forgot her depression.

While Ann was driving her father and aunt home, Mike and Jan and their two children dropped in. The kids watched television while Mary Jo talked with Mike and Jan. Within five minutes Ann returned. She groped through her purse for cigarettes. "I'm out of cigarettes, would anyone like anything from the store?" Ann was about to start out the door again when Richard jumped up from the floor. "Can I go to the store for you?" She gave him the money and walked him to the patio door. "Richard, don't take your bicycle." Richard grinned at Ann. "I won't."

The store was four hundred yards from the house. A two-lane alley ran behind the carports. There was one street to cross at the bottom of a sloping hill. With the skip, gallop, and run gait of an eight-year-old boy, the round trip would take about fifteen minutes, unless the store were crowded.

During an animated conversation it was hard to keep track of time, but after twenty minutes Mary Jo glanced at her watch. Richard should be getting back, if he didn't stop to talk with someone. He often did.

Judie Ann answered a knock at the front door. From her position on the sofa Mary Jo saw Judie listening to someone. She was transfixed. *What in the world was wrong with that child?* Mary Jo thought. *She looked like she was in shock.* Mary Jo got up. A man peered in. "Are you Mrs. Risher?" Before Mary Jo could answer, the phone rang. Ann walked to the phone; Mary Jo stepped to the door. Ann shouted, "It's the woman from the store." The man at the door was ashen. "Mrs. Risher . . . now don't get excited, but your son has been hit. He and his bike were hit by a car."

Mary Jo shook her head side to side. *He was mistaken,* she thought. *Richard didn't ride his bike. But how would this man know my name?* Ann heard confirming news over the phone. "Mary Jo, Richard was hit in front of the store." Mary Jo reeled. "Oh, my God." She looked around the room and ran out the front door. Jan pursued. Mary Jo had circled the row of town houses, running full speed, and was headed down the alley when she noticed Jan alongside her. *I was running as fast as I could and here was little ol' Jan, in high heels, keeping up with me and yakking away:* "Stay calm, Mary Jo. No matter what we see down there, stay calm."

Mary Jo and Jan crested the small hill and started down the incline to the store. Mary Jo stumbled, caught herself, and saw the flashing red lights for the first time. *People all around. Flashing lights. There was the ambulance. Damn that son-of-a-bitch, he said there was no reason to get excited. My God, what was I going to see? All of a sudden I was in a daze. I was moving in slow motion. There was Richard. He was lying on his stomach, his little arms were stretched out. He was lying on the left side of his head. He was in the ditch. I walked up. He had some blood on the back of his head. I walked around in front of him. He looked up and whispered, "Hi, Mamma." He was able to talk.*

Mary Jo cried and moaned. A policeman and ambulance attendant tried to mollify her. It was no use. Mike and Ann drove up with the three kids in the car. Mike stayed in the car with Judie Ann, who was hysterical. Ann pushed her way through the throng of people saying, "That's my roommate's son." The attendants loaded Richard's stretcher into the ambulance. They helped Mary Jo in. One of the men turned to Ann: "The boy's doing fine, you take care of his mother."

The distance to Garland Memorial Hospital was five miles. A half-dozen minutes elapsed. Mary Jo asked over and over,

"When are we going to get there, when are we going to get there?" In Mike's trailing car Judie Ann was sobbing and praying, "Oh, please, let him be all right, please."

At the hospital, Richard was lying motionless on an examining table, waiting for his doctor to arrive. Mary Jo hovered nearby. Ann bent over and spoke to Richard. He whispered: "I'm sorry . . . my glasses, I've lost my glasses. Ann, you know what you've always told us about walking the bicycles across the street. I didn't walk the bicycle, I rode it. I looked out the corner of my eye and I saw this car coming. I tried to outrun it, Ann, but I couldn't do it."

The investigating police officer asked Mary Jo and Ann out into the hall. He told them what the driver of the car and his passenger said about the accident. Richard came out of the alley and they didn't have time to stop. Richard ran into the front fender of the car. It flipped him over the hood, onto the windshield. The back of his head hit the windshield. It gave. Then he was thrown off the car, into the ditch.

The driver would not be charged in connection with the accident. Both he and the passenger came to the hospital. They wanted to see how Richard was doing and to apologize to his mother. While Mary Jo talked with the young men, Judie Ann slipped into the examining room and asked Richard how it felt to be hit by a car.

Richard was taken to X-ray. When he returned he asked Mary Jo if he could move now. "I guess you can, Richard. Why do you ask me that?" "Well, when I had the accident this guy jumped out of the car and yelled, 'Don't move, don't move a muscle.' I haven't moved a muscle since, but my neck is getting stiff." Mary Jo and the doctor chuckled. *Lord, he was lying so still and I thought it was because of his injuries.*

The doctor sewed up Richard's head wound. He had a mild concussion. Mary Jo was doubly concerned. The accident was bad enough, but she was pacing the floor mumbling, "They're going to get him now."

When she got back home she called her attorneys and the court-appointed psychologist. They assured her that "accidents happen to everyone and not to worry about it." Still she did. If Richard's coming home after being pushed into a creek rated a mention in a custody citation as a reason he should be taken away from her, think what impact this accident would have.

Richard, with a patch of shaven head, a dozen stitches, and a concussion, was the center of neighborhood attention that night. He sat at the dining-room table while his friends and neighbors paraded in front of him. The kids walked by one at a time—reverently. Some wanted to see his head wound. All were properly awed and likely were warned afterward by a stentorian parent that it could happen to them, or worse, if they rode their bikes across roads without looking. Mary Jo slept with Richard that night to watch him for any possible complications.

It was a week later when Jimmy called, wanting to know about the accident business; why he wasn't told. Mary Jo said she didn't have to tell him everything that went on at her house.

The next day Doug telephoned about the accident. "He wanted to know why I hadn't called him," Mary Jo recollected. "I said for one thing I wasn't bothered and worried about him at a time like that. And for another thing, Richard never asked me to call him. I had my hands full. If it had been something serious I would have called Doug, definitely. We got him to the hospital, he was X-rayed and stitched up. It wasn't serious." Mary Jo admonished Doug about criticizing Richard for his bike riding. "I remembered when Jimmy had his motorcycle wreck. After he talked with his father about it, he was crying. I told Doug I didn't want that repeated with Richard. He said something and I closed the conversation by telling him to go fuck a tree. He said, 'What did you say?' I said, 'Fuck a tree, that's all you're good for.'

"I think I shocked Doug. I had never talked to him that way before. It just welled up in me. It was awful, pitiful, that I could not completely be thinking of the welfare of Richard alone. I had to be thinking what his father would do to me for something that I couldn't help."

Richard's head healed rapidly. A week after the accident the stitches were removed. Mary Jo got lightheaded watching. "I had to sit down I got so queasy. I had never been that way before, even in an operating room. But watching the stitches coming out, I lost my composure. When your own child is involved, you're no longer a professional person, you are completely a parent."

The first week of December, Mary Jo was contacted by Jimmy's high school. The school nurse said he was running a fever and complained about soreness in his neck glands. On the phone with his mother, Jimmy had already pinpointed the problem. "There are quite a few kids over here that have this mononucleosis. The teacher seems to think that's what I have." Mary Jo cautioned her son, "Let's not diagnose the case before you see the doctor and have blood tests. Go ahead and leave school and let me call the doctor's office and see if you can go right in."

Mary Jo arranged for Jimmy to see Dr. Roy Wagner as soon as he got to the office. A blood sample was taken and sent to a laboratory for analysis. Dr. Wagner told Jimmy to go to bed, stay there, and be sure and eat well. Mary Jo went over to her mother's during her days off and fixed lunch for Jimmy. "Jimmy was a little cold toward me, but he did appreciate it." The report, which didn't arrive until the following week, was negative. Jimmy, well fed and rested, didn't have mononucleosis.

Jimmy's health problem was the first occasion in months when Mary Jo could be around and talk with her son. She was clinging to the theory that the schism could be bridged with talk and a closer proximity. "At that time I felt like my mother was a reinforcement for Jimmy against me. I wanted to have him away from that so that he and I could see each other on a day-to-day basis and try to work our differences out. This was the first time since Jimmy was born that he and I had any major conflict. Now, we didn't have any way to communicate. He was at one house and I was at another. He had my mother around him all the time. There was always that barrier."

Several weeks before Christmas, Ann and Mary Jo spent the evening at Rose's and got home at two in the morning. They were getting ready for bed when someone quietly knocked at the front door. Jimmy was standing there with two young women and a young man. Jimmy's shoes and pant legs were thick with dried mud.

"Hi, Jimmy. What in the world are you doing out this time of night?" Mary Jo queried.

"My car broke down. Something's wrong with the transmission."

"Whereabouts?"

"Oh, just down the road, down Northwest Highway."

"Come on in." Mary Jo opened the door and gestured.

Jimmy hesitated. "Well, really, Mamma, I've got to get these kids home." Ann volunteered, "My car's been wrecked, but you can take my father's car and take your friends home."

While Ann got the keys, Mary Jo told Jimmy that she was off the next day and she would help him, at least take a look at the car. Jimmy, relieved, gladly accepted the offer and returned early in the morning, still dressed in the mud-encrusted outfit of the night before.

Ann was in the car, waiting for Mary Jo to lock the house, when Jimmy confessed that the situation was a little more complicated than he had let on last night. "Mother's going to have a heart attack, but it's really stuck in some mud in the middle of a field."

They were driving on Northwest Highway when Jimmy motioned Mary Jo off the road, over the curb, across a pasture to the top of a substantial hill. At the bottom of the steep slope, Mary Jo spotted her son's car, positioned defiantly like a huge black bug sunning itself in the field. To avoid risking another car, they walked down the hill. "The closer I got the clearer I could see that his car's tires had disappeared into the mud. The car was resting flush against the ground."

The tactic of forcing boards under the tires failed. They were unable to get any lift. Ann reluctantly drove her father's car down the hill and tried fruitlessly to match up the bumpers for a push. Jimmy's car was too low in the mud. Next they tried pulling the car out, using a ski rope that instantly snapped under the stress. Ann went back to the house for a chain and returned with

Mary Jo's full-sized car. The chain, sturdy enough for any tow-
ing, was impossible to manipulate properly, so they devised a
way to match the bumpers to push Jimmy's car out. Mary Jo
climbed on the hood of her car as Ann eased it into position.
After inching Jimmy's car forward, Mary Jo transferred to
Jimmy's trunk to provide better traction for his rear wheels. The
bumpers locked, the engines roared, and the cars rocked and
swayed violently. Mary Jo, spread-eagled on the trunk of
Jimmy's car, yelled, "Whooooo. Whooooo." Jimmy cried, "Ride
'em, Mamma!" After precarious moments of pitching, the fu-
riously spinning wheels took hold. Jimmy's car reared up from
its burial hole spewing pounds of mud in its wake. It lurched
forward. Mary Jo clung to the trunk, breathlessly praying her
metal mount wouldn't buck her. Jimmy and Ann were wild with
laughter. One car was out, another replaced it in the hole. Jimmy
and Mary Jo climbed on the hood and Ann guided Mary Jo's car
back and forth, then up and out of the mire. Later, hoarse with
laughter, Jimmy confided in Ann, "There's not many people that
would have come and got me out of this jam. I knew you would.
I want to tell you how much I appreciate it."

With an opaque logic, Mary Jo viewed the December encounters with Jimmy as significant. "Sometimes I wonder if I didn't
do the wrong thing by not having Jimmy brought back to my
home after the temporary custody hearing. Maybe he was crying
out to me, wanting to show me that he needed me and would accept me telling him what to do. He didn't need to come to me,
there were others around he could have turned to."

To help along this scanty reconciliation, Mary Jo decided to
buy Jimmy his high-school class ring as a Christmas present. She
knew he had made a ten-dollar deposit on the ring; the problem
was locating the jeweler. She and Ann made a number of calls to
disgruntled jewelers who checked their records for a James
Risher. Finally, they located the store. The jeweler, who seemed
delighted at the hint of any intrigue, suggested they leave a note
in the file indicating that the ring had been misplaced by the en-
graver. This safeguard would throw Jimmy off if he happened to
claim the ring before Christmas. Ann and Mary Jo escorted the

children to various stores where they picked out some shirts, socks and belt for their absent brother.

Mary Jo was delighted when Jimmy accepted her invitation to Christmas dinner, and was further surprised when he brought presents for everyone. He was shocked to get the ring, but unrelenting in his refusal to return home. Mary Jo pressed him to return in a private conversation. It was no use.

The potentially ideal day, critically marred by Mary Jo's argument with her son, was capped with a maudlin phone call from Mary Jo's father. Mr. Davidson was spiritless. "He was crying like a baby because the family was celebrating without me. My father was very sentimental about Christmas. For the past thirty some years he would gather everyone around him and say, 'We are all together for another Christmas, that's what my father used to say.' He never explained, but he related our happiness to his own childhood. It was very depressing to hear him cry about our family not being together that year."

Late in the day Mary Jo, Ann, Richard and Judie Ann went over to Mrs. Davidson's with armfuls of presents. This was the first time Mary Jo had seen her mother since the hearing in October. It was as if she was waiting for some type of overture from her daughter. Mrs. Davidson immediately began to telephone daily. This was her custom in the past. She invited Ann and Mary Jo to dinner regularly and started making clothes for the children.

The several months of estrangement had radically altered her behavior toward her daughter; she was warm, attentive and calm. Her views on homosexuality were modified: "I guess everybody to his own. I was never ashamed of Mary Jo. I'd have gone anywhere with her. I thought she really needed my help instead of hatred."

Mrs. Davidson had begun to read magazine and newspaper stories about homosexuals. In the past she had avoided such reading. "It just didn't interest me, so I'd skip over it. Now, whenever I spotted any headline about gays, I would clip the article. Also, you'd be surprised the number of TV and radio shows where homosexuality is discussed. I wouldn't miss a one. I have

to say I learned quite a bit and this played a big role in my accepting Mary Jo."

*   *   *

On January 15, 1975, Mary Jo entered Gaston Episcopal Hospital for minor elective surgery. "I was more worried about
being exposed as a homosexual at the hospital than the surgery
itself," Mary Jo recalled. "As a nurse I had seen hundreds of patients enter surgery, with their wives or husbands at their side,
holding hands, hugging. Ann was there of course, but she had to
act like some disinterested friend. We didn't dare show any
affection. She couldn't reassure me the way I needed for fear
someone I worked with would pick up on it.

"Just her being there in the waiting room caused us some
problems. She told everyone that my mother was working and
couldn't get off.

"I was especially worried that I would say something, call her
name, in the recovery room. Now I know that wouldn't mean a
thing, but at the time it was a real nightmare. That's how fearful
I was of revealing my love for Ann to someone at my hospital.

"Ann would stop by and see me every morning before work.
She would come and have lunch with me and bring the kids to
visit at night. I was in the hospital, as a patient, for four days.
Jimmy came by and visited for several hours. He really seemed
concerned. That meant a lot to me."

Ann presented Mary Jo with a gold ring for her little finger
during the hospital stay. It was a signature ring with Ann's name
as the setting. "Occasionally I would forget to take it off when I
was at work, but no one seemed to notice the name. That would
have been hard to explain, the name of another woman that I
wore as a ring."

*   *   *

The first of the year ushered in mounting expenses in connection with the preparation of the custody trial. The lawyers were
spending more and more time in research and they had already
explored the idea of expert witnesses. That meant money. By

February, Mary Jo grasped the seriousness of her lack of funds. She took a part-time job at a nursing home near their home in Garland. The hours were flexible enough so that she only worked the evenings that she was on duty at the hospital. "Even with my overtime we were just able to meet all of our obligations and save a little for the legal bills," Mary Jo stated. "It was agreed that any expert witnesses had to be paid at the time of their testimony. Plus Frank and Aglaia thought we would have to be evaluated by local psychologists, so they could testify as to our stability and home life. This meant hundreds of dollars. This was out of our reach.

"I was beginning to feel pushed under. When I would put in three sixteen-hour days in a row and then put in an eight-hour day following that, I would drag myself home and fall into the bed and sleep through to the next day.

"A nurse is always on her feet, and your mind has to be constantly alert, because of the importance of correct medications. That last eight hours would completely drain me. I'd get home at midnight. Ann would have something for me to drink; cold tea or even a vodka and tonic. I'd take the drink, bathe, fall into the bed, and be up at six the next morning ready to put in another sixteen-hour day.

"After several sessions with the attorneys where my nerves showed, they began to realize I was under a great deal of pressure, so they would start dealing with Ann. This may have solved our communication problem, but it placed a strain on Ann's and my relationship.

"Ann was handling all the details of the case preparation. She would gather information and yet had to wait until I was in the emotional and physical shape to hear the news. Then everything new would be dropped on me at once. I felt that everyone was very demanding. I was a pawn, being pushed here and there by everyone. I was manipulated, not making my own decisions. I was constantly being told, 'If you want this, you have to pay this much, etc.' Ann would come up to me and say Frank had found a psychiatrist who was affirmative toward gay people and if I wanted him to testify it would cost five hundred dollars plus expenses. But we needed two hundred dollars by the next day. I balked at 'the next day' and questioned her about the suddenness of it all. Then, Ann told me she knew about it several days ago and had waited until now to tell me because she was concerned about how upsetting it would be to hear the news after a sixteen-hour day. Of course, she was right.

"Until this time in my adult life, I had a good standard of living, with fine homes, cars, boats and most of all little or no debts. Going into debt hundreds of dollars a week frustrated me. I was doing all I could. I couldn't work twenty-four hours a day. I was barely holding up as it was. My tiredness dimmed my judgment. Of course we couldn't refuse the attorneys the fees they needed for the case preparation."

Mary Jo felt compelled to maintain all the activities that the children enjoyed. "We believed that any disruption in the way we lived would add to the children's tension. That was one thing that slowly got us into deeper financial trouble. Judie Ann went to a private school. Tuition, transportation and baby-sitters were expensive. Both kids took gymnastics. This was needed to improve their motor co-ordination. Judie and Rich were used to eating out at their favorite restaurants, at least once a week. They went to movies, shows and amusement parks. Both were growing at a rapid rate and their clothes had to be constantly replaced.

"Richard knew that his father was trying to get him. He told us his father kept telling him that it wouldn't be long before he would be living with them. He would come home from a visit to Doug's and be upset for the entire day. He told us that he said he wanted to live with his daddy so they would stop questioning him about it. Then he would cry and say he didn't want to leave. I would tell him that nothing had been decided and he shouldn't worry about those things. Try to enjoy the visits and when he came back we would just take up where we left off, everything would be the same.

"Judie Ann displayed her emotional stress in a different way. She was always coming up with schemes, like mowing lawns and selling things, to raise money for the trial. She pestered us daily to make sure she could go on the stand and testify. We kept telling her it wasn't possible. Frank and Aglaia said no; it would appear that we were using the kids.

"Both children would cry more than usual during this time. The tension was obvious.

"By the end of February I was working three nights a week and often four. I did little talking with the kids or Ann. When I would come home at midnight, Ann would be ready to talk, to tell me what had happened concerning the case. She would stay on the phone every night talking to some person or group about help or how to present the best possible case. When I was sleeping, she invariably would come into the bedroom and have something to do in there. She would even talk on the phone, even though we had two other phones. I guess she just wanted to be near me. The only thing I could think about was rest. My body was crying for rest. And I would hear her talking away on the phone. It was really irritating. I was thinking she didn't really care about me, what I was going through. Here I was working all these hours and all I was asking was to sleep and she was in there talking on the phone. Even on the nights I didn't have to work another shift, the night after three straight sixteen-hour days. I would try to take a nap before dinner. She was in the bedroom rummaging around and yakking. By the time dinner was ready I was furious. I was so mad that I wouldn't talk with anyone. I'd just eat, get up, and head for the bedroom, warning everyone that I didn't want to hear any noise. On the nights they let me sleep straight through to the next morning I became irritated that I had missed a chance to be with the kids and Ann. They couldn't win, I guess."

Ann's composure and pride took a nose dive during the difficult days when Mary Jo worked her two jobs. "I'd help the kids with the homework and I would do the bookkeeping for my daddy's service station. Then I would do the research for the case. I was depressed because Mary Jo was gone so much. I couldn't share all this information I was getting with Mary Jo. It was impossible to brief her on what the attorneys and I were doing.

"At times I would get resentful. Hell, this was her lawsuit. Why was I doing all this and she wouldn't even listen to me about it? She sometimes didn't seem to care, at all. But I would soon get over the hurt. Mary Jo wouldn't know what groups to contact, their background or how to go about finding them."

The many hours taken up by Mary Jo's second job and the absorbing research work Ann was involved with took its toll on the women's sex life. Mary Jo remembered the debilitating effect of the lawsuit: "The night I received the citation our sex life fell apart for a while. It was weeks before I could make love. After that we made love, but it wasn't as much as in the past and not as involved. At one point I even said, 'This is what is causing the trouble' . . . meaning our sex drive. The tiredness of 1975 made things worse. We even slept further apart on the bed. The phone was ringing all night, all the time."

Several weeks after Mary Jo started working at the nursing home, she inquired if they ever hired teen-agers to help the nursing staff. She was told that teen-agers were acceptable as orderlies. Mary Jo told Jimmy, and within a few days he started to work part-time after school.

The night Jimmy began working at the nursing home, Mary Jo was off duty. She and Ann were at her mother's playing cards with Pat and Jack, who were visiting. "Jimmy walked into the house shaking his head. He told me to forget it, he was never going back. I asked him what was the matter. He said we would never believe what he had gone through tonight. I told him I would believe anything he told us, since I had some experience dealing with elderly patients.

"Jimmy started telling us what he saw: 'This guy came out of his room and pulled down his pants and he did it . . . a bowel movement . . . right there in the hall.' I didn't want to discourage Jimmy, but I told him I had seen similar things, nearly every day. He seemed taken aback at that. It confirmed his story. Then he told us about one old man who took his clothes off and tried to crawl into bed with some of the women. I could see that all this really shocked Jimmy. He went on about it for an hour, naming the names of patients and explaining all their little idio-syncrasies in detail.

"I advised him to give it a chance. This was his first night. He would soon adjust. Everybody worked together at the nursing home and the nurses would help him.

"After Jimmy left I told Pat and Jack that he would return. He would make it all right, for one simple reason: he was interested enough to learn the names of over a dozen patients who were on his floor. He knew they needed his help and he recognized them as individuals."

Even though they worked in separate sections of the nursing home, Mary Jo visited with her son during her breaks and got a chance to watch him in action. "I went into the room where he was working one night. The patient, a man, had feces all over himself and the room. Jimmy was patiently cleaning up the man and the room. He was talking to the man in a soothing voice. I was quite proud. At last Jimmy was giving to somebody, not tak-ing. I felt like it would make him a better person."

During an evening in March, Jimmy approached his mother at the nursing home. He was pale and shaking. Mary Jo sat down with Jimmy and asked him what happened. "He told me he went into a room and the man was dead. He said he was by him-self when he discovered the body. I could tell he was an upset young guy, but I had to let him know it wouldn't be the last time he would see someone who had just died. That was the nature of the work. He accepted this, but wanted to know if it would ever get any easier. My answer was no. It never got any easier, no matter how many times one viewed death. I wanted Jimmy to remember that this was a human life and he had a right to be sad if that life was gone. I told him it was not going to be any easier, but he would be able to confront it better. But the hurt would always be there."

* * *

In early March, Mary Jo received a series of forms from the Juvenile Probation Department of Dallas County. That was the agency that conducted investigations into circumstances surrounding child custody cases. After completing the forms and assembling letters of reference, an interview was arranged with Elizabeth Segovis, a domestic relations counselor.

Miss Segovis was housed in the Dallas County Records Building, an ancient gray tomb at the edge of the downtown area. The office where the interview was conducted was barren except for a large, dented gray metal desk and several straight-backed side chairs.

Miss Segovis was cordial and quickly entered the business of the interview. She wanted to know about "the situation with you and this other woman."

Mary Jo tensed. "Miss Segovis, I want you to know I'll answer your questions as best I can, but any reference to that I'll have to ignore, because that has not been in the court record."

Mary Jo didn't need much of an explanation. As soon as she heard that Doug had already been interviewed, she knew where Miss Segovis had obtained her information. The rest of the interview was formal, almost icy.

Mary Jo signed forms releasing Richard's school, medical and dental records. She told about Richard and her activities. Miss Segovis informed her that a home visit was necessary; in fact, she would be visiting the homes of Doug and Jimmy as part of her evaluation process.

The home visit followed two weeks later. The tension, engendered by the homosexuality question, had subsided. Mary Jo and Ann had given the house a meticulous cleaning. Ann stayed home from work. Miss Segovis watched Richard and Judie Ann play the piano, eat, socialize with friends, and interact with Mary Jo and Ann. For several hours she talked with Mary Jo about Richard's education, special needs and recreation.

When she left, Mary Jo was confident they had made a good impression.

*　*　*

Although she had completed her classes in December, Mary Jo's graduation from Abilene Christian College was held May 11. All graduating seniors have what the college calls sponsors. They are family members who sit behind the graduate and drape them with the hood that symbolizes the degree. Mary Jo asked her mother to be her sponsor.

The day of the graduation Mary Jo was dressed in a black robe, with purple and blue trim. Mrs. Davidson wore a white robe. During the ceremonial procession, Judie Ann ran to the corner of the stage and took pictures.

After the degrees were conferred, Ann held a small reception for Mary Jo's friends at the house. Ann and the kids presented Mary Jo with woodworking tools for her hobby of furniture building. Jimmy, who had brought his girl friend with him, seemed proud of his mother. He walked up to her and said, "Well, there's not too many kids in their lifetime that get to see their father's wedding and their mother graduate from college."

❊   ❊   ❊

There was a new flare-up with Jimmy toward the end of June. As often as she could, Mrs. Davidson visited her mother and sisters in Arkansas. Mary Jo attended her high school's twentieth class reunion in Little Rock. Mrs. Davidson rode along and stayed with her family while Mary Jo, Ann, Judie and Richard went to the banquets and picnics of the reunion.

Jimmy stayed home at Mrs. Davidson's. A cousin was spending the summer with him.

"When I got back from Arkansas," Mrs. Davidson recalled, "Jimmy was storming around claiming I hadn't left them anything to eat. I told him there was a ham, bacon, eggs, luncheon meat in the refrigerator. There were over four hundred jars of canned food on the shelves. He had plenty of money, and restaurants were just a few blocks away. If he was too damned lazy to get up and cook for himself, I couldn't help him. He told me he wasn't going to fix meals for himself. I suppose he thought I should have provided him with a cook for the few days I was away."

The furor over the Arkansas trip had just subsided when Jimmy telephoned Mary Jo. "What do you think about me going to Galveston over the July Fourth holiday?" he asked. Mary Jo wanted more information before passing judgment. "Well, Jimmy, where will you be staying?" He was likely going to stay at his aunt Pat's. "Who's going with you?"

"It'll be my girl friend and another boy and girl. I don't know where we'll stay, maybe on the beach." Jimmy quickly added, "Grandma says we can't go."

Mary Jo hesitated a moment. She didn't like the arrangements. "I'm saying you can't go either, Jimmy. One thing, I don't like you going down there with a bunch of young people and not having anywhere to stay. Another thing, it's over a holiday and a lot of accidents happen on the freeway. A lot of drinking and all will be going on down there in Galveston."

"You mean to tell me that you're saying I can't go?"

"That's exactly what I'm telling you. Let me talk to your grandmother."

Mrs. Davidson was standing nearby. "Yes, Mary Jo."

"What is this all about, Mamma?"

"Mary Jo, I told him he couldn't go. He wouldn't take my word for it. He had to call you."

When Mrs. Davidson hung up the phone, she and Jimmy argued heatedly. Two days later, while Mrs. Davidson was at work, Jimmy moved out.

* * *

September was the seminal month in preparing for the custody trial. Domestic Relations Judge Oswin Chrisman had set September 29 as the date he would hear pretrial motions. All parties assumed the actual trial would immediately follow.

Two prominent Dallas psychologists had been engaged to evaluate Mary Jo, Ann and the children and present their findings to the court as expert witnesses for Mary Jo's side. Frank had recommended Dr. Robert Dain, an assistant dean at the University of Texas' Health and Science Center. Ann had found Dr. Dolores Dyer through the recommendation of local leaders in the feminist movement. Both of these psychologists had extensive backgrounds in mental health work and enjoyed top reputations among their peers. Because of their professional standing, Mary Jo's attorneys reasoned, their evaluations and opinions would withstand any assault on their integrity. The big unknown, of course, was how they would view Mary Jo, her partner, and their children.

Even after undergoing an evaluation by the court-appointed psychologist and the probing of a social worker, Mary Jo and Ann were terrified at the prospect of facing Drs. Dyer and Dain. Ann: "We were all scared to death that they might not accept us. We were leery of them finding something that might be wrong with us."

Dr. Dain started his interviews on September 3. It was left to Judie Ann to lighten the anxiety. After her first interview she told the family that Dr. Dain asked her how she loved Richard. "I told him, 'Why, I love him like he was my own brother.'" Judie smiled at everyone and glanced sheepishly at Richard. "I didn't mean it, Richard." Richard laughed.

Mary Jo began her series of visits to Dr. Dyer on September 18. Gradually, the apprehension diminished. "After the first couple of times talking with both of the psychologists, I felt like they were at least interested in us as individual people. We could be open and honest with them. In fact, we did become very open. To me, we answered some of their questions and talked about things that ordinarily we might be protective of."

Ann's lingering doubts were expunged after the attorneys talked extensively with the psychologists to familiarize themselves with the details of their evaluations and the nature of their testimony. "Frank told us exactly what they said about us being a good family unit. Then I felt secure in them." Ann summarized the emotional risk they had undergone: "Your life was in these people's hands. It was like all of a sudden they were going to find out the core of your existence, what you were all about, and whether the public could be brought to understand."

Additional character witnesses were needed, someone that worked with Mary Jo at the hospital. Mary Jo understood the importance of her attorney's suggestion but literally trembled at the quandary it put her in. "How in the world was I going to pick a nurse from the hospital, when they were the very ones I kept my life a total secret from? I thought of Judy Grimes. She was working there when I went to Gaston. We were close. She had left the hospital to have a daughter and had not yet returned full time." The central problem remained the same. Judy Grimes had no inkling that Mary Jo was a lesbian.

After several days of mental haggling, Mary Jo went to Judy's house. She started, awkwardly, by telling her of the custody suit. Judy was puzzled about any grounds that Mary Jo's ex-husband might have. Mary Jo skirted answering directly. "My lawyers think I need someone that worked with me to testify." Judy nodded. "Mary Jo, I certainly know what kind of person you are at work and I've met your family."

It couldn't be delayed any longer. Mary Jo had to tell her. "I have to be fair to you. Doug is claiming that I'm a homosexual."

Judy was startled. "What? If you were, what difference would that make?"

"I am."

"It still doesn't make any difference, Mary Jo. The same goes, I'll testify for you."

"I appreciate that, but why don't you think it over? Talk with your husband about it."

Judy agreed, she should talk it over. Later, after her husband said it was her decision, she called Mary Jo. She would testify.

Shortly after her talk with Judy Grimes, Mary Jo went to the chaplain at Gaston, the Reverend Emmett Waites. At the trial he would testify in her behalf, but that wasn't her intention when she sat down to talk with him in the waiting room of the intensive care unit.

"Reverend Waites, I'm getting ready to go to court within a few weeks. It's a child custody case. My little boy, Richard. My ex-husband is charging that I'm a homosexual." Waites was silent. "I am a homosexual," she continued.

Reverend Waites seemed mildly surprised. "What is it you would like me to do?"

"There's the chance this trial might get some publicity. And if some people in this hospital find out, it will be a pretty rocky ship when I come back. The one person that might be able to calm it down is you."

As they discussed the ramifications of the trial in more detail, the chaplain grew indignant at the ordeal Mary Jo was enduring. He asked her permission to talk with the hospital administrator. In a few days he reported back that it was generally felt what employees did on their own time—their personal lives—was their own business.

Ann wasn't shielded from the ordeal of telling her superiors at work that she would soon be part of a public trial focusing on her homosexuality. While many of her co-workers were aware of her sexual preference, she had a new boss, a vice president of auditing. Her boss accepted the briefing with sophisticated calm. Ann thought she had even shown a sympathetic interest in the outcome of the trial.

With the presumption that the trial would immediately follow the opening motions, Mary Jo arranged for a week of vacation, beginning September 29.

Again, as they had during the temporary custody hearing in 1974, Mary Jo's attorneys prepared a motion to limit the issues and bar homosexuality as a consideration. They were prepared to present expert witnesses to support their contentions.

It is not unusual for dozens of cases to be disposed of during every working day in a domestic relations court. It was midafternoon on the twenty-ninth before Judge Chrisman got around to *Risher* v. *Risher*. He agreed to hear expert witnesses from both sides in connection with the Motion in Limine. The court's docket, however, wouldn't permit testimony until October 1.

Mary Jo didn't take the delay lightly. Her nerves were already balled up in a sinewy lump. The attorneys required an immediate fifteen hundred dollars; they were devoting full time to this case, which was expected to take a week. Mary Jo had less than ten dollars in her checking account.

She had the thin hope that the judge would uphold the motion barring homosexuality as an issue. The attorneys' best assessment allowed that the "signs" weren't good.

Even if the motion was upheld and homosexuality couldn't be

discussed openly during the trial, there was another major problem. Aglaia Mauzy informed Mary Jo, "If the judge does accept our motion, we will be suffering innuendoes, but we will protect you every way we can."

This didn't reassure Mary Jo. It had an opposite effect. She went from a barely containable consternation to choleric terror.

Innuendo? Have you ever been to a so called gay bar, Mary Jo? Yes. I see. Do you like to dance? When you are out dancing, with whom do you dance? Ever dance with a woman, Mrs. Risher? Almost all your women friends are unmarried . . . isn't that so? Most of them have female roommates? You say that each of the children, Judie Ann, Jimmy and Richard, had a separate bedroom? You and Mrs. Foreman share a bedroom? Now, when Jimmy left home, you had a spare bedroom. Isn't that right? Did you move into it? No? Then you still share a bedroom with another woman? Do you have separate beds? One bed? King-size? Very cozy, Mrs. Risher.

But Aglaia will protect me. You can't insinuate those things. You can't say it. No one can use the word homosexual. No one can talk about lesbians. "I'll protect you from innuendoes every way I can." What way, Aglaia? How?

The jury isn't stupid. Look at those prurient smirks on their faces. They know. They get it. It's a roundabout way, but they're in on my secret. Aha, she's a homosexual. Lesbian. Queer. Unfit mother. Unfit. No one will say a word. No labels. The court record is clean. Homosexual? Why, it never entered into our discussions.

Mrs. Risher just didn't wipe Richard's nose enough. She made him fix his own lunch. She allowed some bully to push him into a creek. She let him get hit by a car. Unfit. Dirty, slimy, inhuman bitch. A stinking h——. An obnoxious l——. A degenerate q——. That didn't enter into deliberation. We won't punish her for being one. There's no proof she is. God will take care of her. She'll answer to Him. He'll know what she is. Not us. But it's plain to see she has no right to a son. Overwhelming evidence. Incontrovertible. What she "isn't" will ruin that boy. What no one mentioned will turn him into one. Away. Take him away.

"We will protect you every way we can." Appeal? A higher court? What is there to appeal? Thoughts? What the jury was thinking? Only what's in the record? But there's nothing there. No labels. No words. No homosexuals. No lesbians. No queers. Only smiles. Only leers. Only innuendoes. Innuendoes.

"Mary Jo," Ann whispered. "Mary Jo. Don't sit up in the bed all night. If you can't sleep, why don't you take a Valium?"

"I don't need one, Ann."

"Nonsense. It's after two. That's what we got them for, so you'll be able to hang together during the trial. Please, hon, take one."

"All right, I will."

✿   ✿   ✿

It was shortly after eight when Mary Jo was awakened by the telephone. Ann answered it in the kitchen. The kids were gone. Ann had gotten them up and fixed breakfast. Mary Jo jumped up. Her head was rushing with scrambled thoughts. Her eyes darted around the bedroom, not focusing on anything. Objects startled her. A jewel box. Radio. Everything she gazed at was unfamiliar for a split second. It was as if she had to pause and give her mind time to fathom shapes, sizes, textures.

The water in the sink was loud, torrents of noise. She started to brush her teeth and halted several times to watch the water. She wandered into the bedroom, opened the closet to select some clothes. *Wait. In the mirror on the door. I was already dressed. Different clothes than yesterday. When? How could I have been dressed?*

"Mary Jo, I got up with the kids. I didn't want to wake you. That was Aglaia on the phone. She said there was no need for us to come down to the courtroom tomorrow. The judge is just going to hear the expert witnesses at this time. Mary Jo? What's the matter?"

Innuendoes. I don't even have to be there. "Do you know what they are going to try to do to me, Ann?"

Ann placed her coffee cup on the dresser. "But Mary Jo,

Frank and Aglaia aren't going to let them do anything to you. They said . . ."

"Yes, I know. They said they would protect me all they could. But do you know what they are going to do? Doug's lawyer . . . he's going to insinuate that I am. How are Frank and Aglaia going to protect me against that? Well?"

Ann was perplexed. Her voice was maternal. "Don't worry about it, Mary Jo. They are not going to let anything happen to you."

Ann. What's the matter with you? Why don't you admit it? Why don't you say you know what they are planning to do? We have to do something to stop them. "They can't stop them, nobody can. And you stand there and pretend to me they are going to help me. You don't give a damn. You don't care if I lose Richard."

Ann stammered, "Mary Jo . . . how can you even suggest that? I've been working with them so hard."

"Working with them," Mary Jo shouted. "Working with them." *That's it. They've made a deal. That goddamn Frank and Aglaia got together with Mike McCurley, Doug's lawyer, and arranged a deal. I don't even have to show up. They planned it that way. Frank told me he once had a drink with McCurley. They talked about homosexuals as parents. Frank had a drink with McCurley. They're buddies.* "Hell, they've had more than one drink together."

"Who has, Mary Jo? What are you talking about?" Ann was flushed.

Mary Jo bellowed, "You're with them. You and the whole damn lot of them are selling me down the river. I know you're not behind me. You just wait. As soon as this thing is over I'm getting out of here."

Ann tried to hug Mary Jo. "Come on, Mary Jo, you don't mean that. I love you."

Mary Jo jerked away and walked into the closet. She grabbed clothes off the hook, bending hangers, popping buttons, and hurled them on the bed.

Ann picked them up as fast as Mary Jo tossed them down.

"What are you doing?" Mary Jo glowered at Ann. "I'm packing. Leaving."

By now Ann was angry. Breathing hard. "Look, Mary Jo, we promised Neila and Joline we'd stop over this morning before they had to leave. If we're going to catch them, we have to go now."

"Goddamn those people," Mary Jo screamed. "We have to pull them into the courtroom. The only reason they are going to testify is because they like the excitement."

Ann began to cry. "Oh, Mary Jo, don't do this, please. We're all behind you one hundred per cent."

"The hell you are." Mary Jo stomped out of the bedroom, through the living room, and out the patio door. Ann ran after her pleading, "Where are you going, Mary Jo?" Mary Jo was up the steps to the carport. "To my mother's, to get some rest."

Mary Jo's head was thumping in time to the cross-section breaks in the concrete road as she drove toward her mother's. *Ann just doesn't understand.* Thump. *How can she say it's going to be all right?* Thump. *They're going to get it in.* Thump. *There's no way to fight it. No way.* Thump. *I can't trust her. Anybody.* Thump. *Forget those damn attorneys.* Thump. *They've got nothing to lose.* Thump. *A deal has been made.* Thump. *They'll get the money.* Thump. *Richard is lost. Lost.* Thump.

Mary Jo stopped her car in her mother's driveway, turned off the engine, and removed the keys before it struck her. *Mamma's at work. How could I have forgotten that? That's funny.* She laughed and restarted the engine.

When she entered the restaurant, Mary Jo noticed the clock. It was ten. Her mother poured them some coffee and they sat in a back booth. The lunch crowd wouldn't arrive for an hour.

Mary Jo leaned across the table, almost touching her coffee cup with her blouse. Her hands cradled the hot cup. In a mono-tone whisper she cautiously recanted the story of the innuen-does.

Now, Mary Jo was straightening up. She was getting louder. Several other waitresses drifted over, attracted by the narrative.

Mary Jo was feeding on the attention. Her voice was clarion. She was crying in bursts.

Mrs. Davidson was swept up in the madness. She agreed with Mary Jo. "I've sat on juries, I know what it's like."

"Mamma, the jury will know what I am," Mary Jo sobbed, oblivious to the other waitresses huddled at the booth. "And all this stuff about they have to prove that you are before you are guilty is a bunch of crap."

"That's right, Mary Jo. Once it's out, it's out. Of course they'll know that you are."

Mamma knows. She understands. Why couldn't Ann? "Ann doesn't understand that, Mamma, she doesn't know what they are going to do to me. She said Frank and Aglaia were not going to do anything to hurt me, but lawyers can be bought."

The other women nodded their heads in unison. "That's right," one quipped. "That's for damn sure," volunteered another. "We all know lawyers will do anything for money," Mrs. Davidson said. "We've had some firsthand experience with that in our family."

All the women talked at once. Lawyers, they all agreed, were moneygrubbing, conniving, low-life. After several minutes of this vilification chorus, someone noticed the time. It was getting late, and preparations for the luncheon grind were incomplete.

Rather than leave Mary Jo to cry and brood in the booth, Mrs. Davidson put her to work ornamenting cheesecake with whipped cream; all the while she was sobbing. By the time every last wedge of cheesecake was topped, Mary Jo was lulled into a tractable condition.

"I'm leaving now. I'm going for a drive. Maybe I'll go back home."

While Mary Jo was at her mother's restaurant, Ann had straightened up the disheveled bedroom. Her work therapy quelled a simmering ego. She was worried about Mary Jo. A call to Mrs. Davidson confirmed that Mary Jo had been there, calmed down, and perhaps was on her way back. Mrs. Davidson was still infected with the spirit of her talk with her daughter.

"Ann, you know those lawyers can sell you down the river quicker than that."

"Mrs. Davidson, no one is selling . . ."

"You don't understand," Mrs. Davidson interrupted. "You've never been in any dealings with them like we have."

"Ma'am, they haven't . . ."

"Well, if they are going to ask her what goes on in the bedroom."

"They didn't say that, Mrs. Davidson. That was Mary Jo's imagination."

"Oh, you know they are going to ask that though, Ann. They'll ask that."

"All right, Mrs. Davidson." Ann was soothing. "Please try to calm down, everything is going to be just fine. We don't even know if the motion has been accepted or not. We don't have any earthly idea what our tactics are going to be from this point on. All the lawyers were trying to tell Mary Jo was they were going to protect her and not let her get hurt. I'll talk to you later."

Ann was late for an appointment with her father. He had agreed to loan Mary Jo the 1,500 dollars she needed for the legal fees. She didn't dare leave the house with Mary Jo roaming around irrational. It troubled Ann to take the money from her father; it was the last cent he had in his savings, and the service station wasn't doing much better than paying the utilities and operating costs. *She said she was going to leave me. Should I take Dad's last money? How am I ever going to pay it back if she leaves me?*

Mary Jo walked through the patio door. Ann went over to her, but Mary Jo said only "hello" and walked distractedly through the house. Looking as if she would drop from exhaustion any moment, she slowly eased herself into the armchair. Her arms dangled over the seat cushion, her shoulders were hunched tightly. Ann made some tea and cajoled Mary Jo to accept another Valium. Mary Jo toyed with the spoon and leaned back.

"Ann," Mary Jo barked hoarsely. "Ann." Her voice trailed off as if she didn't expect an answer, even though Ann was just a few feet away.

"Yes, Mary Jo."

"Ann, Richard will be home soon. He's got a half day off at school. Some sort of teacher's conference."

"Yes, I know."

The phone rang. Ann went to the bedroom to answer. She left the bedroom door ajar to listen in case Mary Jo needed her. It was Ann's father calling to see why she hadn't met him. "Something came up," she explained. "No, I won't be able to come over later, either. The money can wait."

Mary Jo caught the snatches of conversation about the money. She stirred, started to get up, then slumped back down. Now, Ann was talking about shipment invoices that her father had misplaced. Service station business. Mary Jo closed her eyes and rubbed her temples. She was exhausted.

Soon Ann was at Mary Jo's side. "Why don't you go and lie down on the bed? You'll be more comfortable."

"No, no, I can't. I can't rest. Do you know what they are going to do to me? Do you realize?" She had snapped again. She was off and pacing. Into the bedroom. Back to the kitchen. Into the bathroom. Back to the living room. Then upstairs. Into Richard's room. The hall. Down the stairs to the landing. Up to the den. Into drawers. Closets. Driven. Seeking. Crying.

Richard bounced through the patio door. Ann scooped him up in her arms and carried him outside. Neila and Joline were walking across the lawn. Joline's classes were ended and she had picked up her three children at school, along with Richard. Neila took a half day off at the pharmacy. They were going to the movies with the kids. Under Ann's urgings they shuttled the kids back to the cars, out of view from the house.

Ann hurriedly explained that Mary Jo was breaking down. "Under no circumstances can Richard see her. Take him with you. Oh, my God. Judie! She doesn't get out until two."

"We can pick up her," Neila suggested. "Do you want us to go in and try to calm Mary Jo down?"

"Yes. Oh, please yes. I can't manage her. She's yelling and pacing. Saying the same things over and over. She's wild."

Neila and Joline found Mary Jo emptying her dresser, gathering up pictures. There wasn't any time for a greeting before Mary Jo began an accusatory harangue. "She's holding that 1,500 dollars over my head. She's teasing me. She's not going to let me have it. She thinks she has control over me with that money. She's not going to get it for me and I can't pay my lawyers. I won't have lawyers."

Ann hadn't done the situation justice. Neila and Joline were stunned. Mary Jo was tossing about snapshots to fall on her head like oversized confetti.

Joline sternly asked Mary Jo, "Do you know what you are doing?" Mary Jo stopped her picture tossing and responded in an ugly, distant voice, "I know what I'm doing. I know what you're doing. What you all are doing. You don't give a damn what happens to me."

That was too much for Joline. "What in the hell is in your mind? Do you realize just what we *are* doing? We are going down to that courthouse and testify for you. We are putting ourselves on the line."

"Putting yourselves on the line? Goddamn it, you're not going to lose your child."

"Mary Jo, listen. Listen. For what we're going to do I could lose my kids. Not one child. But three. Doesn't that mean anything to you?" Joline was furious. She had both hands on her hips. Waiting.

Joline's logic pummeled Mary Jo. It stunted her self-agitation. She lashed out, "Get out of here, get out of this house. I don't want to see either of you again." Mary Jo pushed Neila against the door. Joline moved to the rescue and was shoved back. Mary Jo slammed the bedroom door behind them. Neila and Joline waited on the patio. No telling what might happen. Ann was still in the bedroom with Mary Jo.

Ann sat on the edge of the bed; Mary Jo stood in the far corner of the room, arms folded defensively. "Mary Jo, you shouldn't have done that." Mary Jo's arm flung upward. "What do you mean? Why are you taking up for them now? All you want to do is get back together with Neila. That's right. You want me to have this trouble. Go under. You just want to ruin me. What have you got to lose? When this is over you can go back to Neila." Mary Jo pulled a suitcase out of the closet, opened it, and threw it down on the bed, inches from Ann. "I don't care. I don't need you. All I need you for is the trial. I'm getting out of here. I'm leaving now. I just need you to show up for the trial. I'm going." Mary Jo wrestled an armful of clothes out of the closet and threw them into the suitcase. Ann got up and headed for the door. "If you leave tonight, you're not going to take Richard with you."

Mary Jo ran after Ann, who had fled through the door to the patio. "I want Richard," Mary Jo screamed at the three women. "You can't have Richard," Joline replied. "He's gone to the movies with my kids." Mary Jo eyed Joline in disbelief. "He's done what?" Ann interceded. "Mary Jo, they had planned to go to the movies all week. Daddy took Judie Ann to meet them at the theater. All the kids were very excited."

Mary Jo accepted the movie ploy as a *fait accompli.* "I'll just sit around and wait for him, then. I'll take him with me when he gets back."

Once Mary Jo was inside the three women conferred. Joline was to pick up Judie Ann and take the kids to the movies. Neila would stay with Ann and join them later, at the restaurant, provided Mary Jo calmed down. Unless Neila met them later, Joline was to take Judie Ann and Richard to her house, where they could spend the night.

Mary Jo was on the rampage again when Ann and Neila went inside. This time she was on the phone ranting at Lisa. It went on for a full five minutes before Mary Jo paused. "I'll call you at home." When she emerged from the bedroom, Mary Jo was carrying two large suitcases and piles of clothes on hangers strung over her arm. She shot a quick glance at Neila and Ann and imperiously informed them that she was off to her mother's. "You can bring Richard over there."

Ann was sobbing when Mary Jo left. The desperation had finally caught up with her. Neila tried comforting her, then telephoned Mrs. Davidson and said, "Ann wants to get the 1,500 dollars for Mary Jo. She will get it. But Mary Jo keeps threatening to leave her. Ann's sitting here on the sofa now, in tears. We think Mary Jo's heading toward your house." Mrs. Davidson was more levelheaded this time. "Tell Ann that Mary Jo is not going to leave her. She loves her very much. Maybe I can calm her down when she gets here. Tell Ann to call me in about an hour."

Several hours passed and it was getting dark. No one knew where Mary Jo was. Ann and Neila began to telephone around to see if Mary Jo had changed her plans and gone to Rose's or Lisa's instead of her mother's. Rose hadn't heard from Mary Jo, but promised to talk with her later, when she was located. Lisa was extremely agitated by Ann's call; Ann filled her in on what was happening.

It was dark when Mary Jo walked into her mother's. Mrs. Davidson was in the kitchen frying chicken. She examined her daughter's face for a sign of her condition. Mary Jo's eyes were glazed and bloodshot. Her lips were welded together in a painful grimace. Her hair was blown on end from hours of driving. Mrs. Davidson asked Mary Jo if she was hungry, wanted anything to eat.

"No, I don't need anything," Mary Jo answered. *She could sell me down the river again. She'd like that. I can't trust her. Never.*

Mary Jo walked through every room in the house, peering into closets and behind doors. At first Mrs. Davidson followed her. "Is there anything I can help you find, Mary Jo?" Mary Jo kept on walking, opening drawers, rifling through linens. "No, I don't need your help," she snapped. Mrs. Davidson retired to the kitchen and called Ann. "Yeah, she's really upset. I guess all I can do is humor her and try to get her to eat something. She said she wasn't hungry, but I'll try to get her to eat."

Mary Jo alighted on her mother's bed with the princess telephone across her lap. Her mother was whistling loud and off key in the kitchen. *What is she whistling for? She does that when she's worried. She knows I'm onto her. She's got a reason to worry. I know she's joined them again to get me. This time, I won't be taken in.*

Mary Jo dialed. "Lisa? You told me to call you at home."

"Where are you, Mary Jo?"

"At my mother's."

"What you ought to do is lie down and relax."

"I can't take it easy. I have . . ."

"Well, why don't you come over here, then? We could talk. Ann said you were pretty upset. I can understand why. The pressure has been enough to break anyone."

"Ann? You've been talking to Ann. Probably been planning right along with them, too."

"No, Mary Jo, you don't understand. No one is going to hurt you."

"Oh yes, they are. You too. I see what's up. None of you can be trusted." Mary Jo slammed down the phone.

They are all in it together, even Lisa. They don't care about Richard. I've got to get Richard away from them. Why doesn't that damn Ann answer the phone? Why isn't she home? She's at Neila's. They've gone over there together. They'll start living together before the trial. I knew that would happen.

"Ann? Mary Jo. I'm giving you five minutes to leave her house. I'm ordering you to get back home with Richard. No, bring Richard over here to me."

Ann was adamant. "No way, Mary Jo. Richard can stay here and get a good night's sleep. I'm in no shape to get him to school tomorrow and neither are you. I'm not going home or coming over there, Mary Jo."

"Oh yes, you are. You're coming over here or I'm coming after you. You and Neila are not going to get away with keeping Richard. She'd better keep her goddamn mouth out of it. I've had it with her. All of you. You hear me. She's nothing but a lesbian, a queer. You're a queer too. You're all a bunch of queers. I can't have anything to do with you queers again!" *Don't hang up on me. Don't.* "Ann, Ann."

Mary Jo ran into the kitchen. Mrs. Davidson was whistling full volume and frying chicken. Mary Jo blurted out something. Mrs. Davidson stopped her whistling. Mary Jo stood leaning on the counter, forming words that wouldn't come out. The phone rang. Mrs. Davidson picked it up. Mary Jo grabbed it out of her hand.

"Mary Jo?" the voice was unfamiliar.

"Uh-huh."

"Mary Jo, this is Sandy. Lisa's roommate." Mary Jo sat down. *Strange getting a call from Sandy. Lisa's roommate? Oh yeah. Not a lover, though. Sandy's very "straight." Religious.*

"Lisa is crying, Mary Jo. She told me about you and her. She feels responsible for all your troubles with your ex-husband."

"Look, Sandy," Mary Jo answered, "Lisa's conspiring with Neila and Ann. They don't care about me. You . . . you just don't understand."

Sandy remained tranquil. "No, I don't understand how anyone could get into the mental shape you're in, Mary Jo. There's an answer to all our problems, Mary Jo . . ."

Mrs. Davidson lit a cigarette and walked into the living room, where she could sit down, yet keep an eye on her daughter. After a few moments of argument, she noticed Mary Jo was talking quietly, often repeating snippets of Sandy's conversation, as if to sort it out, absorb it fully. ". . . let Jesus take hold . . . let Him solve it for me . . . place my trust . . ."

For a half hour the catechetical conversation between Mary Jo and Sandy continued. Mary Jo's rage trickled away, atomized by the somnolent voice of Sandy. The combination of her voice and the message produced the perfect response in Mary Jo. She strolled to her mother's bedroom and stretched out on her back. *Lord, I'm exhausted. Confused. I have no control over what I say or where I go. It's like I'm not even doing these things myself. Help me, Lord. I'm so tired of my life.*

"Mary Jo."

Ann. Oh, Ann, you're here.

"Mary Jo, I couldn't stay away when you needed me."

"Hi, honey." Mary Jo looked serene. "I know what happened, Ann."

"We don't have to talk about it, unless you want to, Mary Jo."

"I'm all right now. I am."

"You look better."

"Where are Richard and Judie Ann?"

Ann tensed slightly. "They got in late from the movie and dinner, so I thought they'd better play with Joline's kids and spend the night over there. Is that okay?"

Mary Jo looked into Ann's eyes. They were fearful. Mary Jo smiled, drew a deep breath through her open mouth, turned her face toward the ceiling, and yawned gloriously. "I'm absolutely beat. I don't know if I can walk any more. I'm so exhausted I'm numb."

"You should eat before you go to sleep," Ann suggested.

"Food. Mamma's got all that fried chicken. Let's go."

Late the next morning, Mary Jo and Ann spent over an hour unloading the trunk of Mary Jo's car. Suitcases, shoes, pictures, letters, books, cosmetics, files, records, virtually everything that Mary Jo could cram into the car in her series of autogenic wanderings the day before.

As soon as the car was unpacked, Mary Jo telephoned everyone who witnessed yesterday's madness. No atonement was necessary; everyone knew by Mary Jo's effervescent voice it was over. That was enough.

* * *

On October 1, two days after Mary Jo's ordeal, the witnesses were heard in the Motion in Limine proceedings. Mary Jo and Ann were not present for the hearing.

Mary Jo's attorneys called two psychologists: Dr. Robert Dain and Dr. Dolores Dyer. Doug Risher's attorney put two expert witnesses on the stand: Dr. Roy Austin, a counselor for two Baptist churches, and Philip B. Smith, pastor of Lakeland Baptist Church, in Lewisville, Texas. All of these witnesses would testify in December at the jury trial.

After two days of intricate questioning, Judge Oswin Chrisman made his decision on whether or not homosexuality could be considered by a jury deciding the *Risher* v. *Risher* custody case:

"I overrule the Motion in Limine and instruct the testimony to deal with any acts or events that deal with the emotional environment of the child in the presence of the life style that influences the child—acts, events in the presence of the child or life styles that influence the child—that do or might influence the child."

Homosexuality was to be on trial. Trial date was set as December 16.

*　*　*

The evening of Judge Chrisman's ruling, Mary Jo and Ann were watching the news on Dallas' Public Broadcasting Station, Channel 13. Susan Caudill, a reporter, gave full details of the pending trial and its primary issue of homosexuality. The two-minute synopsis was complete except for the name of the "lesbian mother, who is a nurse."

Mary Jo knew that in less than three months the story would be repeated many times, not only on the PBS station, but every major commercial station in Dallas and Fort Worth. "Next time the names would be there. Mary Jo Risher. Ann Foreman. Richard. Judie Ann. It was a bit scary."

Life stayed on an even keel at the Risher-Foreman household during the months preceding the trial. The children seemed glad that the trial was in the future. Children can barely conceptualize something three months away. They were reassured by distance.

Mary Jo used the time well: "We had constant meetings with groups and individuals that were offering support and advice, but we were more relaxed. We fell naturally into our old mold of everyday living. It gave us a breathing spell.

"I knew I could never go through another crazy event like in September. I couldn't let interior pressure build to that level again. I began to prepare myself psychologically. I visualized the reaction of the people at work and played it through in my mind. The week before the trial I mentioned to one nurse, 'Well, you never know, the next time you hear about me it might be in print.' I said to another nurse, 'Things may happen, statements may be made, but people are generally the same as they were before their public image is changed.' Later they both told me they remembered those comments."

The weekend before the trial Mary Jo and Ann were in the living room discussing the courtroom strategy. Richard came downstairs as they were talking. He walked over to Mary Jo, climbed up on her lap, put his arms around her, and patted her back. "I hope you get me." "Well, darling, I have you," she responded. "You know . . . I hope you keep me." Mary Jo kissed her son's head and squeezed him.

PART II

THE TRIAL

THE DALLAS COUNTY COURTHOUSE building stood poised as a gleaming white concrete intruder on the southern edge of Dallas' most historic square. Facing the courthouse, on the Commerce Street side, was the Kennedy Memorial, a bleak four-sided cenotaph of self-conscious tribute, designed by noted architect Philip Johnson. Farther away, across Main Street, sat a squat, rustic log cabin that once housed the founder of Dallas, John Neely Bryan. The visual irony of the cabin amid the manicured grass and tall, slender-poled translucent globes of the street lights went beyond the anachronism of logs as building material. The cabin was tiny. A child's proportions. The founder of a sprawling plains giant chose to live in an inconsequential wooden box. A hundred yards northwest of the Bryan cabin, across Elm Street, was the old Texas Book Depository building. Notable only for the sanctuary it provided an enigmatic child of violence.

Least significant in this historic acreage, but by far the most active with people, was the county building. The ground floor buzzed with lawyers, taxpayers, clerks, jurors, deputies, dwarfed by the inhuman resonance of the high ceilings and polished marble floors.

In the center of the building was the life line to the upper reaches, a bank of eternally malfunctioning elevators. Dozens of preoccupied people huddled about, waiting. They faced in all directions, not wanting to turn their backs on any door that might open unexpectedly. Their anxious vigilance was like any water hole on the African plain where all manner of animals mixed together at dusk for a life-sustaining drink.

The domestic relations courts were on the fourth floor. It was here that love, the basic binding force of a meaningful human interaction, seemed terminal. While all changes in life were episodic, with beginnings and endings, what dominated this row of courtrooms were the endings. Bitterness, ecstasy, sacrifice, vengeance, or ambivalence—the endings reigned supreme. For husband and wife, parent and child, relative and friend, this was the trauma room of our deepest illusions.

A hall ran the full length of the building. Overhead, every other cluster of fluorescent lights was dim, a forgotten remnant of the energy shortage. No marble here. Instead, there were brown and tan squares of scruffy linoleum dotted with cigarette butts and gum wrappers, an overflow from the sand-filled canisters spaced every ten feet along the wooden benches. A three-inch-wide pane of glass, above the copper hand plates on the double wooden doors, allowed you to peer into the courtrooms. Pressed close to the double door was a small cork board. Pinned to the board was the battle roster for the day, the hour-by-hour court docket. Underneath the board a brown waste container.

Domestic Relations Court Number 4, with the Honorable Oswin Chrisman presiding, was spartan and symbolic. Platforms for the players in this court's dramas were carefully designed to show rank and importance by height. The gradations were simple to comprehend. The judge, distant, high on a wooden tower, surrounded by flags—American flag on the left, the State of Texas flag on the right. Closest to the judge, as if the proximity to the highest authority assured truthfulness, was the witness stand. Off to the left side, but still elevated above the natural floor level, was the jury box. Twelve heavy brown leather chairs were fixed permanently to the floor but swiveled and reclined a comfortable thirty degrees. On the lowest level, directly in front of the judge's tower, was a sixteen-foot rectangular table. Straight-backed leather chairs. No swivels, no rollers. This was the working arena, the "pit." Here sat lawyers and clients. Incidental to the court layout, in fact off to the far right, were a small table and chair for the court bailiff. As a judicial traffic cop, he stood most of the time anyway. The rear third of the room was the gallery. Unyielding, glossy wooden benches for press, friends and assorted voyeurs of human foibles.

On the wall to the left of the gallery was a two-by-four-foot black and white photograph of Judge Chrisman in his robes. The only other odd touch in the courtroom was two laminated "No Smoking" signs prominently fixed on either side of the judge's tower. No Latin inscriptions about equality under the law, no seals of judicial grandeur, no blindfolded statue of a woman balancing the scales of justice in her extended hand, just two disgusting little examples of bureaucratic mindlessness.

"Everyone rise," the stentorian voice of Bailiff Frank A. Taylor signaled the beginning of the first day of testimony, December 16. Taylor, a heavy-set, balding man, with a large friendly face and bemused eyes, handled his major-domo duties with self-assured ease. "I've seen it all," he confided to no one in particular, "but this is going to be a *trial*." His tone was unusually severe, reflecting the proper gravity of the struggle that was about to unfold. Not without a sense of humor—"My friends kid me about my initials, F.A.T."—but he was all business this morning. Stern.

Judge Oswin Chrisman stood courtly atop his wooden tower awaiting the jury's entrance. From the gallery he looked handsome in a boyish way; a shock of neat brown hair, elfish dimples and a warm smile, just the right bench-side manner for such a court.

Sallie Ritcheson, the court reporter, sat motionless. Her dark hair, cut in the Vidal Sassoon style, hung just right in her constant position—head tilted downward over her work. She was never obtrusive in the courtroom; her only act of individuality was always being a few seconds late entering the court. Otherwise she blended with her machinery.

The seating at the lawyers' table in the "pit" was prearranged, with the side presenting its case on the left, nearest the jury, the court-appointed attorney for the children as the neutral buffer in the center, and the Respondent's two attorneys on the right.

All heads turned toward the entrance to the jury room. The jurors filed in, taking assigned seats based upon the order in which they were selected. To a person, they appeared uncomfortable. Now, as throughout the trial, the only emotion their faces registered was discomfort. This may be construed as a positive sign. They respected the ramifications of the fateful decision they would make.

The jury panel: ten men and two women. One black. Median age? Perhaps forty. Their dress was neat, everyday taste. A splash here and there of modish style. If a subjective first impression was valid, the jury was a basic, middle-class collection of Dallas residents. A machinist, toolmaker, accountant, secretary, oil refinery operator, registered nurse, factory worker, real estate salesman, airline mechanic, telephone company employee, retail clerk and engineer.

They were selected the day before. Individually they told the court they either have no knowledge of homosexual life styles (an easily acceptable assertion) or are not prejudiced against such a life style (based upon dominant social sentiment, an incredible example of open-mindedness). Each juror steadfastly assured the litigants he would base any decision upon the evidence and the law.

"Be seated," intoned Judge Chrisman. ". . . Unlike criminal trials this case will be decided on the preponderance of the evidence. A verdict can be rendered if ten members of the jury agree. The party that filed the suit will be referred to as the Petitioner. The party that answered the suit is known as the Respondent . . ."

Judge Chrisman advised the jury that Mary Jo's seventeen-year-old son Jimmy was no longer an issue. By mutual consent, he had elected to live with his father, Doug Risher. The jury would be deciding the custody of nine-year-old Richard Calvin Risher.

While Mary Jo knew Jimmy's preference, she learned along with the jury that the process was final.

The energy level was high as the opening arguments began. Mike McCurley, Doug's attorney, bounded out of his chair and faced the jury. McCurley was short, maybe five foot seven, late twenties, with shoulder-length brown hair. His eyes were dark darts, closely set, small and badly bloodshot. Throughout the trial he would struggle vainly with new contact lenses. His body build was solid (a high-school footballer who was too small for the major leagues of Texas colleges?). Ignoring the precarious balancing needed in his platform shoes, McCurley moved quickly, in a kinetic trot. While others wilted toward the end of eight hours in the pit, Mike never faltered. He thrived on intellectual combat, and it would be entirely in character to hear him cry out after the court is recessed for the day, "Anyone for handball?"

McCurley's opening remarks were brief. "The Petitioner will

show a material change in circumstances that warrant a change in custody. . . . Yes, there has been a life style change. . . ." The opening salvo was clear. The lesbianism of the mother and its impact on young Richard were the prime issue.

Frank Stenger's opening remarks were delivered to the jury in a studied casualness. ". . . We plan to show that Mary Jo Risher is a model mother, cares for, protects, provides for and loves her son . . . goes beyond her duty to provide for the child. Her status as a homosexual has not interfered with her ability to provide a loving, secure home for her son. The environment has no negative connotations. . . . Another issue: if removed, it would be more harmful to Richard, depriving him of a qualified, capable and loving mother. . . ."

Mary Jo was called to the stand as an adverse witness. She was dressed in a skirt and tailored jacket. Her eyes were fearful, but she walked with confidence and was sworn in by Chrisman. For the record she stated her age, address, place of employment, profession, education, marital status and that she was married to Douglas Risher from August 1957 until April 1971.

Under McCurley's perfunctory questioning, Mary Jo responded in a clear, calm contralto voice. She described in detail her everyday life. She had a neighbor care for the children when she was not home, she liked to build toy boxes for children as a hobby, liked to hunt and read, and met her partner, Ann Foreman, in July 1973.

MCCURLEY: "How would you characterize your relationship with Mrs. Foreman?"

MARY JO: "A loving relationship."

MCCURLEY: "At that time when you met Mrs. Foreman, were you a homosexual?"

MARY JO: "I was."

MCCURLEY: "And had you had homosexual experiences with other women at that time?"

MARY JO: "One other woman."

MCCURLEY: "And had you lived with that woman?"

MARY JO: "Never."

Mary Jo explained that she and Ann dated for six months.

MCCURLEY: "Would this be in much the same way as a man would come and call on a lady and take her out? I'm sorry I just don't know how that's done, would you tell me?"

MARY JO: "Pretty much the way you'd say." Her eyes wandered over the jury box. Mary Jo was looking for some reaction. The jury was studying her, but the faces were blank.

MCCURLEY: "Would you call upon her or would she call upon you or who would instigate, who would be the, the one to instigate the meeting?"

MARY JO: "Well, it would sort of . . ."

Frank Stenger objected to the line of questioning. "This has no relationship on her ability to care for the child. She has admitted that she's a homosexual and anything that goes into that would only serve to inflame the jury."

McCurley answered that the jury had indicated a lack of knowledge concerning homosexuality, which he shared. "They have alleged that it makes no difference, it has nothing to do with life style: and I think now is the appropriate time for us to explore that allegation."

JUDGE CHRISMAN: "I will overrule the objection."

MCCURLEY: "Ma'am, the question was when you and this lady were dating or courting one another, who would instigate the date? Who would ask whom?"

MARY JO: "It was a mutual thing since neither one of us went with anyone else."

MCCURLEY: "I see. Well, you all didn't live together at that time, did you?"

MARY JO: "No, we did not."

MCCURLEY: "Well, living in separate residences, someone, I take it, would have to call and ask the other out, how was that done?"

MARY JO: "Like I said, it was a mutual thing." Her voice showed a trace of aggravation. She knew McCurley was fishing for her to admit to role playing. "You know she would call me or I would call her. She would come over to my house since my mother knew and I would go over to her house."

McCurley frowned and paused a long moment. "What type of outing would you all do together?"

MARY JO: "Well, we went to football games together since that was the period of time that, you know, we were seeing one another. We went to Austin to see the Texas football game and by the same token she went to Arkansas with me since I'm from Arkansas. We would go out to eat. That's just about it."

MCCURLEY: "Would you ever go out on the town, so to speak?"

MARY JO: "Sometimes."

MCCURLEY: "Do you drink?"

MARY JO: "Not very much."

MCCURLEY: "Would you and Mrs. Foreman ever have an occasion to go out and have a drink after work?"

MARY JO: "Never after work because we both had responsibilities and I was in school. You know I went to school during the summer too."

MCCURLEY: "Did you and she ever have an occasion to, without that limiting factor of after work, did y'all ever go out and have a drink?"

MARY JO: "Yes, we would go out at night."

MCCURLEY: "What bars would you frequent?"

MARY JO: "At that particular time we went to the Entre Nuit."

MCCURLEY: "Ma'am, I've been to a few bars, but I've never been in this one. Do they dance in this bar?"

MARY JO: "Yes, they do."

MCCURLEY: "With whom would you dance when you were there?"

MARY JO: "With Mrs. Foreman."

Aglaia Mauzy had enough of McCurley's conjuring up spectacles of what goes on in gay bars, and lodged a heated objection. Despite McCurley's innocent pleadings, Judge Chrisman, who looked a bit uncomfortable at this point, directed the questioning back to things related to the child.

Mike probed into the social clubs that Mary Jo belonged to. She was a member of the Order of Eastern Star, a past president of the Dallas County Council of the PTA, a life member of the Texas PTA, a member of the Daughters of Bilitis and a new member of the National Organization for Women (NOW). McCurley cutely asked, "What is the National Organization for Women?" Then he wondered, "Is it a homosexual group?" The gallery, chock full of feminists, roared with laughter. Even some of the stoic jurors smiled. Ole Mike could take a joke. He was primed. The preliminaries were over. "Mrs. Risher, you said that your relationship with Mrs. Foreman was a loving one. Would you explain for me and the jury what you mean by that?"

The slight smile on Mary Jo's lips sagged. "Well, love is, you know, you can expand on it in great depth. You can love to be with a person just for the sheer—for being with them. You can love the conversation that they can have with you. You can love them for the person they are, the ideas they have, the goals they want to attain throughout their lifetime. I love Mrs. Foreman as an individual."

McCurley's voice was rising in volume, with a hint of lurid eagerness. "Ma'am, I know of people that I love in different capacities, I guess would be the way I would phrase it. Everybody from my Uncle Hap to my mother. In what capacity do you love Mrs. Foreman?"

Stenger objected. Mary Jo, who knew what was coming, flashed a hostile glance at the judge. Chrisman allowed McCurley to continue. Mike sensed Mary Jo's hostility and backed off slightly. His control could be astounding when it served his objectives. "My question to you is, in what capacity, in what manner—and I'm not asking you about sexual activity at this point, I'm asking you about feeling—how do you, in what capacity do you love this woman?"

MARY JO: "I love Ann Foreman more than anything in this world. That does not mean that I do not love Jimmy and Richard, you understand."

MCCURLEY: "Then let me ask you this. Do you love Mrs. Foreman more than you love your child Jimmy?"

Mary Jo looked sick. Her head nodded from side to side. "That would be like asking me at the time I was married to Mr. Risher if I loved him more than I loved Jimmy."

MCCURLEY: "Well I may ask you that question in a moment.

But my question to you now is, do you love Mrs. Foreman more than you love Jimmy?"

MARY JO: "I love Jimmy and I love Mrs. Foreman the same."

MCCURLEY: "And that would go the same for Richard?"

MARY JO: "Yes."

MCCURLEY: "Then maybe a better question would be, you do love them in a different capacity, is that true?"

MARY JO: "I love Jimmy and Richard as a mother."

McCurley pounced. "All right. I'm not trying to trap you ma'am, I'm trying to find something out. Do you love Mrs. Foreman as a mate, as a spouse?"

Mary Jo didn't hesitate one beat. "I would have to say I do."

MCCURLEY: "Do you consider her as a mate?"

MARY JO: "I live with her."

MCCURLEY: "Yes ma'am, but I mean, maybe I should make that clearer. When two people get married you take that spouse, and I believe the phraseology still goes 'for better or for worse until death do us part', but we all know it doesn't work that way sometime. Do you feel that way about this woman?"

MARY JO: "I would have to say yes."

MCCURLEY: "Do you have sexual intercourse with anyone else but Mrs. Foreman?"

MARY JO: "Never." She looked relieved.

MCCURLEY: "Now directing your attention back to your present home life, ma'am, do you show your affection for Mrs. Foreman in your home?"

MARY JO: "Never in the presence of Richard Calvin."

MCCURLEY: "Who does little Richard think Mrs. Foreman is?"

MARY JO: "A lady that we live with."

At that point McCurley began a not too subtle tactic. His voice took on an unctuous, just-a-down-home-Texas-boy-fightin'-evil tone. He didn't pull off the mood, but the questions were as sharp, blunt and skilled as an orthopedic surgeon's chisel. "Sitting here today, if you had one wish . . . would you be homosexual or heterosexual?"

MARY JO: "I would be exactly what I am."

MCCURLEY: "Then my next question, which you almost answered in advance, is, do you feel any remorse or guilt about what you are?"

MARY JO: "I do not."

MCCURLEY: "Do you think the status of homosexuality is anything that we should discourage in society today?"

MARY JO: "I think a person should be himself. You've got to live out your life . . . we should be happy while we're here."

MCCURLEY: "That's fine. But my question is, do you think the homosexual life style is something that should be discouraged or encouraged?"

MARY JO: "I don't think it should be either. I think it should be the choice of the individual person."

McCurley posed a series of hypothetical questions about how Mary Jo would handle Richard's sexual preference, especially if at a future date he informed her that he was a homosexual. Her summary response: ". . . As a parent I still have an obligation to see if that is truly what he wanted. I would have him counseled."

Religion, quite understandably in a Dallas population that was over 50 per cent Southern Baptist, would play an important role in trial testimony. Mr. McCurley was particularly inclined to equate sin with crime. He was hardly alone in the "amen chorus." The Texas legislature, a notorious cadre of ethical cretins, had seen fit to wholly deny the U.S. Constitution and insert in virtually every law about child welfare that the children must be raised in a religious home.

MCCURLEY: "Mrs. Risher, do you believe in God?"

MARY JO: "I most certainly do."

MCCURLEY: "Are you a Christian lady?"

MARY JO: "I am."

MCCURLEY: "Do you have any religious qualms or misgivings about being a homosexual?"

MARY JO: "I do not."

MCCURLEY: "Do you believe it's immoral?"

MARY JO: "I do not."

MCCURLEY: "If you had the opportunity at this time, are there any circumstances that you would change your life style from a homosexual to a heterosexual?"

MARY JO: "I would not."

MCCURLEY: "Pass the witness."

Before Mary Jo's attorney cross-examined her, there was a break. Judge Chrisman was partial to frequent breaks. They served a dual purpose in the trial. It permitted a long courtroom day, from 8:30 A.M. until 5:00 P.M., and surely was a pressure valve for overwhelming emotions and frayed nerves.

Besides, the hall outside the courtroom was a valuable study with its microcosms that transcended the opposing camps in the litigation. There were members of the gay community, feminists, friends, excused witnesses, a small corps of journalists, attorneys and a large, hourly changing mass of persons, awaiting their moment in the domestic relations court.

Every conversation, however private, had an audience. There were just too many bodies in too small a space.

"How are we doing?"

"There's a fund raiser Saturday night."

"Is he a minister, too?"

"I know how much this means to you."

"Where's court number one?"

A cacophonous deluge of human voices. Chain-smoking tension. Furtive looks. Bursts of strange laughter. Huddled conferences. Pacing. Robert Altman's camera could weave through the hall and capture another quintessence of America. This film might be called *Endings*.

Supporters of Mary Jo formed concentric circles around her or anyone who had a salient point or argument to make. Better to hear it firsthand. Penetrating those clusters, leaning over a shoulder, was fruitful for information, insights and just plain gossip.

"Hello, Doctor. It's pretty rough in there. Yeah. When are you slated to testify? I see. Are you going to be able to say . . . ?"

Always aside from the activist crowd around Mary Jo—in fact, usually down the hall—sat Doug Risher, his wife Delaine, and sometimes a witness or a friend. Body count was smaller in the Doug Risher camp. The conversation there was minimal, subdued. Either of the Rishers would respond to questions from reporters or the curious. Polite. Their answers were succinct and they never volunteered anything more. It might have been a combination of things that restrained Doug and Delaine. Attorneys' orders, the rather burgeoning size of the throng that attended Mary Jo, natural shyness, distrust of reporters, or, more likely, a genuine sense of dismay over the startling notoriety the custody suit engendered. The resulting reticence limited the scope and depth of reporting on the feelings and motivations of Doug and Delaine, perhaps to their satisfaction.

The first recess of the trial ended and the questioning of Mary Jo resumed, this time by her attorney. She poignantly recalled how Jimmy got his car and how she tried unsuccessfully to get him to return home. Mary Jo was ashen. She cried openly.

STENGER: "Define what you mean by your being a homosexual. What are your feelings in that regard."

MARY JO: "I have feelings for Ann Foreman; I have feelings of wanting to be with her, of making a life with her."

STENGER: "Have you ever allowed your homosexuality to interfere with your ability to care for and provide for Richard?"

MARY JO: "No."

STENGER: "Have you ever performed any sexual acts in front of your children?"

MARY JO: "I have never performed any sexual acts in front of my children."

STENGER: "Have you ever taken Richard to a bar?"

MARY JO: "Never."

Systematically led by Frank Stenger, Mary Jo talked about the warmth and love in her home, shared by all members of the "family unit." She told of having psychological evaluations for everyone to assure the family stability. Stenger prompted her to clarify her feelings toward Ann and Richard that McCurley raised in his direct examination.

"It's hard to describe a love for an individual that you want to spend the rest of your life with . . ." Mary Jo was sobbing. She paused often, overcome by emotion, but clung to her train of thought. ". . . You love your child . . . you protect and care for him. I love Richard so much. I love Richard as a mother. I also love Ann . . . as a person I want to spend my life with."

STENGER: "Is there any sort of conflict in your opinion between your love for Ann and your love for Richard?"

MARY JO: "No conflict whatsoever."

Stenger sought to illustrate how much Mary Jo loved Richard and wanted to retain custody. This series of questions escalated Mary Jo's distress until she cried out in agonizing hoarseness, "I wouldn't be here today if I didn't want him!" It was several minutes before she could continue. The jury didn't stir. Only the elderly man in the front row, nearest the witness stand, looked away. The others stared at Mary Jo constantly.

Stenger's voice startled everyone. "Did you consider carefully the fact that you were going to expose the fact that you were a homosexual when you decided to go and fight for the retention of Richard?"

MARY JO: "I did, because Mr. Risher told me, 'I'll show the world what you are.' . . . I'm a mother, and I'm a good one. I have done everything for Richard and Jimmy. I feel that Mr. Risher has labeled me, but that doesn't mean that I'm not a good mother. I love Richard very much, very much."

On redirect examination, McCurley brought up Jimmy's motivation in leaving Mary Jo's home in September of 1974 and moving in with his grandmother. Mary Jo believed Jimmy was seduced away by the promise of a car from his father.

McCurley was incredulous that Jimmy would put a car above his mother in priorities. Through a series of questions he sought to establish another motive for Jimmy's departure. "At the time he left did he know you were a homosexual?"

MARY JO: "He did."

MCCURLEY: "Had he ever stated to you that perhaps it became a problem with him and his friends?"

MARY JO: "Never. In fact he had boys that came in to stay the night; I'd even have to walk over boys' legs when getting ready to go to work, they'd all be down in the living room."

MCCURLEY: "Did any of those boys ever question why you lived with another woman?"

MARY JO: "Never."

MCCURLEY: "No comments concerning that at all?"

MARY JO: "Jimmy brought his girl friends into the house also."

MCCURLEY: "And no comments from the girl friends?"

MARY JO: "No."

MCCURLEY: "So as far as you know, until Jimmy left in September of '74, the fact that you were a homosexual and living with another homosexual had never been any problem whatsoever for that boy?"

MARY JO: "Jimmy never related to me it was a problem. In fact on my graduation, which was May the 11th of this year, he brought his girl friend to my graduation and also attended the reception afterwards."

MCCURLEY: "Okay now, I'll ask you one more time and then I will move away from this. Is it your testimony here today that the reason your son left you is because of the purchase of a car?"

MARY JO: "There is that possibility."

MCCURLEY: "Is it possible that he left you because you are a homosexual, ma'am?"

MARY JO: "I don't think so."

As the detailed questioning, nit-picking ad nauseam, continued, the animosity between McCurley and Mary Jo became more pronounced. Both had short fuses and were set on painting different portraits for the jury to consider. Mike saved his least endearing moment until just before the break for lunch. "All right ma'am, I hate to ask you this, but I feel I have to. You testified to us about how you loved your children. Does little Richard know you're a homosexual?"

MARY JO: "He does not."

MCCURLEY: "If you found out that the car wasn't the deal that's causing these problems, that one of your sons left you, but in fact it was very seriously related to the fact that you are a homosexual and living with another homosexual and it came to the choice of the son you've got left and being a homosexual, which would you choose, ma'am?"

Barton Bernstein was on his feet, objecting. Throughout the trial, he, as court-appointed attorney for Richard, would be the balancing factor between the stringent advocacy of the two sides. Bernstein maintained a proper neutrality and often focused issues and resolved semantic haggles. He was a moderate man, favoring corduroy suits. Using a soothing, pleasant voice, he asked useful questions designed to elicit answers for the jury's aid in making the proper determination. Bernstein, by carefully following up answers left dangling by both sides, served his role well, safeguarding the rights and interests of young Richard.

McCurley's last question strained the boundaries of fairness inherent in Bernstein. "Your honor, I'll object to the hypothetical nature of the question. He's calling for this witness not to recite any facts involved in this lawsuit, but for the witness to respond to a hypothetical question which may or may not ever . . ."

JUDGE CHRISMAN: "I'll overrule your objection."

Next, Aglaia Mauzy entered for the record her objection to the question and its speculative nature. Again, Chrisman overruled. Mary Jo's mouth was drawn tight. Her eyes flashed hatred at the judge. She had been pushed to her limit. The court reporter was asked to read back the question: ". . . If it came to the choice of the son you've got left and being a homosexual, which would you choose, ma'am?"

MARY JO: "You know, as an individual I should not have to answer a question like that . . ."

MCCURLEY: "No ma'am, but as a mother you should. My question to you as a mother is this, if it comes down to a choice between your homosexuality and the son you've got left, which are you going to choose?"

MARY JO: "I'm not going to lose the son I have left."

Judge Chrisman jumped in immediately. "All right, let's break for lunch."

Mary Jo was livid as she left the stand. She accosted her attorney. "They're pushing me into a damn corner. It's not right to ask me that question." Aglaia nodded her head affirmatively and shrugged her shoulders. Someone from the gallery had joined the huddle. "Don't you know," she offered bitterly, "in Texas they can take away your sexuality. How asinine. What would they have you do, become a eunuch?"

Ann walked into the courtroom with Charlotte Taft. Charlotte, an artist and feminist, was the catalyst for the community support that Mary Jo had garnered. She had been in Dallas for less than a year and was jabbering in disbelief about Mike McCurley's "sickening politeness." That had escaped Mary Jo, who was so accustomed to Southern etiquette she hadn't noticed McCurley slipping on the thin ice of social convention. His endless "ma'ams" had degenerated into epithet. Charlotte began a full-blown parody, less to amuse than to distract. "Ma'am, won't you sit here? Are y'all comfy, ma'am? Let me strap y'all into this little ole chair, ma'am. Here's a darlin' little metal cap for y'all's head, ma'am. Now, ma'am, I surely do hate to do this, but I'm going to pull the lever, ma'am, and electrocute y'all."

Lunch in the packed cafeteria in the basement of the county building gave Mary Jo and Charlotte time to fill in Ann on what had transpired. More accurately, to expand on what she had learned in the restroom during the morning break. The women's restroom at the end of the hallway on the fourth floor, became the command post, so to speak, where witnesses on the stand could relay testimony to those waiting outside. That was, strictly interpreted, prohibited by the court, but at least the retinue of Mary Jo's supporters posted a guard outside to warn of any approaching strangers who simply wished to urinate. If they fudged on the court's gag order, at least they were concerned enough to be discreet.

By the time they had savored the cremated cuisine of the underground lunchroom, the first edition of the afternoon newspaper was in the coin boxes. On the front page, there it was. "Lesbian Mother Fights to Keep Son." No more lingering doubts about publicity. Those reporters and photographers upstairs weren't idling away their time.

Ann, who had already devised an imaginative scheme to keep her elderly Aunt Kizzie from learning of her homosexuality, via the trial, was faced with another obstacle. Newspapers. She hurriedly telephoned a friend to arrange for some minor thievery. The friend was to go to her aunt's house every morning and afternoon and swipe her papers. That, coupled with the evening news blackout, should effectively cut her aunt off from the outside world. News blackout? Every night, at six and at ten, when the local television news was on, one of Ann's friends would telephone Aunt Kizzie and absorb her in a lengthy discussion. Likely it would be some time before Kizzie would become suspicious of this unparalleled attention.

The final stage of the lunchtime strategy game was how to recover from Mike McCurley's last question about giving up her homosexuality or her son. Mary Jo debated her companions, then scribbled something onto a piece of paper. Her memory wasn't trustworthy at this juncture.

The trio's precaution in discussing the last McCurley question was providential. In the reconvened court he started again. "Now ma'am, are you saying if it comes between your sexuality and your son, you will give up your homosexuality?"

MARY JO: "I believe that I can be a homosexual and be approved as a fit mother also."

MCCURLEY: "All right, now that's not the answer to my question, ma'am, that's what you've alleged in this lawsuit, but my question again to you is . . ."

STENGER: "Your Honor, I would once again object to this question. It is speculative and it's impossible for her to answer. She's answered it the best she can. There's simply no choice, she cannot be forced to choose one way or another in terms of a speculative answer."

JUDGE CHRISMAN: "I'll overrule your objection."

MCCURLEY: "Ma'am, would you answer the question? Do you not understand the question?"

MARY JO: "I understand the question." She tugged at the lapels on her jacket.

McCurley's voice was bitter. "Would you please answer that?"

MARY JO: "Mr. McCurley, that is like asking one of these jury members to make a choice between their wife or husband against, for their child."

MCCURLEY: "Ma'am, I'm asking the questions now and I want to know the answer to that question, and I think these people . . ."

Bernstein interrupted. "Your Honor, I would object to Counsel pursuing that question. She has answered the question to the best of her ability and she says that she cannot answer it."

JUDGE CHRISMAN: "I'll overrule your objection."

MCCURLEY: "Thank you, Your Honor. Ma'am, would you please answer that question?"

MARY JO: "The situation has not arisen."

MCCURLEY: "No ma'am, that's not what . . ."

MARY JO: "But should it arise, I would have to meet it then. It has not arisen and I don't think it ever will. I don't think that I've lost Jimmy . . . There was too much between a, a son and mother . . . one day when Jimmy is older . . ."

MCCURLEY: "Ma'am, excuse me for interrupting you. I hate to be abrupt, but this is a very important lawsuit and it's a very important topic of discussion. Now I have asked you a question, and I will rephrase it, and I would like a 'yes' or a 'no' or 'I refuse to answer,' not a speech."

MARY JO: "I refuse to answer."

For the next thirty minutes, Mary Jo answered routine questions about how the visitation arrangement was working, the stability of her job, and the emotional health of her children.

The questioning ended. Mary Jo walked stiffly to her seat. Her four hours on the stand left her distracted and exhausted. She glanced at the gallery. Charlotte Taft clinched her hands together and smiled. Her lips formed the words, "You did fine." Mary Jo sat down.

Ann Foreman was called to the witness stand as an adverse witness. The shortest route to the witness stand from the courtroom door was a diagonal path from the right side of the gallery, in front of the judge and past the court reporter. Ann started to walk that way. Bailiff Taylor stopped her. He whispered and pointed the proper route. Behind the lawyers' table, past the jury. Apparently this bit of decorum was intended to give the jury a walk-by view of each witness. The men on the jury perused Ann indifferently. The two women's eyes roamed up and down several times. Hypercritical. The look that you see some women give new arrivals at a cocktail party. Petty, distrusting, competitive. Ann stared them down. After a few preliminary questions, McCurley employed a new surprise.

MCCURLEY: "During the past five years have you resided with anyone other than your child and Mrs. Risher?"

ANN: "Yes, sir, one other woman."

MCCURLEY: "And who was that?"

After an objection from Aglaia Mauzy, McCurley withdrew the question. It had served its purpose. Mike was structuring for the jury a picture of instability in homosexual relationships.

MCCURLEY: "Have you had a homosexual experience with any other women except Mrs. Risher and this other woman, we'll refer to as Jane Doe?"

ANN: "No, I haven't."

MCCURLEY: "What happened to your other . . . excuse me what would you call a homosexual that you lived with? Do you call them a mate or a . . . what do you call them?"

ANN: "It depends. It varies." Ann looked at the jury. She obviously didn't want to say the wrong thing. "Mostly you call them the person you live with."

MCCURLEY: "The person you live with. Okay. What happened to this other person that you lived with? Jane Doe."

ANN: "She's still a good friend."

MCCURLEY: "Y'all, of course you wouldn't, you weren't married at that time, you didn't get married to that woman, did you?"

Ann's face registered "fool." She gave McCurley a sardonic grin and answered: "No. I don't believe the law would allow that."

Frank Stenger's objection was overruled.

MCCURLEY: "When y'all parted the ways, did you just part ways?"

ANN: "Yes."

MCCURLEY: "No formality about it at all?"

ANN: "I don't understand what you mean by formality."

MCCURLEY: "All right, let me drop that line of questioning and I'll come back to it. How did you feel about Miss Doe?"

ANN: "The same way I felt about my ex-husband."

MCCURLEY: "We don't know your ex-husband or how you felt about him."

ANN: "All right. I loved my ex-husband very much. He's still probably my very best friend."

MCCURLEY: "How do you feel about Miss Doe?"

ANN: "I loved her also."

MCCURLEY: "Do you love her now?"

ANN: "She is a good friend."

MCCURLEY: "Has your feeling for her changed, since the termination of y'alls' living arrangement?"

ANN: "Well, sir, I think when you're not living in the same situation that your feelings do change; your type of love changes; you transfer affections."

MCCURLEY: "Let me ask you this, how do you feel about Mrs. Risher?"

ANN: "I love her very much. That should be obvious, I'm here."

Ann was steady as McCurley delved into morality. "Do you feel there's anything wrong with being a homosexual?"

ANN: "No, sir, I don't."

MCCURLEY: "Do you feel there's anything wrong with raising a child in a homosexual environment?"

ANN: "No, sir, I don't."

MCCURLEY: "Do you think that perhaps homosexual environment is a coming thing in today's society?"

ANN: "I wouldn't know whether it's a coming thing, I think it's already been here, sir."

MCCURLEY: "Well, do you think it's becoming something more recognized?"

ANN: "Probably."

MCCURLEY: "Do you think it's something that should not be discouraged, but admitted?"

ANN: "Yes, sir, I do, for your own peace of mind that you should be able to openly admit it."

MCCURLEY: "Do you hide it from your daughter?"

ANN: "No, I don't."

MCCURLEY: "Ma'am, let me ask you this, as a mother can you

foresee any potential problem for a young man child or a young woman child growing up in a lesbian home?"

ANN: "No, sir, I can't."

Mike McCurley, again, grappled with the idea that any homosexual could be well adjusted and productive without haunting reservations.

MCCURLEY: "Ma'am, were you to have a choice, would you prefer today to be a homosexual or a heterosexual person?"

Ann gave him a tolerant smile. "I'm happy in my homosexual life style, sir, so I definitely would prefer to be what I am now."

MCCURLEY: "Would you prefer that your children be homosexual or heterosexual?"

ANN: "I would love them no matter what. I would probably, since there is a bit of ridicule in being a homosexual, would prefer that they be heterosexual so they wouldn't have to experience that, but I think my child could cope with the situation whatever it was."

MCCURLEY: "Of course you'd love your child wouldn't you, you'd love your child whatever?"

ANN: "Right, but of course, I wouldn't want her to be put in a situation like this."

MCCURLEY: "You say, you'd prefer that she would be heterosexual so she won't have the problems of being a homosexual?"

ANN: "Right, so society wouldn't cause her the problems, which I also believe by the time she has grown society will change considerably."

MCCURLEY: "Do you think society is changing its acceptance of this life style?"

ANN: "I think society is probably letting a lot of people live like they want to live so long as it doesn't hurt anybody else."

MCCURLEY: "Well, I take it that you mean society is accepting it? Do you think that's a good thing, that ought to be encouraged?"

ANN: "I didn't say that."

MCCURLEY: "Well, I'm asking you?"

ANN: "I don't think anything should be encouraged. I think you should be what you want to be, what you are."

MCCURLEY: "Ma'am, when did you first become aware that you were a homosexual?"

ANN: "I have no earthly idea. I mean, it's like when did you learn how to breathe or when did you start learning how to read, I don't know. It's just there."

MCCURLEY: "What caused you to be a homosexual, ma'am?"

ANN: "I have no idea. It just happened."

Aglaia Mauzy conducted the cross-examination. In a husky voice, barely modulated, she filled in the gaps left by McCurley's selective questioning. "Does the fact that you're a homosexual affect your ability to work?"

ANN: "No ma'am, it doesn't."

MAUZY: "Does anyone at work know you're a homosexual?"

ANN: "Yes, they do."

MAUZY: "Without giving me any names, would you tell me what relation these people have to you at work?"

ANN: "They're probably some of my best friends. My supervisor knows, and I was a supervisor for three years and the people under me knew. I didn't have any problems. I probably had a very good rapport with them."

MAUZY: "Did they act as though they had an aversion to you because you were a homosexual?"

ANN: "No, as a matter of fact, some of them were my close friends and one of the ladies had a child, I've forgotten her . . ."

MAUZY: "Did that lady trust her child to you?"

ANN: "Yes."

MAUZY: "Did you ever keep that lady's child?"

ANN: "Yes, I have."

MAUZY: "Your ex-husband is going to testify at this trial, is he not?"

ANN: "Yes, he is."

MAUZY: "How long has he known that you are a homosexual?"

ANN: "Ever since we divorced. And he knew of the possibility before we were married."

MAUZY: "Does he come to your home now?"

ANN: "Yes, he does."

MAUZY: "Does he keep your daughter?"

ANN: "Yes."

MAUZY: "Does he have children?"

ANN: "He has two more children now."

MAUZY: "Does he allow his other children to come to your home?"

ANN: "Oh, yes. They all love each other and they also love Richard."

MAUZY: "Has your ex-husband expressed to you his views about whether you or he should keep your child?"

ANN: "Yes, he has."

MAUZY: "What are those?"

ANN: "He believes that I'm a good mother and I love our daughter very much and she should stay with me. And he loves his daughter very much and doesn't think she ought to have any more trauma or problems than she already has."

MAUZY: "Do you consider yourself, your child and Mary Jo's child as a family unit?"

ANN: "Yes, I do."

MAUZY: "Do you do things together and act as a family unit?"

ANN: "Yes, we do."

MAUZY: "How do you feel about Richard?"

ANN: "I love Richard very much."

MAUZY: "What kind of little boy is he?"

ANN: "He's great. He's a doll. He's intelligent, he's quick, he's loving, extremely loving, he's . . ."

MAUZY: "Do you want, along with Mary Jo Risher, to help raise Richard Risher along with your daughter?"

ANN: "Yes, ma'am, I do."

Aglaia examined the permanence of Ann's relationship with Mary Jo. "Ms. Foreman, have you and Mary Jo Risher done anything, in a financial way, that indicates that your relationship is permanent?"

ANN: "We have insurance policies on each other in the event that something should happen to one of us."

MAUZY: "Have you purchased any property together?"

ANN: "Yes, we have some lake property so that the children can have recreation as well as the family."

Mrs. Mauzy was wrapping up her cross-examination. "How do you feel about Mary Jo Risher?"

ANN: "Words can't express how much I love Mary Jo. I want to live with her. I just want to be happy and live my whole life with her . . . with our children."

MAUZY: "You were aware before you got up on this stand to testify that it would mean publicly you are a homosexual and have deleterious effects on your life?"

Ann was weeping quietly. "Yes, I knew."

MAUZY: "And that didn't make any difference to you?"

ANN: "No." Ann looked at Mary Jo. Both smiled faintly. It was over.

One of the pivotal witnesses was Dr. Robert Gordon, the court-appointed psychologist. His evaluations would be given substantial weight by the jury for two reasons: the aura of neutrality, and he was the only professional who conducted diagnostic interviews with members of both families.

Dr. Gordon was a slightly built man, with close-cut black hair and the "obligatory" Vandyke beard. His clothing was bland, blues and blacks. Off the witness stand he appeared self-conscious, ill at ease and slightly defensive about his role, even though he spent a lot of time as an expert witness. On the stand, Gordon was extremely articulate, answering in a forceful baritone voice and ultracareful to give proper qualifications where needed.

MCCURLEY: "After your investigation and as a result of your interviews and investigations concerning the home life of these children, of both the home of Mr. Risher and the home of Mrs. Risher, did you come to an opinion as to who would be the best managing conservator for Richard?"

DR. GORDON: "Well, the word managing conservator is a legal term. . . . I didn't see it as part of the framework of what I was up to. What I did see my purpose was to evaluate the family in general and the parents in particular; and I do have a, I did reach a conclusion and judgment as to whom I thought might be the most effective parent or home for Richard Risher to live in."

MCCURLEY: "All right now, Doctor, that is perhaps well put.

Without the use of the legal word, who did you find to be the best parent?"

DR. GORDON: "Well the word best parent troubles me too. If I may elaborate. I did find, as my report to the Court reflected, that Mrs. Mary Jo Risher was a warm and loving parent, and that she cared very much for her son and her son expresses warm feelings towards his mother. I satisfied myself that she had been responsive and was responsive to his educational and medical needs as of the time I interviewed her. I found that Mr. Douglas Risher had a long history of emotional stability, that he was part of a traditional family, that he had a warm relationship with his wife Delaine and with her child, Michael [*sic*], who was four years old at that time. It was my conclusion that Mrs. Mary Jo Risher had exhibited poor judgment in a number of instances which made me conclude that Mr. Risher would provide the child with the best opportunity to develop into a healthy, normal young man."

Since Dr. Gordon had already made a written report that all parties were aware of, there were no visible reactions from Mary Jo or her attorneys. Mike McCurley was ebullient, strutting like a peacock marking his territory. "Doctor, WHAT, in your opinion, were some of the examples of this POOR JUDGMENT?"

DR. GORDON: "The instances of poor judgment that I was especially concerned with, was information that I gleaned from interviewing the entire family. In particular, the older son Jimmy Risher, who was of course at that time sixteen years of age and able to verbalize and explain his feelings and thoughts in a way that the younger child was not, of course. Based on these diagnostic interviews, I was concerned with the way Mrs. Risher was handling her sexual preference in her family life; and I was also concerned about the effect it might have on Richard Risher as I had observed and noted the effect that it had on the older boy. To be specific, when I first saw Jimmy Risher as the result of the relationship which the mother had engaged in he was mentally confused, he exhibited homosexual panic, uh, he felt depressed and in an irrational and unconscious way it was my judgment that he felt guilty or responsible as if somehow he had caused these problems. And while that is not realistic it is not uncommon for adults to feel that way. In particular Jimmy related to me instances of mother dressing up in attire that was masculine in nature and taking him to bars, or a bar, that was either known for or understood to be a place where individuals who were homosexuals or bisexual or transvestite in nature had an interest in going to this particular establishment. I can't give you a name, I don't think I ever inqured about it.

"The boy's own sexual identity which was undergoing a state of flux and confusion as an adolescent concerned me and alarmed me. When I examined Richard I did not find these symptoms. Richard at this time was eight years old and he, he was in what we call a latency state of development, which means as a youngster he has not yet gone into puberty, so that his mother sharing a bedroom with another woman or them both being amorous in his presence would not have the impact that we would expect it to have on someone who himself was aware of the cultural significance of the family life."

After this lengthy monologue Gordon made sure he redeemed his credentials as an enlightened psychologist by volunteering to the jury that he didn't criticize Ann and Mary Jo and that homosexuality was not a form of mental illness. Gordon maintained he deplored discrimination, then went on to suggest a dual standard for homosexuals in matters of raising children that mocked his rhetoric. He cited two other examples of Mary Jo's poor judgment that weighted his assessment.

"Now something in particular that struck me was his attire [Richard's]. He was wearing a particular suit of clothes, I think they were jeans or denim material, and I complimented him on them and he explained, he thanked me for the compliment and he told me that those were Judie Ann's clothes, that is Ann's daughter that also lives in the home. The day in September when Richard Risher was brought to my office by his dad with apparently no knowledge to the mother, which I regretted and I was not aware of, but at any event, Mr. Doug Risher had brought Richard to my office from his mother's home and he was wearing a T-shirt which had inscribed across the chest YWCA."

Mary Jo's arm dropped from her chair and she shook her head in disbelief.

Gordon apparently caught sight of this; his face flushed. He continued, "Now, typically with the changing clothes within our society I don't suppose I would think too much about it; but in this particular case where the identification of this child is so critical I thought that too was an example of poor judgment."

As to the causative factor of homosexuality, Dr. Gordon recited three prevalent, unclearly defined theories: heredity, through chromosome differences in genes; the second theory is hormonal, it deals with endogen and estrogen imbalance; and the third theory deals with psychological factors, i.e., early childhood development and competition between the same sex parent and child.

During Aglaia Mauzy's cross-examination, Dr. Gordon readily conceded he saw the family members less than six hours and never as a unit. He concurred there was little or no evidence to suggest that a child raised by homosexuals would become a homosexual. Indeed, the vast majority of homosexuals were raised by heterosexual parents, as in the case of Mary Jo and Ann.

Aglaia, armed with details of an incident that Jimmy related to his mother, asked Dr. Gordon about one of the sessions he conducted with Jimmy. "Did you ever take Jimmy Risher with you to a barbershop and counsel with him there?"

DR. GORDON: "Yes, Mrs. Mary Jo Risher refreshed my memory and on one occasion, when I officed on Stemmons Freeway on the tenth floor, I had a barbershop appointment and since my haircuts take a very short time I told Jimmy to come on down with me, I was going to get a haircut and we would go back upstairs and talk."

MAUZY: "Did you talk to him about his personal life there in the barbershop?"

DR. GORDON: "I am sure that I did not. If there was any conversation it might have been how is school, or what are you doing this weekend, or something superficial, I'm sure."

Aglaia zeroed in on where Gordon had gained his knowledge of Mary Jo's poor judgment. "What was your source?"

DR. GORDON: "The sources of information were accumulative; by that I mean there were overall impressions from interviewing all the parties and there were also very specific examples which grew out of conversations with Jimmy Risher and Richard Risher and observational data of those two children."

Aglaia held up her arm. "Let me stop you there because I want some very specific examples. The information you gleaned both from Jimmy and Richard, starting with Richard, what if anything did he say or do that led you to the opinion that Mary Jo had mishandled her sexual preference?"

DR. GORDON: "With regard to Richard, his attire, the fact that he was wearing Mrs. Foreman's daughter's clothes as he explained to me . . ."

MAUZY: "Let me stop you there a minute. Describe those clothes to me."

DR. GORDON: "My recollection of the clothing is vague; the incident was profound. The . . ."

MAUZY: "Would you please answer my question and then go on . . . Let me, if you will, lead you through the attire, Doctor. What sort of shoes was this nine-year-old boy wearing?"

DR. GORDON: "I do not recall."

MAUZY: "Were they high-heeled pumps or anything outlandish? You would recall that?" Snickering in the courtroom.

DR. GORDON: "I do not recall that the shoes were high-heeled shoes."

MAUZY: "If indeed he had on very feminine shoes, given your training and experience, would that not have made a permanent impression on you?"

DR. GORDON: "Perhaps."

MAUZY: "But you don't recall what sort of shoes that boy had on at that time?"

DR. GORDON: "That is correct. I do not currently recall after a year has passed what sort of shoes he was wearing."

MAUZY: "Now, what sort of pants did he have on?"

DR. GORDON: "I have a memory trace which is only a recall that it was a jean suit, blue jeans and a jean vest; I believe that's what it was, but I'm not sure."

MAUZY: "Were they girl's clothes?"

DR. GORDON: "Apparently they belonged to his sister. They were not feminine in attire so that I was concerned that he was being dressed as a female."

MAUZY: "Is it uncommon for children who consider themselves siblings, as you have just stated, I believe, or Richard considers Judie Ann as a sibling, to exchange clothes if they are about the same age, height and weight?"

DR. GORDON: "And of the same sex?"

MAUZY: "Do children, do girls now to your knowledge, often dress in jeans which are for either girls or boys?"

DR. GORDON: "Yes, it is quite common for girls to be dressed in jeans today."

MAUZY: "And if indeed those were Judie Ann Foreman's clothes, were they not also appropriate for a boy?"

DR. GORDON: "The clothing themselves could be worn by a youngster of either sex."

MAUZY: "I have to find out the source of the child's displeasure with his clothes because the impression I'm getting from what you're saying and I think probably the jury is getting the same impression, that Mary Jo Risher because she is a homosexual tried to dress this boy in drag or girl's clothes. Now is that what you're telling us?"

DR. GORDON: "I am reporting to you observational data; you can make of it what you will. In my view it was an instance of poor judgment on the part of the mother."

MAUZY: "Doctor, do you know that it was the mother who caused the child to be dressed that way?"

DR. GORDON: "As opposed to whom?"

MAUZY: "Doctor, does a nine year old child normally need assistance in dressing?"

DR. GORDON: "Not generally."

MAUZY: "Do you have any indication that this child wasn't capable of dressing himself?"

DR. GORDON: "No, I do not."

MAUZY: "Okay, I have to, I have to understand and I think the jury does, where did you get the impression that his mother made him wear his sister's clothing?"

DR. GORDON: "Well, let me say this. If a child gets up in the morning and he puts on a garment that is inappropriate, whether the garment is too heavy because it's warm outside or it's too light and it's cold outside, it is obvious that a parent will intervene and say, 'Honey, or son, you'd better put on a heavier jacket because it's cold outside;' and that is the kind of intervention that I would expect from an effective parent."

MAUZY: "Doctor, I am again confused. You just told me that it wasn't an inappropriate set of clothing that the child had on."

DR. GORDON: "It was inappropriate in this case. It was an instance in my view of poor judgment because of the special facts that we're dealing with. If you have a parent who has a sexual preference that is homosexual and that parent has a desire of course, nevertheless, for that child to grow up if he is a boy, to be a man, or if he is—or she is a girl, to become a woman, that the parent must take special care, that there are special responsibilities to nurture the biological destiny of that child."

At one point in the cross-examination Dr. Gordon stated that he "gave great weight to my interview with Jimmy." Aglaia Mauzy suggested it was very common for an adolescent to undergo an identity crisis. Dr. Gordon agreed. Gordon could not say whether or not Jimmy had actually been taken to a gay bar by his mother, nor could he pinpoint the amount or extent of affection Jimmy alleged occurred between Mary Jo and Ann. Dr. Gordon said it was unimportant if the incidents had actually occurred; what was clinically significant was that Jimmy perceived that it had happened.

Throughout the trial the rules of evidence in law would be abridged when so-called experts were on the stand. All courts allowed what amounted to hearsay testimony when given by psychologists and psychiatrists. Both sides in the *Risher* v. *Risher* custody case encouraged experts to delve into matters that would be inadmissible if offered by laymen. The only attempt to alter this procedure was a tactical move by Mike McCurley to try and keep the expert witnesses called by Mary Jo's attorneys from commenting on what Richard told them in regard to his preference in staying with his mother. That motion was over-ruled.

Aglaia Mauzy returned to the matter of "inappropriate" clothing.

MAUZY: "Doctor, you made allusion to the fact that Richard Risher came to your office wearing a YWCA shirt, did you not? And from that incident you drew the conclusion that that was poor judgment on the part of Mary Jo Risher?"

DR. GORDON: "I certainly did. I thought it was ridiculous."

MAUZY: "Would it surprise you to know that Richard Risher goes to the YWCA to take gymnastic lessons?"

DR. GORDON: "No, it would not."

MAUZY: "Would it surprise you to know that he wears a YWCA shirt to go there?"

DR. GORDON: "I have observed him wearing it. But I must say that when you're dealing with this particular issue, and I'm not criticizing sexual preference, but the manner in which the parent is dealing with it. I think that is most ill-advised."

MAUZY: "So it would have been better advised if he was told not to wear his YWCA shirt to the YWCA where he is to wear it?"

DR. GORDON: "No. It would be much better for him to have matriculated into a YMCA program. And it would be much better for a mother to encourage those kinds of masculine identifications."

MAUZY: "Doctor, are you aware or do you know that there are programs offered at the YWCA centers for boys?"

DR. GORDON: "I was not aware of that, but it doesn't change my view of things one whit, if you're dealing with a child with special problems. Now, I don't see anything wrong in the ordinary sense with a boy attending programs at the YWCA or a girl attending programs at the YMCA; that's perfectly fine as far as I'm concerned. But when you have the particularly sensitive issue here that Mrs. Mary Jo Risher is cognizant of—she is an intelligent, sensitive, bright lady—she owes the responsibility in my judgment to try to meet this special need, and not advance in my view the YWCA experience."

The court-appointed attorney for Richard, Barton Bernstein, jousted with Gordon over why he didn't simply inform Mary Jo that the inappropriateness of her son's apparel was causing some consternation. Gordon responded that he didn't have the rapport with Mary Jo to initiate such a discussion, even though they exchanged several telephone calls after the evaluations were completed.

Bernstein wryly asked Dr. Gordon if he had ever heard of the "cut-it-out" school of psychology, suggesting that simply informing Mary Jo of the problem would have ensured the proper behavior modification. Gordon's sense of humor didn't extend to anyone making tongue-in-cheek jabs at the hallowed tenets of psychology and he artfully avoided a direct answer. The final rupture occurred when Bernstein demanded to know if Mary Jo had corrected the judgment errors cited by Gordon, would he have changed his opinion. Gordon, pleading fatigue at the grueling afternoon, hinted that he may have, but that was too late and after the fact. Dr. Gordon was excused and the court recessed for the first day of testimony.

In Judge Chrisman's chambers, Mike McCurley expressed alarm over what he saw as prejudice in favor of Mary Jo shown by Barton Bernstein. Frank Stenger disagreed, insisting that, as an attorney ad litem, Bernstein would have to take a role in cross-examination. Judge Chrisman said the credibility of Bernstein would rest to a great extent on whether or not the jury thought he was impartial and it should be left up to the jury to weigh.

Bernstein said there were questions that he wanted answered and they were, to his thinking, proper questions. He said he assumed he could take the same position in cross-examination of the other expert witnesses. Bernstein declined to take any other position at that point. "I don't intend to make an argument which says I'm the attorney ad litem and this is what I want."

Everyone went home.

On Wednesday, the second day of testimony, Mary Jo and Ann arrived at the courtroom shortly after eight to confer with

Frank and Aglaia. Despite their ordeals on the stand and lack of sleep because of late night telephone calls, both women appeared refreshed.

Subject to recall as a witness, Ann was not permitted inside the courtroom during testimony. She was consigned to the benches outside, along with friends and supporters who wished to talk with her.

Waiting down the hall for court to reconvene, Doug and Delaine Risher chatted with a well-dressed blond-haired man who carried a Bible. He was Dr. Roy Austin, the family counselor for two area churches.

Dr. Austin was not a Texas-licensed psychologist, and after considerable bickering between attorneys he was limited to the area of counseling in his testimony.

MCCURLEY: "Is there any nomenclature for the phenomenon we see for a little boy putting on his dad's hat or a little girl trying to wear her mother's high-heeled shoes; is there a nomenclature for that?"

DR. AUSTIN: "The nomenclature is used at various times, the term that is used most by people in my field is modeling."

MCCURLEY: "It's called modeling."

DR. AUSTIN: "Modeling or sexual identification."

MCCURLEY: "This seems like an obvious question, but I must ask it: Would you explain to us, in your own terms, what the learning phenomenon of modeling is, sir?"

DR. AUSTIN: "The concept of modeling is that the child learns in the early stages of his life before adolescence the important roles and functions that he is to play in society as an adult, as well as the roles and functions as a child in his growing-up days from his parenting figures.

"And you will notice that I use the words parenting figures as it does not necessarily have to be his biological parents. It can be anyone who plays the role at all of a parent for the child.

"But the parenting figures have long been, and I contend still are, according to all literature and experiences of the people in the area now, very important factors in the child's emotional development for the rest of his life.

"He follows those particular examples that are given to him by the people who parent him; and this has been carefully documented as one of the primary factors in the child's development."

Dr. Austin was asked his opinion about the merits of a homosexual family unit versus a heterosexual family unit. ". . . I believe in our society, the interest of the heterosexual family is primarily the ideal model, because it is basically—(inaudible)—and by statistical majority, the common mode of living in our society.

"And so, under normal circumstances, the heterosexual family, I believe to be the best modeling concept for children to prepare them to live in the society in which we live."

Cross-examining, Frank Stenger pointed out that Dr. Austin had never met Mary Jo or any member of her family, thus could offer no valid insights into the suitability of her home.

During a hypothetical line of questioning Stenger highlighted a viewpoint held by Dr. Austin that later, in posttrial discussions with the jury, would prove to be the majority sentiment. It revolved around single parents.

STENGER: "Doctor, if we were to have a situation in which all the elements of family living were equal, in terms of food, clothing, shelter, care, affection, in two families—one being a single woman or a widowed woman or a divorced woman living with children; and one being a married couple with children—are you saying that the married couple would necessarily be a better home to put the child in?"

DR. AUSTIN: "All things being equal, yes."

STENGER: "Would you say in the same regard to a single male or widower living with a child as opposed to a heterosexual couple?"

DR. AUSTIN: "Yes."

STENGER: "And given the alternative of one or the other, are you saying that since one is better—that is, the heterosexual couple living together—that if a child had a choice, he should go to the heterosexual couple?"

DR. AUSTIN: "For his sake, yes." Dr. Austin was excused.

A break was called and the attorneys met with Judge Chris-

man in his chambers. Mike McCurley formally filed a motion to
have Barton Bernstein removed as Richard's attorney. The motivation was obvious. A new attorney would not have any preparation time and couldn't effectively serve as an advocate. Bernstein
defended his role. "I do not have a preconceived conviction at
this time of what should be the ultimate choice in this case. It is
my duty to cross-examine the witnesses to elicit information not
elicited by other counsel; and ultimately, it is not my intention to
make a personal recommendation to the jury . . ." Judge Chrisman refused to replace Bernstein.

Chrisman postponed ruling on another motion, to keep Richard from testifying on the stand. The judge did narrow questioning concerning Richard's preference as to which parent he
wished to live with. Only the psychological witnesses would be
allowed to answer questions about any preference the child may
have expressed to them.

The next witness called by McCurley was Elizabeth Segovis, a
former domestic relations counselor with the Juvenile Probation
Department of Dallas County. Her job was to investigate the issues where the custody of children was in dispute.

MCCURLEY: "Did you reach a conclusion as to where the children should be placed?"

SEGOVIS: "At that time, my conclusion was that in the balance—
if the educational needs of Richard were available or Mr. Risher
could make them available, and if Mrs. Mary Jo Risher's schedule and work responsibility continued as it was—that Richard
would be better off in his father's home."

Miss Segovis did not consider the sexual preference of Mary Jo
in formulating her recommendation. On cross-examination Frank
Stenger wanted more specific detail about her assessment of the
custody assignment.

STENGER: "In your evaluation of Mrs. Mary Jo Risher, since, in
fact you found that she had a very warm and loving relationship
and was caring for the needs of Richard, especially his special
education needs, what were the reasons that you felt that he
should be placed with the father?"

SEGOVIS: "I think the primary reason and my concern was that given the schedule that Mrs. Risher had at that time, the fact that she was working two jobs and that the bulk of Richard's care at that point on a day-to-day basis appeared to be assumed by Mrs. Foreman and that she simply didn't have the time, as much time to give him as he would have had, had he been spending time in his father's home."

McCurley called Violat Tonnemaker as an adverse witness. She had known Mary Jo for twenty years and testified that to her knowledge no overt sexual activity was ever displayed in the home or at parties that Jimmy may have attended with his mother. Violat also denied that Jimmy had ever been taken to a homosexual bar by his mother. She was excused.

Thirty-year-old Delaine Risher, Doug's wife of three and a half years, was by her own definition a full-time housewife, who had a child by an unhappy previous marriage. She was a pert, auburn-haired woman, with a round, pretty face. Both in and out of the courtroom she had an anxious half-smile on her face. She always seemed a little overcome by the hullabaloo surrounding the custody battle. Delaine told the court she spent all her time "looking after the house." Her hobbies were mostly "family things."

Mrs. Risher dutifully identified eighteen pictures of her home and family events, presented as exhibits. It was hard to speculate if the photos were solicited by Mike McCurley or if Doug and Delaine were infected with our society's desperate need to record every segment of our lives on photo paper to capture proof that we still enjoy fleeting moments away from our loneliness and alienation. If visceral insecurity was our symptom, mass "polaroidation" was the prescription.

The jury leaned forward, showing great interest, as Mike McCurley laid out the photos one by one on the railing of the jury box. How many of them have paused in the middle of some joy to watch a photograph develop, checked it for the reality it confirmed, before returning to their life?

It's hard to photograph piety, so McCurley asked, "Do you raise your child, Shane, in a religious atmosphere?"

DELAINE: "I do."

MCCURLEY: "Do you teach him the difference between right and wrong?"

DELAINE: "Yes, I do."

MCCURLEY: "Kids have a way of being mischievous sometimes, and we all say dirty words occasionally; do you chastise him for that?"

DELAINE: "Yes, I do."

MCCURLEY: "If Richard is placed in your home, would you and Mr. Risher raise him as a Christian?"

DELAINE: "Yes, I will."

MCCURLEY: "Do you love Richard just like you love your own child?"

DELAINE: "Yes, I do."

While cross-examination was being conducted by her attorneys, Mary Jo scribbled a note on Frank Stenger's legal pad. He glanced at it, whispered to her, and began a new line of questioning.

STENGER: "Mrs. Risher, I take it from this custody battle that, in general, you and Doug both like children and like to have them around?"

DELAINE: "Yes."

STENGER: "And do you see them as a source of stability for the family life; they give you something extra in your life?"

DELAINE: "Yes, they're a joy to us."

STENGER: "And they help you in terms of your relationship with Doug and doing things together and going out and having a generally good time with the children?"

DELAINE: "Yes."

STENGER: "Something to live for and work for?"

DELAINE: "Yes."

STENGER: "Mrs. Risher, have you and Doug had any children of your own between you since the time of your marriage?"

DELAINE: "No."

STENGER: "Do you plan to have any children of your own?"

DELAINE: "No."

STENGER: "Is there any reason why you will not, do not plan to have any children of your own?"

DELAINE: "Well, I have one and he has two, and we figure that's all we need."

STENGER: "Is it possible for you to have children of your own?"

DELAINE: "I can, yes."

STENGER: "Has not, in fact, Doug Risher had a vasectomy?"

DELAINE: "Yes, he has."

STENGER: "Well, doesn't that make it fairly impossible for you to have children of your own?"

DELAINE: "Yes, yes, it would. I'm sorry, I'm a little upset, I'm nervous. I'm sorry."

STENGER: "Do you think that Doug and you would have pursued this lawsuit so vigorously to obtain his children, if, in fact, you could have had children of your own between you?"

DELAINE: "I don't understand. I'm sorry."

STENGER: "Let me phrase it this way: Would you prefer to have your own natural children through Doug rather than children that he had through a prior marriage?"

DELAINE: "That doesn't make any difference, no. The answer is no. I love his children whether we had the children together or not"

STENGER: "But it would have been nice, I take it, in your opinion, to have been able to have children together?"

DELAINE: "If we had so desired, yes."

STENGER: "And that was, perhaps, one of the motives behind your trying to seek custody of his children through a former marriage?"

DELAINE: "I don't know."

On further redirect examination by McCurley, Delaine said that she signed a consent paper for Doug's vasectomy after they were married. She was excused.

There was a shuffling of the chairs at the attorneys' table, so that Mary Jo was placed nearer the center, in a clearer line of vision to the witness stand. This new seating arrangement was explained when McCurley called seventeen-year-old Jimmy Risher to the stand.

James Douglas "Jimmy" Risher was a tall, thin young man with long brown hair that swept down over his forehead to his eyebrows. His features mirrored his mother and father. He sat well forward in the witness chair, speaking directly into the microphone in a typically adolescent voice. Throughout his testimony he would glance at his mother, who was crying. Jimmy appeared well rehearsed and confident in his answers. There was a strong trace of triumph and a lesser hint of contempt in his voice when he commented on his mother's homosexuality.

MCCURLEY: "Did living with your mother present any problems to you on a day-to-day basis, Jimmy?"

JIMMY: "Well, it brought up problems between my friends, and they seemed to kind of steer clear of me. They seemed not to have anything to do with me after they found out WHAT my mother was."

MCCURLEY: "Did any of your friends inquire to you about your mother?"

JIMMY: "Well, on several occasions, people asked me about mom living with somebody else and I really didn't want to discuss it with them, but they, you know, asked me."

MCCURLEY: "Was your mother's homosexuality a source of embarrassment to you, Jimmy?"

JIMMY: "Yes, sir, it was."

MCCURLEY: "Does it embarrass you today?"

JIMMY: "Yes, sir, it does, to know that my mother is a homosexual."

Mary Jo dabbed a tissue to her eyes. Jimmy avoided her stare; he was becoming quite uncomfortable. He tossed his hair and shifted position in the chair.

MCCURLEY: "Have you ever seen any pictures depicting her as a lesbian?"

JIMMY: "Yes, sir, I have."

MCCURLEY: "And would you describe for us that picture?"

JIMMY: "Well, there was one occasion that my mother showed me a picture of her in a tuxedo and Ann in a formal, and it was on New Year's Eve."

MCCURLEY: "When you say tuxedo, are you talking about a man's suit of clothes?"

JIMMY: "Yes, sir."

MCCURLEY: "Did it have a necktie and all that?"

JIMMY: "Yes, sir, it did."

MCCURLEY: "And a vest?"

JIMMY: "Yes, sir."

MCCURLEY: "And it was clearly a man's suit of clothes?"

JIMMY: "Yes, sir, it was."

MCCURLEY: "Okay, now, was there also another picture of Ann in a lady's formal or were they both in one picture?"

JIMMY: "They were both in one picture together."

MCCURLEY: "How were they posed?"

JIMMY: "Well, they were standing next to each other with their arms around each other, I believe. It's been so long since I've seen the picture, I don't remember that part."

Jimmy related how his mother and Ann expressed affection for each other: "There were several occasions they would hug each other and kiss each other on the cheek and things like this, like they'd be in the kitchen and they'd come in and whenever Ann or mom would be at home and the other one would come in, they would hug each other or something to that effect."

MCCURLEY: "From your observations, could you ever decipher which one—your mother or Ann—played the masculine role?"

JIMMY: "Yes, sir, my mother played the masculine role and Ann played the woman's role."

MCCURLEY: "Have you ever been in the presence of your mother or Mrs. Foreman and/or other homosexuals at a party or anything of that nature?"

JIMMY: "Uh, there was an occasion . . . They (some friends of my mother's and Ann) had a get-together, and they invited friends of theirs over, and I walked in there one evening and there were two guys on the couch necking on each other."

MCCURLEY: "Two men?"

JIMMY: "Yes, sir."

MCCURLEY: "Does it bother you to be around homosexuals?"

JIMMY: "Yes, sir, it does."

McCurley directed Jimmy to his present life at his father's house and how it differed from his days at Mary Jo's. "Whenever I first came out there," Jimmy recalled, "I was nervous and I just, uh, you know, was uptight about everything. And since I've been living out there, I've felt at ease, I've done things that I was used to doing, going hunting, fishing, things like that, just you know, going, being able to go out to the pasture out back and be able to hunt.

"And it just seems like a more suitable environment, you know, to be where man and wife live together than to have two women or two men, as I've been living with for six months."

For his final question on direct examination, McCurley asked Jimmy why he came into the court to testify.

JIMMY: "Well, I felt that I had a chance to get out of what I was living in and I felt that Richard shouldn't have to live with what I lived in."

Mary Jo gasped out loud. McCurley had concluded his direct examination and Aglaia Mauzy took over. Always low keyed, she handled Jimmy in an especially tactful manner.

MAUZY: "Did you say at the earlier hearing that you left your mother's home because she was a homosexual?"

JIMMY: "That wasn't the only reason."

MAUZY: "Just try to go along with me and just answer the questions. At that earlier hearing, you didn't say that, did you?"

JIMMY: "Would you please clarify?"

MAUZY: "You did not say at that earlier hearing that you left your mother's home because she was a homosexual, did you?"

JIMMY: "Well, at that hearing, that wasn't relevant, at that earlier hearing."

MAUZY: "Okay, Jimmy. Whether or not it was relevant, did you say that was the reason that you left your mother's home when you were asked that question?"

JIMMY: "No, it wasn't."

MAUZY: "Do you recall testifying at the earlier hearing that you loved your mother?"

JIMMY: "Yes, ma'am, I do."

MAUZY: "Do you still love your mother?"

JIMMY: "Yes, I do."

MAUZY: "Do you remember testifying about the car being very important to you?"

JIMMY: "Well, the car wasn't the most important thing in my life, but, I mean, you know, I did want one."

MAUZY: "Did you want your mother, hadn't you been asking your mother to buy you a car prior to the time you moved out?"

JIMMY: "Well, I asked her, but I had a motorcycle, and I had use of the Mustang on the side."

MAUZY: "Did you want your mother to buy you a car?"

JIMMY: "Yes, I did."

MAUZY: "What did she tell you when you asked her?"

JIMMY: "Well, she told me she couldn't afford a car, which I understood."

MAUZY: "Didn't your father buy you a car?"

JIMMY: "Yes, he did, about a month and a half or two months after I had moved away from mother."

MAUZY: "Can you honestly tell this jury that your father buying you a car, or promising to buy you a car, had nothing to do whatsoever with your moving out?"

JIMMY: "Yes, I can say that."

MAUZY: "Jimmy, I want you to think very carefully, because there is a record of the last hearing. Are you sure that is what you said at the last hearing?"

JIMMY: "Yes."

Aglaia Mauzy was trying to illustrate to the jury that Jimmy's story had changed in rather significant fashion. Her problems in impeaching Jimmy were multifold. She didn't have the transcript of the last hearing with her in the courtroom; Mary Jo was resisting the idea of having her son appear to be a liar, and Mike McCurley was likely to fight the introduction of past testimony into the current proceeding.

Later, when the jury returned and the verdict was final, the foreman would indicate that Jimmy's purported change in testimony escaped the consideration of the jury.

MAUZY: "Jimmy, did you, during the time you lived with your mother, bring your girl friends to your mother's house on several or many occasions?"

JIMMY: "A few occasions, I did."

MAUZY: "And you and your girl friend and your mother sat down and talked and chatted, didn't you?"

JIMMY: "No, we didn't. We might have sat down once or twice . . ."

MAUZY: "Did your mother, did she do anything that shocked your girl friend?"

JIMMY: "Well, she kept it pretty well concealed from my friends but she still, they still asked questions and wondered about it, because they had noticed a change in her, you know, or, you know, if they knew her."

MAUZY: "Let's talk about that. Your earlier testimony just a minute ago on direct examination was, you were embarrassed because all of your friends knew and asked you questions. Now, do I understand, you are saying that she kept it from your friends?"

JIMMY: "She kept it from them, but she couldn't hide the fact that she was one because they would ask why is she living with another woman?"

MAUZY: "Well, Jimmy, don't a lot of women live together just as a matter of convenience?"

JIMMY: "Yes, but not in a queen-size bed together and share the cars together and things like that."

MAUZY: "Did your friends have access or knowledge to the fact that your mother and Ann shared a bed?"

JIMMY: "Yes."

MAUZY: "Explain to me how that happened."

JIMMY: "Well, they'd ask me, whenever I had, on a couple of occasions friends would come over to the house and they would ask me where your mother sleeps. And I would say that she slept in the same room with Ann, and so . . ."

MAUZY: "She didn't point it out to them, you told them?"

JIMMY: "Well, they were asking me the questions and, you know, I didn't want to lie and I told them the truth."

All during the questioning of her son, Mary Jo was crying and moving her head from side to side in pained disbelief. The final questioning by Richard's attorney, Barton Bernstein, caused

Mary Jo to fall forward in her chair, gasp, and cover her mouth with both hands.

BERNSTEIN: "Are you angry at your mother?"

JIMMY: "No, sir. It's just that I'm ashamed of the way she is."

BERNSTEIN: "And does that bother you a great deal?"

JIMMY: "Yes, sir, it does."

Jimmy was excused, subject to recall. The court adjourned for lunch.

Mary Jo was stunned. Everything that had gone before: the arguments with Jimmy, his leaving home, his role in informing Doug of her lesbianism, his electing to live with his father; all of this was diminished by what he said on the stand. Jimmy's vindictiveness, the way he characterized her as an odious degenerate appalled her. "Jimmy had more than betrayed me, he twisted words to kill me, destroyed all the years of love and care I had built up in my boy. My heart was pounding in my chest, missing beats literally, and the pain, the pain was unimaginable. My stomach knotted up. I was literally sick, I wanted to vomit. He was so cold, up there. I didn't know him, anymore. I went back and forth between crying and wanting to kill him. How could he have done that to me? What made him say those things? He seemed to enjoy it, sticking in the knife. Why? Why?" After an hour-and-a-half break for lunch, Mary Jo was barely composed enough to re-enter the courtroom.

The next witness for Doug Risher's case was Dr. Philip Smith, pastor of the Lakeland Baptist Church in Lewisville, Texas. Dr. Smith was impressed by the Doug Risher family; he called them "clean-living Christian-type folks."

Mike McCurley got to the point quickly. "Sir, do you know whether or not the Bible addresses itself to the topic of homosexuality?"

DR. SMITH: "It does."

MCCURLEY: "When it addresses itself to that topic, is it favorable or unfavorable toward homosexuality?"

DR. SMITH: "It's unfavorable toward the practice. Toward the relationship."

MCCURLEY: "I'm referring now to the Bible, the unabridged

version, to the Book of Romans, and I would like to, for you to read to us what is said by the Lord on this topic."

DR. SMITH: "Paul is writing to a lot of Christians at Rome—and in the first chapter of Romans, verse twenty-four, he said: 'Wherefor, God gave them up to the lusts of their hearts and impurities to dishonor their bodies among themselves because they exchanged the truth about God for a lie and worshiped and served the creature rather than the Creator, who is blessed forever. Amen. For this reason, God gave them up to dishonorable passions; for their women exchanged natural relations for unnatural, and the men likewise gave up natural relations with women, and they were consumed with passion for one another. Men living in shameless acts with men and receiving into their own persons the due penalty for their error. And since they did not see fit to acknowledge God, God gave them up to a base mind and to improper conduct."

On cross-examination, Frank Stenger prodded Dr. Smith to a greater showing of his theological wares; the traditional fundamentalist beliefs of Southern Baptists.

STENGER: "Could you give us your feelings in regard to the morality or immorality of smoking, for instance?"

DR. SMITH: "Well, I think that the Bible teaches that the body is the Temple of God, and that it houses the Spirit of man in which the Spirit of God can dwell. And any habit that contaminates that Temple is a bad habit."

STENGER: "So in a sense, then, smoking would be immoral because it could cause bodily harm?"

DR. SMITH: "Because it harms the body, yes."

STENGER: "What would be your feelings as to the morality or immorality in regard to the drinking of alcoholic beverages?"

DR. SMITH: "The same thing."

STENGER: "What would your feelings be about the morality or immorality of abortion?"

DR. SMITH: "There are extenuating circumstances. Personally, I think it's against the law of God. There are certain conditions in the Old Testament which allow this to be."

STENGER: "Are there any explicit sexual acts that the Bible

would prohibit within the context of a marriage relationship in the privacy of one's own bedroom?"

DR. SMITH: "Between a husband and wife?"

STENGER: "Yes."

DR. SMITH: "I don't know that the Bible prohibits, uh, in a declarative statement the acts of a man and woman during marriage."

STENGER: "Does this include all sexual acts?"

DR. SMITH: "Well, between the two parties . . ."

STENGER: "And so, in your opinion, the performing of oral sex, for instance, between two married partners in the privacy of their own bedroom would not be immoral?"

DR. SMITH: ". . . The man is instructed to love his wife as Christ loved the church, and that is a predicated love relationship. And the woman is instructed to love her husband and be submissive to him. . . . I think all sex acts should be governed by the worth of the individual and their mutual esteem for each other."

STENGER: "Would you consider dancing in public places a moral or immoral act?"

DR. SMITH: "I think it can lead to immorality."

STENGER: "Can you describe what sort of dances you might consider to be immoral?"

DR. SMITH: ". . . I think any relationship that throws men and women together with music and vibrations, this kind of thing, that it lends itself to the excitement of the emotions, and those emotions are Holy and should be reserved for one's mate."

Dr. Smith was excused.

Dorothy Bennett, who lived five miles from Doug and Delaine, told the court, "That as friends and neighbors, I find them to be some of the nicest people I know. They're clean-living people."

Douglas L. Risher, Jr., took the stand in his own cause. He was thirty-eight, a high-school graduate, Air Force veteran, built his own home, and worked as a $1,700-a-month mechanic for an airline.

Doug was stone-faced, no glimmer of emotion when he talked.

His hair was razor cut and just a whisper lower than the top of his earlobes. Not one strand of his vivid red hair was ever out of place. His clothes were contemporary, wide-lapeled, colorful, and hardly showed any wrinkles. A hint of perfectionism. Risher spoke *sotto voce*. There was no audible spillover of the strong emotions that prompted him to file the suit. As with many people who have red hair and fair complexions, Doug's face was flushed in proportion to the stress he was experiencing. It stayed red during his entire time on the stand.

Early in the questioning McCurley asked his client: "Have you received any threats from your ex-wife, Mary Jo Risher, concerning this thing of homosexuality and bringing this lawsuit?"

DOUG: "Yes, I have. She told me that if I pursued this suit to get custody of the boys, that she would take it so far that I would be financially ruined. That she had—that she had all the support in the world that it would take, even if I won this trial; that she had enough financial support to take it on and on and on until I was drained of all resources and eventually, I would lose my home and my wife and everything."

MCCURLEY: "Did she tell you from where these resources were to come?"

DOUG: "Yes, she did."

MCCURLEY: "Where from?"

DOUG: "She said there were over two hundred and some odd thousand people in this area and each one of them was going to contribute a dollar apiece and that would be more than sufficient to fight me with."

MCCURLEY: "Did she refer to any organization in particular?"

DOUG: "I don't remember specifically, uh, there was some mention of Feleabus, (phonetics); I'm not just exactly sure of the pronunciation of this."

Doug said he noted a change in Jimmy after he came to live with him a few months ago. "There's just been such a change in Jimmy and his disposition that there's, that it's very pleasing to me. Because, when Jimmy moved in with me, he was very much uptight, he was, uh, he was distressed and emotionally, uh, what

I would consider, in my opinion, to be an emotional state. He was very depressed."

MCCURLEY: "Does he seem better now?"

DOUG: "Yes, sir. His grades have improved a great deal, from failing and barely passing student to the honor role since he moved in with me."

MCCURLEY: "Did you purchase a car for your son?"

DOUG: "Yes, sir, I did. I went and bought the car with my resources and gave the car to him. And the reason why I did this, I did it after some close consideration of the situation that I found him in there at his grandmother Davidson's."

MCCURLEY: "What situation was that?"

DOUG: "There was not a car in the family there. They were the only ones living there. Jimmy was in the band and he had no way, he had no way of getting up to the school and back and forth, and he was trying to hold down a job and go to school early and practice band and hold onto the job and participate and keep his school lessons up. And he was having to more or less, pardon the expression, bum rides, and him and his grandmother had no way of going to get groceries at the grocery store."

MCCURLEY: "Now, when did Jimmy move in with you?"

DOUG: "June the 30th of this year."

MCCURLEY: "And the car was bought and the check dated on what date?"

DOUG: "September the 15th, 1974."

MCCURLEY: "And Jimmy moved away from his mother on or around August the first, he testified to; and he moved where?"

DOUG: "To Mrs. Davidson's."

MCCURLEY: "And he moved to your home, when?"

DOUG: "June the 30th of this year."

MCCURLEY: "Hardly the sole motivation for a lawsuit."

After Judge Chrisman sustained her objection to "the grossest sort of testimony by an attorney," Aglaia Mauzy cross-examined Doug. She was clearly out to destroy the model image that Doug's attorney had constructed for the jury.

MAUZY: "Do you drink?"

DOUG: "Very seldom."

MAUZY: "How often?"

DOUG: "I can't recall at this moment the last time I had even a drink of beer."

MAUZY: "You're a very temperate man with regard to your intake of alcoholic beverages?"

DOUG: "Yes."

MAUZY: "Do you recall having a matter set in the County Criminal Court here in Dallas in 1972?"

DOUG: "Yes, I can. I learned a very valuable lesson."

MAUZY: "You were convicted or you pled guilty to a charge of driving while intoxicated?"

DOUG: "Yes, I did."

MAUZY: "Were you drinking when they picked you up?"

DOUG: "I was, I was single at the time . . ."

MAUZY: "You'll be able to expound on that later. I want to know if you were drunk when they picked you up?"

DOUG: "No."

MAUZY: "Why did you plead guilty?"

DOUG: "Pardon?"

MAUZY: "Why did you plead guilty to driving a car while intoxicated. You did plead guilty?"

DOUG: "I did plead guilty, yes."

MAUZY: "You got a year's probated sentence, didn't you?"

DOUG: "Yes, I did. My lawyer told me that I employed, that if this was my first time this ever happened to me, which it was, that this would be the cheapest and most economical route to travel."

MAUZY: "Are you telling this jury, under oath, that you weren't drunk when you were picked up by the police for that offense?"

DOUG: "I didn't feel that I was drunk, no."

MAUZY: "All right. Let's leave your drinking habits for awhile. Are you a violent man; are you given to temper outbursts?"

DOUG: "I, uh, I think I have a moderate temper."

MAUZY: "Do you hit people when you get mad?"

DOUG: "No, not as a daily rule, no, ma'am."

~ 183 ~

MAUZY: "Were you breaking that daily rule on October the 9th, 1969 when you hit Mary Jo Risher in the face and broke her nose?"

DOUG: "When?"

MAUZY: "In October of 1969."

DOUG: "I don't recall this."

MAUZY: "Let me refresh your memory. Do you recall back in October of '69 preparing to go on a camping trip with the two boys, Richard and Jimmy?"

DOUG: "October of 1969; and I'm supposed to have hit her and broke her nose? I'm sorry, I don't recall this, no."

MAUZY: "Are you telling this jury, under oath, that you never hit this woman in the face and broke her nose?"

DOUG: "On October of 1969?"

MAUZY: "Whenever. Tell me when you did it, if I've got the wrong date."

DOUG: "In Savannah, Georgia in 1959, she spit in my face and slapped me; and I lost my temper and hit her immediately thereafter. And I'm sorry that I did this ever since, that I lost my temper."

MAUZY: "Your boys were there, weren't they?"

DOUG: "Jimmy was a baby. This was 1959."

MAUZY: "How old was he?"

DOUG: "I don't know, maybe a year or so, I don't recall exactly."

MAUZY: "But you did hit her in the face and you did break her nose."

DOUG: "I don't ever remember breaking her nose."

MAUZY: "Do you remember hitting her in the face?"

DOUG: "I didn't hit her in the face."

MAUZY: "Where did you hit her?"

DOUG: "I think I hit her on the cheek."

MAUZY: "Who paid for the subsequent operation to have her nose fixed? Did you pay for that?"

DOUG: "I know nothing about that. I know nothing about a broken nose."

MAUZY: "Did the police serve you with a warrant for that assault?"

DOUG: "In '59?"

MAUZY: "The one we're talking about."

DOUG: "Yes, she called the police."

Aglaia steered Doug into the area of morality and asked if he agreed with his minister, Dr. Smith, that sex should be reserved for people who are married. He agreed.

MAUZY: "What are your feelings about abortion?"

DOUG: "About abortion? I have wondered about this. It is something that has entered my mind and I have wondered if, how God, if he was here with us, how He would look at it."

MAUZY: "Have you ever had anything to do with an abortion?"

DOUG: "No, I have not."

MAUZY: "Have you ever impregnated an unmarried lady?"

DOUG: "Not to my knowledge."

MAUZY: "You don't recall the impregnation of an 18 year old girl, who was the daughter of one of your co-workers in 1972?"

DOUG: "I was told that I was the one, yes."

MAUZY: "You had been having intercourse with this girl, hadn't you?"

DOUG: "Only once."

MAUZY: "How old was she?"

DOUG: "She was married and divorced and had a child."

MAUZY: "How old was she?"

DOUG: "I don't know, 18, 19, 20 years old. I don't know."

MAUZY: "What did you do after you found out you had impregnated this girl?"

DOUG: "I never found out that I had impregnated this girl."

MAUZY: "What did you do . . ."

DOUG: "She had been running around with a number of people."

MAUZY: "What did you do after you were told that you had impregnated this girl?"

DOUG: "Of course, I was, uh, I was told I was, uh, the one and I questioned it. I saw the girl one time."

MAUZY: "And you had sex with her?"

DOUG: "Yes."

MAUZY: "She was the daughter of one of your co-workers?"

DOUG: "I knew her father, yes."

MAUZY: "She was under 20 years old?"

DOUG: "This girl? If you say so. I don't know."

MAUZY: "Did you feel a moral obligation to help this girl that you might have impregnated?"

DOUG: "There's a long chain of circumstances and things which evolve around this, which I couldn't . . . I can't answer that question by saying yes or no."

MAUZY: "What did you do?"

DOUG: "When her dad asked me if intercourse did exist between me and the girl, I admitted it. And he said she had had an abortion. You see, this was a long period of time after the incident happened."

MAUZY: "Umm-hmm."

DOUG: "And he said, 'She has had an abortion.' And the girl never did point me out as the one; but when he said this, I did go ahead and give him some money."

MAUZY: "How much?"

DOUG: "Uh, I don't recall."

MAUZY: "Well, give me a ball-park figure, a hundred dollars, two hundred dollars?"

DOUG: "Maybe $150.00. And then, I found out through other sources that this girl had been pretty loose and that she had been running around with other people. She had been married and divorced and had a background, which I didn't even know existed."

MAUZY: "What would you have done? Would you not had sex with this girl if you had known she had been married and divorced?"

DOUG: "That is a question I can't answer."

MAUZY: "Nonetheless, you paid for the abortion, didn't you?"

DOUG: "Only part of it, when I found out that I may not have been the guilty party."

MAUZY: "But you may have been?"

DOUG: "There is that slight possibility."

~ 186 ~

Back to the car. Aglaia Mauzy reminded Doug Risher of the date the car was purchased, September 15, 1974, and the date of the temporary custody hearing, October 25, 1974.

MAUZY: "The car, of course was bought before the hearing?"

DOUG: "Yes . . ."

MAUZY: "Did you and Jimmy talk about that car much before the hearing?"

DOUG: "Yes, I bought him a car before the hearing, of course."

MAUZY: "And hadn't you talked to him about the car before September the 15th?"

DOUG: "He told me he wanted a car, yes."

MAUZY: "And he told his mother that he wanted a car, too, didn't he?"

DOUG: "I had reason to believe that he did."

MAUZY: "And he wanted that car very badly, didn't he?"

DOUG: "Yes, I can remember I wanted one very badly when I became his age."

MAUZY: "It was a really important event in Jimmy's life, wasn't it?"

DOUG: "If you want me to measure how important it was to him, I don't know how I would do this to your satisfaction. I know that it was important to me when I became old enough to get a driver's license to have a car; and I'm sure it's very important to Jimmy."

At one point in his questioning of Doug, Barton Bernstein asked if it was in the best interest of Richard for him to be awarded to his father.

DOUG: "There are a number of reasons why I feel that Richard would be better off in my home. Uh, I think that it is beneficial to him that my wife could be there to attend to him and his needs on a 24-hour basis, as she is with my stepson, Michael Shane. That is one reason foremost in my mind. Another thing, he will have a mother and father image to be portrayed before him, for him to see and model himself after. And since I do like the outdoors and sports and fishing and this sort of thing, I think these things are valuable in the upbringing of a young boy, as it was with Jimmy, even though I was, we were separated and divorced when Richard (sic) was eleven, this sort of activity that existed while me and my ex-wife were married stuck with him and he still enjoys a sort of clean type of recreation."

BERNSTEIN: "Mr. Risher, is there anything that you can think of that would make a change of custody at this time ill-advised? In other words, is there anything that, any harmful effects that you can think of that there might be because of a change in custody?"

DOUG: "I don't think there is any, no, sir."

BERNSTEIN: "You think that Richard would be happy in your home?"

DOUG: "I think this adjustment could be made very well. He is at ease in my home."

After a brief conference with his client, Mike McCurley announced, "The Petitioner rests." Court was adjourned until Thursday morning.

Since both Mary Jo and Ann had already appeared as adverse witnesses, Frank Stenger opened the Respondent's case with the Reverend Emmett M. Waites, chaplain of the hospital where Mary Jo worked.

STENGER: "I would like your personal impressions of Mary Jo Risher."

REV. WAITES: "Okay. Mrs. Risher is a hard-working nurse. I have observed her putting in eight hard hours; she's not a person who loafs; I don't see her hanging around the desk. She is attentive to her patients and she is well liked by her patients. She gets along very well with her associates. She's all business as a nurse and is a very compassionate person and a very sensitive person."

Frank Stenger asked Waites about the time he visited with Mary Jo, Ann and the children at their home. The Reverend Waites told the jury he was impressed with the children and the home.

STENGER: "What was your impression of the relationship between Mary Jo and Richard? Did you observe anything that gave you an impression as to how they interacted?"

REV. WAITES: "Yes. Uh, to me, there was a relaxed relationship between mother and son. Uh, went through the usual thing after supper and after the kids had played the mechanical piano for me and showed me their rooms, uh, I think it was Mrs. Risher who said that 'It's time to get ready for bed;' and there were the usual delays.

"'Well, let me just show him this and show him that,' and finally she said, 'Okay, that's enough, go upstairs and get your bath.'

"There was a relaxed degree of obedience there. I liked what I saw, and I went there wondering what, exactly, what the situation would be."

When pressed for a personal evaluation of Mary Jo, as a result of his counseling with her, the Reverend Waites called her "honest." ". . . She is a person that I would trust. I don't know what she thinks of me, but I regard myself as her friend."

STENGER: "Do you have any feelings or opinions as to whether that relationship, [between Mary Jo and Ann] is a moral relationship?"

REV. WAITES: "Let's leave the word morality out of it right now, may I? As a . . . and I have Mary Jo's permission to say this—I asked her two questions when she revealed this relationship to me. I asked her, I said: 'Were you, as a married woman, faithful?' And she said: 'I was never unfaithful to my husband;' and I believed that. And I asked her if she had a commitment and a sense of responsibility that she felt in this relationship with Mrs. Foreman; and she said that: 'I can say the same thing for this relationship.'

"So I believed their relationship to be a relationship in which there is a commitment and responsibility. I am not going to judge the morality of it; because Mary Jo has never asked me to.

"She has, uh, she has not asked me for my moral judgment, and I feel there are possibly some relationships which belong in the area of the privacy of a person and his or her conscience, and his or her God. And she seems to accept this, so that is none of my concern. Does that answer your question?"

STENGER: "Do you think that there is any correlation between her relationship with Ann Foreman and her ability to raise her child Richard? That is to say, in her relationship . . . being a homosexual . . . affect the child morally?"

REV. WAITES: "The relationship, as I have seen it—and there are some or certain types of homosexual relationships which, I would say, would be unhealthy for a child—but her relationship, as I have seen it, I would say is one in which the child could grow and grow normally."

STENGER: ". . . Can a blanket statement be made that all homosexuals are immoral?"

REV. WAITES: "No I can't do that."

STENGER: "Then, how would you embark on judging whether they are or are not?"

REV. WAITES: "Uh, the degree of selfishness or unselfishness in the individual; the degree of commitment in the relationship. There are some homosexuals who hop from bar to bar every night. There are some who are terribly selfish and destructive and dishonest. They are like heterosexuals."

STENGER: "Would you, then, say on a judgment basis that they are the same as heterosexuals?"

REV. WAITES: "Absolutely."

On cross-examination, Mike McCurley insisted on a literal interpretation of the Bible: "From your studies of the Works of God, do you have any knowledge as to whether or not the act of homosexuality is against the instructions and law of God?"

REV. WAITES: "Okay, Mr. McCurley. You, we can draw out several texts from the Bible that speak of that act, of homosexuality, as an abomination before God, that's the Biblical word. The Bible is written in an historical context, and I believe the Bible to be the word of God. But I am not a fundamentalist. And the Bible is written in an historical context.

"Society changes; and I feel that the, many of the things which we have . . . for instance, the Bible says after woman has borne a child and she is still in the state of maturity, that she should offer two ewe lambs or offer two doves as a sacrifice. That act would simply have no relevance to me."

MCCURLEY: "Society changes and we all know that, but at least, and I am out of my area, and I apologize; but as far as I know, the word of God doesn't. And what I would like to ask you is: Do you know whether or not the act of homosexuality is against the teachings of God?"

REV. WAITES: "And I answered you the best I can, Mr. McCurley. I'm talking as a man. Okay. Under certain circumstances, I cannot say it is immoral. Under many circumstances, I say it is immoral."

MCCURLEY: "Okay. Do you know what God says about it? Now, we've heard what you say about it; but do you know what God has said about it?"

REV. WAITES: "God hasn't spoken to me about it."

McCurley wasn't prepared for any humor when he was thumping the Bible issue. His voice hardened into a distasteful reproach for a man of the cloth who couldn't see the miasmic doctrine of fundamentalism as an eternal absolute.

MCCURLEY: "Do you believe that God addresses us through the Bible?"

REV. WAITES: "Yes, I do."

MCCURLEY: "And has he addressed us through the Bible on the topic of homosexuality, sir?"

REV. WAITES: "I am not a fundamentalist, Mr. McCurley. Yes, historically, there are, there are many, many references to homosexuality in the Bible."

MCCURLEY: "Okay. You used the word abomination and I believe that there is a portion of the Bible or one particular section that uses that word, that it says: 'I am the Lord' at the end of it and some place else it says: 'The act of homosexuality or homosexuality is an abomination to the Lord,' does it not?"

REV. WAITES: "That's in the Old Testament, right."

MCCURLEY: "What does the word abomination mean, sir."

Rev. Waites was exasperated at Mike's condescending tone. He wasn't about to attach the same ex-cathedra interpretation to a singular passage of the Bible that McCurley demanded. "It meant, in the time of the Jews, in the morality of the times, that it was abhorrent to the Jewish society at that time."

MCCURLEY: "And if I understand you, you say that its morality or immorality depends on such things as commitment to one another, is that your testimony, and other factors?"

REV. WAITES: "In a relationship where there is responsibility and commitment and where other people are not hurt, I think it is the business of the two people involved."

The Reverend Waites was excused. His good nature returned immediately; and he left the courtroom, his theology unswayed and, by the looks on the faces of the jury, unswaying.

Catherine Jo Crittenden was called. She was an acquaintance of Mary Jo's. Aglaia Mauzy anticipated the usual practice Mike McCurley employed and she asked Miss Crittenden if she was homosexual or heterosexual. She replied, "Heterosexual."

After several unsuccessful attempts, by Mike McCurley, to quash her testimony, Aglaia was allowed to ask Miss Crittenden's impressions of Jimmy Risher's relationship with his mother.

MISS CRITTENDEN: "My individual impressions were that he in no way was ashamed of his mother's living arrangement; that he had no reason to be ashamed to his friends or anyone else, because of the fact that if they were to accept him, they had to accept his mother and her life style also, and that was a very definite impression that he gave me."

MAUZY: "Did you have an impression that he was embarrassed or ashamed of his mother?"

CATHERINE: "Not at all."

MAUZY: "There has been testimony by Jimmy that he came to a party at a neighbor's house and that there were two male homosexuals there and that they engaged in some sort of sexual activity. Have you ever been to a party where there were two homosexual males at a neighbor's house?"

CATHERINE: "I have been to a party where they were present, yes."

MAUZY: "Did you, at any time, see any display that you would describe as sexual in nature between these two men?"

CATHERINE: "Absolutely not."

MAUZY: "How would you describe their conduct while you were there and they were there?"

CATHERINE: "I guess the only suitable word would be respectable. They just sat around and nothing in the way of hugging or kissing or anything like that at all."

MAUZY: "Did you come with these men and leave with these men?"

CATHERINE: "Yes."

Miss Crittenden was excused.

Mary Jo's lawyers would put three psychological witnesses on the stand. The first was Dr. Dolores Dyer, a state-certified clinical psychologist specializing in child and family relations.

Dr. Dyer was a petite, handsome and cordial woman. Although her clothes were attractive, they seemed to have been selected for utilitarian value; she always appeared slightly disheveled, coat unbuttoned, lapel pin askew, the belt of her dress avoiding several loops. Wisps of blond hair kept falling across her forehead. Her perpetual state of motion—meetings, seminars, encounters, lectures and therapy—was transmitted physically through her wind-blown appearance.

Unlike many of her colleagues, Dr. Dyer was cognizant of the mystique surrounding her profession and avoided, where possible, the "psycho-babble" that hindered communication between psychologist and layman. That quality, alone, was enough to endear her to the jury.

Dr. Dyer spent thirteen to fourteen hours evaluating the Mary Jo Risher family unit.

STENGER: "Do you feel that in that 13 or 14 hours, you were able to come to a professional evaluation and also, a personal evaluation of the interrelationships of that family and of the individual personalities in that family?"

DR. DYER: "Yes. Of course, as a psychologist, I did reach my own conclusions. I saw the relationship between the two women as a respectful one. They were able to meet their children's needs, uh, emotional needs, physical needs, and I also found out how they handled their children.

"I observed the children coming to each one of them for assistance. I watched the children interact with each other in a comfortable way.

"And my conclusion about this family was that after all questions, that they were people who could make a stable commitment, who could solve problems, could openly communicate with themselves and the children, and, in general, compared to most of our modeling, which are heterosexual, that they had an extremely good relationship."

STENGER: "Let's start with the respondent, Mary Jo Risher. Did you come to any conclusion after talking with her and counseling with her as to her personality, her stability, uh, her emotional state and things of that nature that a psychologist evaluates?"

DR. DYER: "Yes, I looked at her relationship historically, in the sense that she had a marriage and had been able to make a commitment to this marriage until such time that it was no longer possible; that she then made a commitment to the present relationship and is a devoted partner, so to speak, and that she is able to express affection both in observation and conversation toward her children; that she was very open and willing to listen to things about being a good parent as well as to be aware of the great many things that it took to be a good parent and to answer those questions for me.

"Now, I based this on her past history and I based it on her responses to me and on her capacity to show emotion. And I based it on her with her child and, in part, I based it on what her child said about her."

STENGER: "Were you able to come to any conclusions as to her emotional fiber or her stability . . . could you address yourself to that aspect of Mary Jo's personality?"

DR. DYER: "To me, she is an emotionally stable person with no psychosis—that is my thinking. And what I mean by that is: I do not see her as being in need of treatment. I saw her under stress and have had a chance to observe her and feel that she is dealing extraordinarily well under a stressful situation."

STENGER: "What are some of the specific things that you observed about her that made you reach the conclusion that she was emotionally stable . . . ?"

DR. DYER: "Well, one of the things is that even during this period, she's been able to cope with her children and to consider them. She has not demonstrated any sort of, you know, how should I put that, unreality. She's able to assess the situation and come to conclusions and behave accordingly."

STENGER: "Did you come to any conclusions as to her ability to provide for and care for her son, Richard?"

DR. DYER: "Yes. She talked about how she cared for him in the sense of the day-to-day living arrangements. She works and the child is cared for after school. She's with him, and I found out that she attends to his needs, special needs. He is taken to the doctor and he is taken to school to a special reading class; that she attends to his needs in this way. And, as I say, I personally observed the child coming to her and she did respond to him when he came in an affectionate and warm manner."

STENGER: "Was there anything, in terms of your observations of Richard, physically, that would make you come to the conclusion that she was providing for him and caring for him?"

DR. DYER: "Yes. He was an average, healthy, bright, alert youngster. He was able to verbalize and behave according to his age expectations."

STENGER: "What was your evaluation of Richard, as a nine year old boy, after you had several sessions with him, in terms of his emotional stability?"

DR. DYER: "I found him to be an emotionally stable child in keeping with his age limits. I checked him out on several factors and I found out that he could see things as they really were. He was okay psychologically in the sense that he is not crazy and is not disturbed in the sense we talk about children."

STENGER: "Okay. In terms of intellectual capacity, did you note any serious impairment of his intellectual capacity?"

DR. DYER: "No. I did not see any signs or responses that would cause me to say, 'Let's determine an IQ on this child.'"

STENGER: ". . . Did you come to a conclusion that he was . . . a normal nine year old boy?"

DR. DYER: "Yes. And specifically, you know, when I knew we were coming to trial, I asked the child a number of questions about himself and his own identity. . . . People's sexual identity are set usually between 18 months to about two or three years.

There's usually a difference between the boy and the girl. Usually by age four, they are able to distinguish certain toys and certain occupations as being male and/or female.

"I asked the child a number of questions like this and he gave me a very typical male stereotype, actually. He wants to be a policeman; he plays with bicycles . . . He wants to be a lion. That may not mean a lot to you personally, but in our way of looking at children, it helps us to know what roles they are adopting and playing.

"And this did come up and I was asked to look at it, and I did in this manner. And I think, if you read any of the books on child identity, you will find that this is one way of ascertaining if a child sees himself as a boy or a girl."

STENGER: "Did he ever relate to you directly what he felt about his mother and his living environment?"

DR. DYER: "Yes. The only, as I have said, concern that I had about Richard was the second time that I saw him, when I specifically asked him questions. Again, he appeared to be quiet and more subdued. The first time I saw him he was spontaneous and he was laughing and playing.

"All right. When he was asked, he said he knew he was going to court, uh, or he said that he knew his father wanted him, he didn't say anything about the courtroom actually. He just said he did not want to tell his dad that he didn't want to live with him. And, uh, you know, that's of course, one of the reasons that I volunteered to come down here today, because of my interest in children.

"And I don't know, but I did advise Mary Jo Risher, and I have to say this, not to put the child or make him decide between his parents. And I felt it was important that he should not be put on the stand, and I said so at the time. He said that he did not want to have to say this, but he said he was happy where he was."

STENGER: "Was the indication to you that he felt close to his mother?"

DR. DYER: "Yes, he said that he felt close to her and that he wanted to live with her."

STENGER: "In regard to Ann
lives with Mary Jo Risher. Cou
selling you provided for her or s
she might have had?"

DR. DYER: "All right, let me clarif
selled with, I saw these people ori
they were asking me to make a pro
emotional and mental health and sta

"I did not see any of these people a
peutic counselling. I did, when I evaluat
of this case give them back some answer   , let
me make that distinction.

"I did evaluate Ann Foreman and the   nation then was
conveyed back to my clients. I found her, again, like her partner,
to be a stable, emotional person and was able to form bonds in
relationship to other people. And in the interaction, I found her
respectful of her partner and I found her respectful and warm
toward her child and the other child, and all sorts of things."

STENGER: "Do you have any recollection as to what it was that
you gathered from your conversations with Ann Foreman that
made you come to the conclusion that she was emotionally stable
and that she could provide for and care for her child and have
a proper environment for her child, Judie Foreman?"

DR. DYER: "Specifically, the fact that they took these children
to school, and here again, when one had a reading problem, they
saw that the children got the proper attention. They saw that
they were provided for with afterschool care; they were well
clothed; they looked healthy. She expressed her concern about
her child; and they showed me that they had the best interest
of the children going for them, even under the stressful periods
—(inaudible)—when she expressed herself to me, she expressed
emotion in her voice and behavior.

"She was able to face the reality of this situation and not only
cope with it, but I think be fairly realistic."

STENGER: "Let me get into Judie Foreman, since she has, of
necessity been brought into this trial, and since she does, in fact,
live in the same environment as Richard lives.

describe for me and for the court what sort
...ad with Judie Foreman; first of all, describe Judie
...terms of who she is and her age and things of that

DYER: ". . . She's ten years old and she's a very pretty little
girl with long blond hair and she smiled and she was very charming. She made funny faces . . . when she came in, she was sitting
in my office, in my waiting room, and working on needlepoint.

"And when she came in, she seemed comfortable with herself
and to be a rather poised young lady, which you know, they get
to be around that age. And she was spontaneous in her speech;
by that, I mean she talked on her own; she is not quiet and shy
and I did not have to reach out and ask her every word; she
talked about herself.

"I, again, asked her some questions in terms of her own identity
and the kind of life that she led. I asked her about such things
as school and when she gave answers to that, I asked her what
her favorite toys were and she talked about playing dress-up and
modeling; she talked about a particular doll that she liked; and
she talked about her playmates, her needlepoint and she talked
about liking to play dress-up and modeling.

"I asked these questions, because these are one way which psychologists have of looking at how a person sees herself, what her
identity is as a person. I asked her who she got along with best.
And she said she got along best with her mother. I asked her
who she got along worst with, and she said her mother."

There was hearty laughter in the courtroom; even Judge Chrisman smiled knowingly.

STENGER: "Was there any indication during these sessions or
during your evaluation of Judie Foreman that she had any problems as a result of the environment in which she was living?"

DR. DYER: "No. Again, I do know that both of these children
needed some special help in reading, and that this was being
taken care of. So I do not address myself to that. I saw no problem
in her intellectual functioning that would cause me to test her
or anything like that."

STENGER: "Would it be fair to say that in psychological terms or as a result of a psychological evaluation of Judie Foreman, that she appeared to be a normal ten year old girl?"

DR. DYER: "Yes, within my evaluation, yes. I spent more time with Richard than I did with the little girl. I simply checked out, and in my observations and through my questioning, I did not hear or see anything which caused me to continue to probe in any given area.

"Now, I also will state that I did not attempt a whole, complete evaluation on this child quite in the way that I did Richard. But, on the other hand, I saw nothing there that concerned me."

STENGER: "Can you give me a summary of your conclusions, your professional conclusions, derived from your observations of these four people as to how they interrelate as a family or what their interactions were like?"

DR. DYER: "All right, I'm afraid I'm repeating some of the same things. I looked at how they, as a family, worked together, who assumed what responsibility in the household and I found out that they shared, they both worked, and they shared many tasks about the household as well as the tasks toward the children. That economically they shared their funds and economic concerns with each other. In terms of with the children, I felt that either one of the people could act as a parent to the children on any given occasion.

"I found that the children both seemed happy and comfortable; and my final conclusion was that this seemed to be a family."

STENGER: "Give us your opinion as to what you felt about that situation [homosexuality] and how it affected Richard."

DR. DYER: "I felt like it had not hurt him in the development of his identity or his sexual identity or his emotional stability as a child."

STENGER: "What are your feelings in regard to homosexuality, in general, and what would be your position as a psychologist in regard to homosexuality as a mental illness?"

DR. DYER: "As a psychologist, I go along with the position of the American Psychological Association which no longer endorses homosexuality as a mental illness in that we no longer consider a homosexual a deficient in stability of judgment or impairment of their ability to function and that we encourage that people do not discriminate against people who are of homosexual orientation any more than they would on the basis of race or color. That is my position in that regard.

"In regard to fitness of who the child is living with, in a household like this, I think, I believe that, along with this opinion, that these people are capable of being good parents.

"Again, on my own, I adopt personally the position of the American Psychological Association, which has passed a resolution from the Board on Social and Medical Responsibility, we say we encourage the rights of parents to retain custody of their children regardless of sexual orientation. And in the case of foster parents, then this should no longer be an issue in determining the fitness of parents. I go along with this position. I am not unaware that, uh, people who differ from us have special difficulties and I would be a fool to say otherwise."

STENGER: "Did you, in your professional capacity, and based upon your training and your experience as a psychologist, come to any conclusions as to what effect might occur in regard to Richard as a result of removing him from his mother and the environment in which he now exists?"

DR. DYER: "Yes. They were similar conclusions to ones I might make for any child. That is, if the child is comfortable and happy and part of his own identity has to do with what he has learned from his mother, that he is an all right person, and to him, she is an all right person.

"And as a psychologist, I see no reason to remove the child from the situation in which he has been living. To remove the child would be to say that something is wrong with his mother. And this would certainly affect how he sees himself."

STENGER: "And could you give us your professional opinion as to what emotional problems might occur as a result of a son being removed from his mother on the basis that she is a homosexual and a bad parent?"

DR. DYER: "I think that a child's identity depends upon the

kind of feelings that he gets about himself from both his parents, and he must value himself in order to accept their opinions.

"And if we, as society, devalue his mother or father, then we are, of necessity, bringing the child to be in conflict. And I think you know, from what I observed, that he feels his mother to be all right. I don't want to exclude fathers, either."

On cross-examination, Mike McCurley was in good form—tough, abrasive questions posed with subtle innuendo. He and Dyer would quibble endlessly over finite meanings of words and just what information he was trying to uncover. Dr. Dyer was a strong witness and wouldn't be trapped by McCurley's sometimes specious arguments and the oldest of legal tricks, convoluted logic. He was a formidable courtroom advocate, but she was a resolute professional with a gyroscopic tranquillity. A standoff.

McCURLEY: "Tell us what possible problems Richard might face being raised in a lesbian family unit?"

DR. DYER: "If we, as a community and as a society, accept the differences of other people then I see no problem. If we, as society, make it difficult for people who are different from us, then I can see that society could also punish the child. And that would create problems for him."

McCURLEY: "To narrow this question in scope, we're not litigating society, though it sometimes seems so. We're litigating this child. As society is today, December of 1975, do you anticipate that this child is going to have problems?"

DR. DYER: "I'm as anxious to know the truth as . . ."

McCURLEY: "Ma'am, don't tell me that. Just answer the question. Now, will you tell us what those problems are?"

DR. DYER: "I think that there will be people who, uh, will not like his mother and maybe his father, too; I would anticipate that there will be people who will disagree with either of those life styles."

McCURLEY: "You don't know of any other problems? You can't anticipate any other problems except someone might not like his mother?"

DR. DYER: "I can anticipate that someone would run into the whole range of human problems."

MCCURLEY: "All right then, let me be more specific. Can you conceive of any problems that our hypothetical little Richard might have or might anticipate that someone else who is not raised in a lesbian family unit would have. Or stated in the affirmative, is he going to have any additional problems?"

DR. DYER: "I can anticipate if he were removed from his mother . . ."

McCurley was apoplectic. "No, ma'am, that's not my question. Wait, wait, wait . . ."

DR. DYER: "I'm sorry, I'm really trying to help you."

MCCURLEY: "I think you are and I'm trying to get an answer to a specific question. If you'd like for me to ask something else about removing the boy or whatever, I'll be glad to do it. But my question to you is this: As a psychologist, do you anticipate that little Richard might experience some problems in addition to whatever problems everybody else on the street experiences because he is raised in a lesbian family environment?"

DR. DYER: "No, I guess I don't."

MCCURLEY: "What? You say that . . ."

MAUZY: "Your honor, this witness has answered that question. She's just made a specific answer and she's just now answered it again. Now is the counsel going to try to testify to these questions until he gets the witness badgered into answering what he says?"

JUDGE CHRISMAN: "What is the answer?"

DR. DYER: "As I understood the question, it was: 'Would he or might he have some special problems because of his mother's life style,' and I specified under what condition this might occur, and then he said: 'He might have other problems,' and I said: 'He might experience a whole range of problems, but that I did not see any other specific problems,' and I answered 'No.'"

Later, in the cross-examination, McCurley asked Dr. Dyer about her marital status and family situation. She had a thirty-year-old son and a grandson. That was startling, only because Dr. Dyer looked in her mid-thirties.

MCCURLEY: "Do you have any preference, as a mother, whether your son is a homosexual or a heterosexual?"

DR. DYER: "Can I answer that as . . ."

MCCURLEY: "Just answer yes or no."

DR. DYER: "That's the only answer I can give?"

MCCURLEY: "That's it."

DR. DYER: "I can't answer."

MCCURLEY: "You what?"

DR. DYER: "I can't answer yes or no."

McCurley was petulant. "Well, let me ask you this, ma'am: It matters not to you whether your son is a homosexual or a heterosexual, is that true?"

MAUZY: "That is the same question restated."

JUDGE CHRISMAN: "I'll overrule your objection."

DR. DYER: "Say it again."

MCCURLEY: "All right. Let me ask you this: Does it not matter to you at all whether your son is a homosexual or a heterosexual?"

DR. DYER: "I can't give a blanket yes or no to that."

MCCURLEY: "Well, ma'am, it either matters or it doesn't."

MAUZY: "She said: She can't answer the question, your honor."

DR. DYER: "It matters in some ways and not in others; I can't give a blanket answer, yes or no."

MCCURLEY: "All right, are you telling me you can't or you won't? You can't answer that question: 'I care' or 'I don't care.' Your Honor, I think this is very important."

MAUZY: "Your honor, I think this witness has answered that she can't answer yes or no. If he wants to let her explain her answer . . ."

A jumble of loud voices.

JUDGE CHRISMAN: "I believe the question is: Whether or not it matters, is that correct?"

MCCURLEY: "Yes."

MAUZY: "And she said: She can't give a yes or no answer."

DR. DYER: "I don't know what you mean by matters."

MCCURLEY: "All right let me ask you: Do you know what I mean by prefer? Do you know what the word prefer means?"

Dr. Dyer hesitated. Finally, she realized that McCurley wasn't just being sarcastic, he actually wanted an answer. "That I would pick one over the other."

Just as if he were congratulating a schoolgirl McCurley continued. "Yes, that's one definition of prefer. Okay. Would you, in any way, prefer your son to be a heterosexual as versus a homosexual?"

DR. DYER: "Of course."

MCCURLEY: "Of course. Now, how about your grandchildren? Are your grandchildren male or female?"

DR. DYER: "Male."

MCCURLEY: "Would you prefer your grandchild to be homosexual or heterosexual?"

DR. DYER: "Heterosexual."

MCCURLEY: "All right. Heterosexual. Would you prefer your grandchild to be raised in a homosexual home or a heterosexual home?"

DR. DYER: "I don't care."

MCCURLEY: "You don't care? You want them to be one or the other, but you don't care which they are raised in?"

DR. DYER: "That's right."

McCurley slumped into his chair and passed the witness. Someone had just introduced the color gray into his black and white spectrum. Court was recessed for the lunch break.

Before the court reconvened, Mike McCurley and his legal assistant brought several armfuls of books into court and neatly arranged them on the lawyers' table. Most were texts about psychology and human sexuality. Words and phrases like "lesbian, abnormal psychology, women in love," were interspersed among the titles. The collection must have been more for show than substance, for McCurley never opened them during the testimony of the two psychologists. The array may have been a billboard to remind the jury of the central issue of homosexuality, but the unused references only amused Drs. Dain and Dyer; they weren't in the slightest intimidated.

Dr. Robert N. Dain was an assistant professor of psychology

and assistant dean for academic affairs at the University of Texas Health and Science Center in Dallas.

Dr. Dain was a sociable man of average build, with an unevenly cropped short beard, glasses and large, piercing eyes. His manner was precise and iconoclastic. A wry sense of humor saved him from the pedagogic boorishness that overtook so many academic psychologists.

Frank Stenger conducted the examination. "With regard to Richard Risher, did you make an evaluation of whether his emotional development was age appropriate for a nine year old boy?"

DR. DAIN: "My assessment was that it was age appropriate for a normal nine year boy."

STENGER: "Because this is so important, may I ask you what you remember about the interview with Richard Risher that led to your conclusion that his development was age appropriate for a nine year old boy?"

DR. DAIN: "The major . . . the major things that I remember about it was that he was able to discuss his own life and his home life and his school life with me in an appropriate way. I was mainly concerned with his attitudes towards his home life and towards his . . . towards himself or his self-concept."

STENGER: "What sort of self-image or self-concept did you determine that the boy had?"

DR. DAIN: "I determined that he had a very positive self-concept and that he was realistically aware of some of the difficulties that he was having academically; that he felt, uh, secure, and that he felt well supported by the adults with whom he had contact; that he seemed to believe that he would continue or be able to remain in that environment, he seemed to be very comfortable with that knowledge on his part."

STENGER: "Did the question of whether or not Richard Risher might leave his mother's home come up in the interviews or evaluations that occurred between you?"

DR. DAIN: "Yes, it did."

STENGER: "Did you discuss this with him?"

DR. DAIN: "Yes. And, uh, he had . . . he was quite . . . well, he was concerned that there was a possibility that he might be removed from that home. But he did not consider it as a probability; he did not wish to leave that home, and he seemed to feel more hopeful rather than certain that he would be able to remain."

Dr. Dain's assessment of Mary Jo was similar to Dr. Dyer's. "She seemed to me to be a very intelligent and stable, well-put-together person, who had a secure self-concept; who thought well of herself and her capacity to deal with whatever problems she might have to deal with. She related very warmly and we discussed at some length her concerns relating to the problem that this trial was about; and she believed that she would be able to cope with that, as well."

STENGER: "Did you discuss or were you aware that Mary Jo Risher is, by preference, a homosexual?"

DR. DAIN: "Yes, that was immediately apparent because she told me."

STENGER: "And can you tell the jury whether or not her homosexuality was well-integrated in her personality and character?"

DR. DAIN: "Extremely well integrated."

STENGER: "In your opinion, after having interviewed and evaluated Richard Risher, does he or are there other males in his family, males with whom he can relate to in various aspects of his life outside of his home?"

DR. DAIN: "Well, he certainly relates with his father; as I understand it, he visits with his father very often, perhaps weekly. There is Ann Foreman's husband, who comes into the home. And, of course, in this society, there are a multitude of males who provide roles."

STENGER: ". . . Would you say he has as many male contacts outside of his immediate family as a child of a divorced family would have?"

DR. DAIN: "Certainly."

STENGER: "Do you have a professional opinion as to whether or not the existing relationship between Ann Foreman and Mary Jo Risher will have an effect on Richard Risher in that because of that, he may become a homosexual or have a homosexual choice of some kind?"

DR. DAIN: "I think the major consideration, generally, is one of the extent to which he is loved or cared for. The evidence about who, in fact, becomes homosexual is that almost all homosexuals come from heterosexual, normal, regular heterosexual families.

"There is very little evidence about what happens to children who are reared in homosexual settings; but such evidence as there is, would suggest that they tend to be heterosexuals as one would suspect, since that is the way most people become in this society."

STENGER: "Did you see any evidence that Richard Risher was developing other than that way?"

DR. DAIN: "No."

STENGER: "Do you have an opinion . . . as to what the effect would be on Richard of taking him away from his mother and his present home?"

DR. DAIN: "Well, given, of course, I have no knowledge except very indirectly about the status of the father's home, so I couldn't comment on that.

"But my assessment was that this was a very good home and a very warm and loving and supportive home, and that Richard saw it as such and that he strongly desired to remain in it. And were he to be removed from it, that he would have considerable disturbance over that fact.

"And, of course, the question is: How could one cope with that disturbance, since many of us do encounter unfortunate disastrous events in our life, and given my assessment of Richard, I would have to say that I think he probably would survive it, but I don't think that it would be a desirable thing to impose on him."

STENGER: "You don't think it would be in the best interest of Richard Risher to take him from his mother's home?"

DR. DAIN: "No, I do not."

Frank Stenger asked Dr. Dain what effect would the eventual realization of his mother's sexual preference have on Richard.

DR. DAIN: "I think that most likely, assuming and it's very

hard to assume the manner in which this knowledge will come to him, but I don't believe right now it's possible for him to incorporate all of the different kinds of negative things that some people hold about homosexuality.

"But as he becomes aware of it, hopefully, gradually, that impact will be one which he will simply or essentially accept that as a viable life style with whatever disadvantages there may be as a result of the publicity of this trial.

"And he will have, probably, a good deal less prejudice or homophobia, as it is called, than the general population has. In the same way that a child from any family has some prejudice, religious or racial or so on, about a life style that is somehow different from the absolute norm."

STENGER: "Hypothetically, if Richard is taken away from his mother will he have to, at some period, probably during his teenage years, have to deal with the fact that his mother is a homosexual?"

DR. DAIN: "I expect he will have to deal with that, yes."

STENGER: "Will he consider her his mother, in your opinion, whether or not he lives with her?"

DR. DAIN: "Certainly."

STENGER: "Will the impact of discovering that his mother is a homosexual be greater, lesser, better or worse, if he discovers it after having been removed from his mother's home?"

DR. DAIN: "Well, I think that if he discovers it after having been removed, that he won't have the same kind of opportunity to continue to see his mother as a good person (inaudible) than he would if he were to continue in her home."

STENGER: "Then, it would be a correct statement that Richard's discovery of his mother's homosexuality would be better dealt with if he is in his mother's home?"

DR. DAIN: "I would think so."

Mike McCurley had some difficulty refuting the testimony of the psychological witnesses and sometimes used novel, if inconsequential, rebuttal. He introduced into evidence a newspaper feature story, written several years ago, about Dr. Dain. The sole excerpt he wanted the jury to consider was the following:

"Doctor Dain admits that he's opinionated, but it's the business I'm in. Actually, I'm opinionated as hell, but the difference is, I realize my opinions aren't truth.

"Academic administration is a stereotype stocked with stodgy, old kooks stuffed away in their offices. So I guess I'm a little odder than most people. That is what I believe all the things that make Dr. Bob Dain perfect for his new job."

Using that fragment of a newspaper article, Mike McCurley thought to impeach the testimony of Dr. Dain. Actually, the bulk of the piece was about Dain's family life; incidental to his job as college administrator.

Before he left the stand, Dain sought to correct a misquote, not that it really mattered. "What I said was that 'there are stereotypes of academic administrators as being rather stodgy.'"

Judy Grimes, a thirty-two-year-old postgraduate practical nurse at Mary Jo's hospital, took the stand to testify that she was a friend of Mary Jo's and regarded her as "an excellent nurse." According to Mrs. Grimes, Mary Jo, "took care of her patients physically as well as emotionally and mentally. . . . She gets along well with the other nurses that she works with; and also with her superiors, like the head nurse and supervisor. . . . She's a very professional person, very intelligent, gets along with people very well, especially if they are in trouble. She can really talk to people in depth." Mrs. Grimes was excused. The midafternoon break was called by Judge Chrisman.

The lawyers met in Judge Chrisman's chambers and conferred on the record. The topic for discussion was Mike McCurley's library, on the lawyers' table.

Barton Bernstein: "Your honor, I didn't object to Mr. McCurley coming into the courtroom with all those books on the desk earlier today, because I assumed that these would be used for the impeachment of either Dr. Dyer or Dr. Dain.

"Both have testified and he hasn't used the books. I would like the books removed from the desk and I think the jury should be told it's because the books will not be used in evidence; and if so, that they will be offered one by one.

"I think the case is prejudiced by having the trial with 20

books, all containing 'abnormal psychology, women love women,' in full view of the jury."

Mike McCurley: "If the court suggests that I remove the books, then I will. There are, as I understand it, two other psychologists to appear . . ."

Aglaia Mauzy: "One psychiatrist."

McCurley: "I don't know but what I might want to use them then. I don't know what I'm going to use."

Bernstein: "Well, I'll say yes if you're going to use the books. I was under the impression that all those books were out there for was the purpose of impressing these two people."

Mauzy: "Do you know that they weren't?"

Bernstein: "I don't know that they weren't at all. I'm just saying that they should be removed until they are used."

Finally, after more dialogue, Judge Chrisman made a ruling: "Let the record reflect that the court instructed the counsel for the petitioner to place his books outside of the jury until . . . or I would allow him to use them, of course, when an expert witness is called."

Thus, the psychology section of the Dallas Public Library, bare for a few hours on December 19, was replenished.

When the trial resumed, Carolyn Miller, a mother of three children and neighbor of Mary Jo's, testified about the excellence of the home, how well taken care of Richard appeared, how fine a person Mary Jo was, and how no overt sexual activity was ever exhibited by Mary Jo and Ann. She reiterated that proper food, clothing, education, understanding and love were evident in the Risher domicile.

Richard's family physician, Dr. Roy A. Wagner, took leave from a hunting trip to testify. Dr. Wagner, a relaxed and congenial man, apologized to the court for his casual dress; he had driven directly from a hunting lodge to appear. He certified that "all medical needs have been met by the mother." Dr. Wagner pronounced Richard "well cared for, well nourished, clean and always appropriately dressed."

Casandra Keys, a special education teacher in the Garland, Texas, school system told the court how she had tutored Richard for his reading problem during the summer of 1974. After working with Richard three times a week she observed that his sight vocabulary, essential to reading, was increased.

Laurie Jopling, a teacher at a private school in Dallas, testified that she spent the summer of 1975 tutoring Richard in sound blending and in sight vocabulary expression and as a result he had improved to within one half year of the norm for his grade level.

The reading tutors concluded the witnesses planned for Friday, and Judge Chrisman recessed the court until Monday.

Despite the protection of Mary Jo and Ann, the children, Richard and Judie Ann, were being affected by the rigors of the trial. They had not been exposed to any newspaper, radio or television accounts of the proceedings, but sensed acutely the anxiety and pain of their parents, who came home every night exhausted and preoccupied. Judie Ann, especially, demanded a recounting of the trial day. Her frustration at being shut out grew into a major problem.

Mary Jo and Ann, still able to focus on their children, arranged for Mike and Jan Foreman to keep the children during the weekend, and if necessary until the jury made a decision. It was presumed that being away from the endless phone calls, interviews and emotional afflictions of their parents would benefit the children, give them a chance for some needed recreation without the constant reminder of the trial.

Saturday night the Dallas County chapter of the National Organization for Women (NOW) held a benefit auction for Mary Jo. It was NOW that had spearheaded the support shown Mary Jo nationwide. NOW's National Task Force on Sexuality and Lesbianism had passed a resolution endorsing Mary Jo's right to retain custody of her son, and primarily through the efforts of Dallasites Marge Shuchat and Martha Dickey, both national officials, the organization's Legal Education and Defense Fund was planning to make a sizable contribution.

Mary Jo's custody problems were the impetus for formation of a Dallas County task force on sexuality and lesbianism, headed by Leah Sherman. This task force examined the problems of gay women locally and co-ordinated a statewide campaign of consciousness raising.

Although there were the usual grumblings, by a minority, Mary Jo's plight coalesced the feminist organization locally and clearly gave it an unquestioned leadership role in the diverse women's rights movement.

In return, Mary Jo was uplifted by this unparalleled, at least for Dallas, show of support for homosexual rights. The auction raised over one thousand dollars for attorney fees.

The auction also had an unsuspected, positive effect on Mrs. Davidson, who was still in the midst of a maturation process concerning her daughter's sexual preference. "It really did me good to see all those men and women openly support Mary Jo. I finally could see for myself that I didn't stand alone; there were many, many others who understood and wanted to help. It was great."

The auction was important in another respect. The organizers were to form the nucleus of a separate group that would continue to raise money and promote publicity for Mary Jo's cause once the trial was ended.

By Monday morning, the afterglow of the auction had worn thin as Mary Jo and Ann prepared for the week that would decide Richard's fate. The inevitable sense of dread was never worse as they drove to the courthouse in silence.

The mass of humanity inside the courthouse never changed; even the new faces took on characteristics of the old. Litigants came and went; their visages of fear, anguish and frustrations lingered to haunt their replacements on the wooden benches.

Jan Foreman was the lead-off witness for Monday. A thin, pleasant woman with a whispery, husky voice, she had been married to Ann's ex-husband, Mike, since 1969. They had two children. After establishing Jan's personal data for the jury, Aglaia Mauzy asked the present Mrs. Foreman about Mary Jo's home.

JAN: "It's a very nice home. To me, it's warm, uh, both the children that live together love each other very much, and it's obvious that both mothers love the children and the children their mothers.

"It's always clean when I've gone there and the children have beautiful rooms."

MAUZY: "Have you ever seen Mary Jo Risher and Ann Foreman act inappropriately in front of Richard Risher?"

JAN: "No, I never have."

MAUZY: "Do you love your children?"

JAN: "I love my children very much."

MAUZY: "Have you taken them into the home of Ann Foreman and Mary Jo Risher?"

JAN: "Sure."

MAUZY: "As a mother, do you feel that they will see or hear anything that will harm them?"

JAN: "No."

MAUZY: "Would you describe the relationship between Mary Jo and Richard to be a good and loving relationship?"

JAN: "Very definitely. It's very obvious to me each time I've seen them together that they love each other very much, it shows, their affection."

MAUZY: "Having observed Richard and his mother on numerous occasions, do you, personally, have an impression as to where the child wants to be, and you mustn't go into what the child has told you or said."

JAN: "The impression I get is I feel he loves his mother very much and he wants to stay with his mother." Jan was excused.

Michael J. Foreman was sworn in. He was a bank equipment salesman. Mike was lean, with refined, handsome features, light brown hair and mustache, soft hazel eyes and a bright, animated voice.

STENGER: "Would you describe what sort of situation, to your knowledge, she [Ann] is living in with Mary Jo Risher?"

MIKE: "Well, I've been very close to the situation since our divorce, because there was a time when I considered trying to get Judie Ann back again.

"Of course, as in most divorces, it was fairly bitter. So I kept

~ 213 ~

pretty close, pretty close watch over how they treated Judie Ann and how they took care of her.

"Judie Ann is a very mature child, and she's very well taken care of. We get to see her every weekend practically, and some time during the summer time and on holidays, she would spend a week or two weeks at a time with us, so I kept a very close watch on the situation. And as far as medical needs and other needs, she probably gets a little more medical attention than I would have given her, because every time she coughs or sputters or spews, she's taken to the doctor. So as far as clothing and medical attention and her special education needs and that sort of thing, she's very well taken care of."

STENGER: "In your opinion, has she been totally properly cared for?"

MIKE: "Yes."

STENGER: "And would you say that you, as a father, love her and recognize and are concerned with her best interests?"

MIKE: "Yes."

STENGER: "If there were anything in her environment at the present time that you felt would be detrimental toward her, would you try to do something about it?"

MIKE: "If I felt that there was some basis or some reason for doing that, then I would try . . ."

STENGER: "But at this time?"

MIKE: "But at this time, I would not try, and I don't think any father that loves their daughter or children would put them through this type of situation."

STENGER: "During your frequent visits to their home, have you ever had occasion to notice that either Mary Jo or Ann were engaging in any conduct that would be inappropriate for the children?"

MIKE: "If they had engaged in any such activity, to my knowledge, I would have already had them in court. Judie Ann is very, very outspoken. If there is any kind of problem at home or she has anything that she's unhappy with, then she tells me or my wife, because she and Jan are very close together."

STENGER: "What made you come to the decision that you

would not embark on a custody matter of this nature to get Judie Ann?"

MIKE: "Like I say, I had, at one time, I had my doubts as to what the situation was and so a little over a year ago, with Ann's permission, she didn't know, of course, my ulterior motives, I asked for Judie Ann to have her evaluated; she had had some problems in school.

"She had gone to Scottish Rite and been evaluated, and the school had evaluated her, and all of these different people had evaluated her, and nobody ever really told us anything.

"So I paid for her to go to a child psychiatrist to have all of this testing evaluated and to have her evaluated to see if he could tell us, in plain language, what she needed in special schooling and what is or was her problem.

"And of course, it was still in the back of my mind that possibly it was this situation over there that maybe there was something over there that was influencing this child.

"After about six months in this therapy situation where she would go to the doctor and they would play together and they would talk about her family at home and he interviewed Ann, my ex-wife.

"And he explained to us, basically, what her learning disability was and what she needed to do.

"And he said that her and her mother had a very strong, close situation, that she had no identity problem, and that there was, or that it seemed to be very healthy for her because there was no homosexuality or any influence in that area brought directly into the home.

"If they had not told me, I would not have known they were homosexuals. If they had not told me, I would not know but that it was anything but two women sharing an apartment, sharing a household.

"So he said, in his opinion, that it would have been much worse on Judie Ann to try to remove her from her mother, because she would not be able to understand. It was more important for me and Jan to accept her mother as we have for the person she was and to go on and love Judie Ann and let her love her mother and let her love me."

STENGER: "You have sort of inadvertently been brought into this lawsuit because of the fact that your daughter's name has been mentioned several times; because of the fact that the family unit that's being discussed here consists of—one of the members consists of your daughter, Judie Ann.

"What are your feelings in regard to what's happening and the fact that your daughter has been brought into this lawsuit and the idea, itself, of trying to take a child away from that home?"

MIKE: "In the first place, had this not have happened, there was no reason for any peer pressure on Judie Ann. Her friends didn't know about what happened in the privacy of Mary Jo's and Ann's bedroom, any more so than my children know what is happening in the privacy of my bedroom.

"But now, because of this, it's being brought out, and it's in the papers and it's in the schools and just anybody that wants to know, can know about it.

"I just hope that we are at such a time in the world that they're not going to have the same kind of pressures and the same kind of harassment because of this type of situation that I would have had if I had been in this situation when I was a child."

Mike McCurley conducted his cross-examination. In a fatuous voice he asked Mike: "Mr. Foreman, you came in here this morning and told us about your being the father and how you thought everything was fine and you were glad your child was in that home, is that right?"

MIKE: "No. I'm not glad that she's in that family."

MCCURLEY: "You had no objection to it?"

MIKE: "Yes, sir."

MCCURLEY: "Okay, now, you do not remember your date of marriage to Mrs. Ann Foreman?"

MIKE: "No, and there's a reason for it."

MCCURLEY: "All right, we're going to go into that reason . . ."

McCurley offered a court document as Exhibit Number 25. It

was the record of Mike's and Ann's divorce pleadings. He read a portion of it to the court: "Plaintiff alleges that one minor child was born prior to this union, to wit; Judie Ann Davis, and plaintiff hereby alleges that he is the natural father of said child and plaintiff alleges that he is a fit and proper person to have custody . . ."

Aglaia Mauzy jumped from her chair. "Your Honor, Your Honor, although we're not hiding anything from this jury, we would object to this man's bringing the additional issue of this child's legitimacy into this trial, and we feel that it has no relevance at all, except to do further harm to the children in question."

MCCURLEY: "This man came in here and testified that he was the father of this child and that he had made an investigation into what a fit and proper place it was that this child was living in, in a lesbian environment; and he is not that child's father at all."

Aglaia screamed, "That is the crassest . . ." McCurley, Mauzy and Chrisman all spoke at once. The judge restored order.

FRANK STENGER: "Your honor, I will object on the following basis: Number 1, that document does not say that he is not the father of that child; Number 2, the fact that the child was born prior to the marriage has no bearing on this lawsuit and only serves to further injure what has been, already, a very injurious situation to all the children involved in this home. It is only a very crass tactic on Counsel's part to demean this family. I have very strong objections that, first of all, he would say that he is not the father of this child when, in fact, this document does not allege it. Secondly, that he would bring it before this court when it has no bearing to the issue at all."

Judge Chrisman asked to see the document, read it, and then instructed the jury, "Disregard any statements made as to the paternity of the child; and I will allow the documents to speak for themselves; and I will allow the cross-examination to proceed."

McCurley then produced a second document and handed it to the judge to look over while he continued. McCurley requested that Mike Foreman read along with him and correct him if he misstated anything.

McCurley read aloud, "Plaintiff alleges that one minor child was born prior to this union, to wit: Judie Ann Davis; and plaintiff hereby alleges that he is the natural father of said child and plaintiff alleges that he is a fit, a fit and proper person to have the custody of said minor child, and that the best interests of the child would be conserved by awarding the child to the plaintiff. That's you, is that true?"

MIKE: "That's true."

MCCURLEY: "Next, I would like to direct your attention to your wife's Original Answer and Cross Action, filed in that same divorce. . . . Now, Cross-plaintiff is your wife and she filed against you. . . . 'Cross-plaintiff, Ann E. Foreman,' your wife, 'denies that said child is of issue of cross-defendant,' that's you. . . .

"That's your ex-wife talking?"

MIKE: "No, that's two lawyers talking."

MCCURLEY: "I pass the witness."

BARTON BERNSTEIN: "Mr. Foreman, it is your testimony today, is it not, that you are the father of Judie Ann Foreman?"

MIKE: "Yes, and I would even go further . . ."

JUDGE CHRISMAN: "Excuse me . . ."

BERNSTEIN: "Just a minute. Now, you are the father of Judie Ann Foreman?"

MIKE: "Yes."

BERNSTEIN: "And during your marriage to Mrs. Foreman, did you take care of the child and support the child?"

MIKE: "Yes, I did."

Barton Bernstein went on to clearly establish that Mike provided for the care and support of his daughter even after the divorce. Then he asked about Judie Ann's knowledge of her mother's sexual preference: "Does she know what a lesbian is or that her mother is a lesbian?"

MIKE: "Uh, due to the situation, we thought it would be best to be honest and open about the situation, and so, she understands as well as she can understand."

BERNSTEIN: "Has it affected her adversely in any way?"

MIKE: "No."

BERNSTEIN: "Are you sure?"

MIKE: "Yes, I'm positive."

BERNSTEIN: "Has it affected the relationship between Judie Ann Foreman and Richard Risher?"

MIKE: "No."

Bernstein's examination of Mike plodded on for several more minutes, then Frank Stenger had a chance for redirect.

STENGER: "For purpose of clarification, Mike, could you please tell the jury the circumstances surrounding your marriage to Ann Foreman and the birth of Judie Foreman?"

Mike's voice was steely and he looked directly at the jury.

"We had gone together since the first year of high school, and, in fact, we only dated each other exclusively through high school, and we wanted to be married, but we were under age. And when Ann became pregnant, we didn't know what to do. I consulted with an attorney, and to see if there was any way, you know, that we could go to Arkansas or some place where we could get married. And he said, in the state of Texas—the state of Texas is a common-law state and . . ."

McCurley was rapaciously objecting: "Your honor, I object to this man testifying about the law."

JUDGE CHRISMAN: "I'll sustain the objection."

STENGER: "Your honor, I believe he's not testifying as to the law, but as to what he was advised and the reason he embarked on the course he did."

MCCURLEY: "Then, that would be hearsay."

JUDGE CHRISMAN: "I'll sustain that as hearsay."

That picayune exchange was too much for Mary Jo's supporter, Charlotte Taft, who abruptly left the gallery muttering. McCurley turned in his chair darting his glance behind the woman who walked out on his objection. Frank Stenger, more accustomed to pompous displays of lawyers' prerogatives, merely turned casually, with a sullen look on his face. He continued:

"What was your understanding?"

MIKE: "It was my understanding that if we could, if we set up household and profess to be man and wife, then we would be legally married in the state of Texas."

STENGER: "And is that what you embarked on doing?"

MIKE: "Yes. And then, when we were legally of age, then we did go and get married, but we did live together as man and wife. I signed Judie Ann's birth certificate and I was there since her birth."

STENGER: "And you subsequently got married through a ceremony?"

MIKE: "Yes."

STENGER: "Is there any doubt in your mind but that Judie Ann is your daughter?"

MIKE: "No, sir."

STENGER: "And you are the natural father of that child?"

MIKE: "Yes, sir."

STENGER: "And you are the legal father of that child?"

MIKE: "Yes, sir."

STENGER: "Could you please describe for the jury what your feelings are in regard to that child?"

MIKE: "She's my first born. She's always been one of the first things on my mind in respect to everything I do. I've given her the best I could then as well as now."

During the recess Mike went out into the hall where his wife Jan was waiting. A reporter who had left the hearing had told her about Mike McCurley's line of questioning. She was crying, being consoled by Ann and several friends. Mike and Jan embraced. "I can't believe they brought that up," Jan said. "I know," Mike replied, "I know."

In Judge Chrisman's chambers, McCurley introduced a motion "to instruct counsel for respondent and counsel for attorney ad litem not to make any suggestions or allude to any comment by the court concerning any elements of the temporary hearing." Judge Chrisman sustained the motion.

The precise purpose of the motion was unclear, since it would have been impossible to keep the actual transcript of the temporary hearing out of the trial record if Stenger and Mauzy used it to impeach anyone.

Likely, McCurley wanted to keep out comments by the judge that may have been damaging to Doug Risher's case. At the time of the temporary hearing Judge Chrisman had ordered Jimmy's auto returned to Doug and suggested that Mr. Risher refrain from any further gifts that might constitute a bribe.

McCurley was aware that Stenger and Mauzy were considering recalling Jimmy to the stand and confronting him with his earlier statements, word for word. And the instructive remarks by Judge Chrisman about the gifts might prove more damaging than any attempt at impeaching Jimmy. Since it is usual procedure to strike any side-bar remarks by the judge from court records, McCurley's motion was upheld.

The concluding witness for the Respondent was Dr. Neville Murray, M.D., a San Antonio psychiatrist with a long list of professional attainments.

Neville Murray was a striking-looking man, with angular features, a modest beard and short, wavy black hair, styled to follow the natural contours of his hairline. His manner was mildly patrician; inoffensively elegant, due perhaps, to his being born and educated in Scotland. He spoke in a felicitous voice with the lyrical locution of the land of his birth. Dr. Murray wore a hand-tailored cashmere and wool blue suit, attesting to his Continental flair, more than the prosperity of his psychiatric practice.

Dr. Murray didn't know either party in the lawsuit and would offer testimony only in a hypothetical context. After a background briefing in the presence of the jury, Frank Stenger started his questioning.

STENGER: "Would you please give your professional opinion . . . as to the effect, if any, the offering of a car to a 17 year old boy might have on his choice as to which parent he would desire to live with?"

DR. MURRAY: "Well, one could say that it might have a profound effect. The circumstances depending, of course, on the child's value system and the environment from which he comes and how much importance he places on material objects and so forth.

"And certainly, at 17, he's at an impressionable age. The adolescent is very much conscious of status and material objects, especially an automobile. One would think that it must have a rather seductive effect upon whoever receives the car, in terms of motivating their decision as to which of the parents they wish to go to."

STENGER: "Jimmy has also testified that one of the reasons he has elected to go live with his father is that his mother's homosexuality is a cause of embarrassment to him and that, at times, he is embarrassed to bring his friends to his mother's house.

"I would like for you . . . to address yourself to whether or not Jimmy will have to understand and deal with his mother's homosexuality whether or not he lives in the home that she provides or in the home that the father provides."

DR. MURRAY: "Well, one would have to consider the fact that the child's present solution to the problem is to run away from it, not to face it, but to deny its existence, as it were, by abandoning his mother and presumably affiliating himself with his father's cause.

"That's not, in a psychological sense, a rational solution to the problem. Eventually, he has got to deal with the problem, sooner or later. He cannot deal with it internally by merely ignoring it or affiliating himself to a contrary cause, as it were. So escape or running away from the problem is not considered to be a very elegant type of solution and one would not approve of that as being a psychologically healthy way of dealing with the situation.

"He's going to have to work it through presumably in his relationship with his mother and not away from his mother. And the working through probably will take place within the context of that relationship and not without that relationship.

"In other words, if he ceases to have anything to do with his mother, then, I presume he's going to have difficulties later on, because of his escape."

STENGER: "If we were to show you that there was a homosexual environment in which the evidence showed or indicated that the homosexual relationship between the two women involved was a respectable relationship, a stable homosexual relationship, a relationship in which sexual acts were not performed in front of the children and a relationship in which all the basic needs and all the special needs of the children were provided for, and a relationship in which the children related very strongly to the mother and had close emotional ties to the mother and were loved and cared for and, in turn, were loving and caring for their mother, given that context, what, in your opinion, would be the effect of the removing of the child from that home because his mother is a homosexual?"

DR. MURRAY: "I think the effect would be deleterious, because the child would, obviously, be very confused as to the justification for any such separation.

"The effect would be confusing, puzzling and, I think, detrimental to the psychological stability of any such child who was removed for any such cause without that cause being apparent to the child."

STENGER: "What would be the effect on the child in terms of his image of his mother, in your professional opinion?"

DR. MURRAY: "I think he would be very confused and perplexed, and would be driven between what would be some kind of social condemnation of his mother, as opposed to his own feelings, which are support and approval of his mother; and, as I said, it would be very confusing and stressful on such a child, who has to undergo this kind of removal, a reaction.

"On the one half, he would have to face up to the fact that society has deemed that his mother was unworthy, and then, he would have to equate that with the fact of his own feelings of approval and worthiness of his mother. And it would be very difficult for him to come up with some kind of adequate solution to these two diverse opposing forces."

STENGER: "Are you saying that it would go toward or have a detrimental effect on his own self-esteem?"

DR. MURRAY: "Certainly."

STENGER: "And more explicitly, could you explain why, just for clarification purposes?"

DR. MURRAY: "This child is currently in the home with a mother, whom he loves and adores and admires and supports, and as far as he knows, there is no reason given why he should not do this. He is not aware of anything deviate about his mother's behavior, because whatever her private sexual activities are, they are private, and they are not common family knowledge.

"As such, he is then faced with the kind of stress, which would be involved where a child is suddenly told that his mother or father was guilty of some socially despised or disapproved of behavior.

"And it would be very painful for him to have to come up with that kind of conflict. On one hand, the feeling that he does love his mother, and on the other hand, learning that society does not share in that feeling."

On the judgment question, concerning Richard's dress when he visited the court-appointed psychologist, Dr. Murray saw the genesis differently than Dr. Gordon: "It probably is a function of convenience rather than judgment. I think one has to understand that nowadays, articles of dress, such as blue jeans, are unisexual and they are merchandised as such. And the differences, I believe, are the cut and the style and they are indistinguishable, it's not very easy to tell.

"However, the wearing of clothing is very much a question of individual preference on the part of young people. They very often put on what they want to put on, not what they are told to put on.

"My own daughter has a proclivity for borrowing my shirts. I, when I was a young boy, wore skirts in Scotland that they called kilts. I don't really think that the dress of a young child is very much a matter of great import because it changes so much from time to time.

"If the child puts on the sister's jeans or the other girl's jeans by preference, then one would have to think that there might be some kind of relationship between the two in terms of sharing and so on and so forth, that that might have to do with the cause of the action on the part of the young man in wearing his sister's —or whatever she is to him—presumably sister in this family.

"Uh, it may be, as I say, a sharing experience rather than

merely an attempt to identify as a female. I really don't think that that, in and of itself, is indicative of judgment on the part of the mother, because she's presumably not likely to intervene in this situation because it is after the fact.

"That is to say, after the child puts the blue jeans on, then she may or may not realize that he has gotten the other child's jeans on, and she may decide to ask him to change or not.

"But, in any event, since they are unisexual garments, I really don't think it's of much consequence. So, so far as T-shirts are concerned, people wear all kinds of emblems on T-shirts, and I don't think that they are necessarily attributable to the wearer. And if the child is attending the YWCA, I see no reason, no real reason why he shouldn't have a YWCA T-shirt.

"I don't think that one could consider these things as aspects of parental influence; what the child wears, the jeans or the T-shirt, as I say, it may or may not be a function of parental influence, and I rather imagine that it was not. So, in a sense, the wearing of these objects cannot necessarily be a reflection of parental judgment."

STENGER: "If we had two psychologists testify that . . . Richard is, at the present time, a normal nine year boy and age appropriate in terms of development and the mother . . . Mary Jo Risher, is mentally and emotionally stable and an integrated individual, not in need of therapy . . . and the family has strong emotional ties . . . should Richard be removed?"

DR. MURRAY: "In my professional opinion, he should be allowed to continue to live in his present environment."

STENGER: "And could you give us some reasons why . . . you have come to that conclusion?"

DR. MURRAY: "Well, primarily, the stability of the household, the atmosphere of sharing and love and warmth and security that's provided by such relationships are really what, what family life is made up of.

"The question as to the sexual preferences of either one or both parents is really not relevant to the growing of the personality, and I don't really feel that there's any evidence to suppose that homosexual activity is any more transmittable within a family, as is heterosexual activity.

"In a sense, one could say that the majority of homosexual persons come from heterosexual parents.

"There is no reason for us to believe, then, that homosexual parents are likely to bring forth or develop homosexual children any more than heterosexual parents can guarantee that their children will be heterosexual. So the relationship, then, as to the sexual preference and parental attitudes is, apparently, not an established quantity.

"And therefore, to remove someone from a homosexual parent on the grounds that the individual's homosexual behavior seems to be ill-founded and illogical. There is no reason to believe that any such homosexual activity would, in any way, infringe upon the personality development of the child in such a home.

"I cannot understand the justification of such a removal, unless it could be the mistaken idea that the homosexuality in some way would be epidemic or endemic in the family, and there is no evidence to support that, and I cannot agree with any such removal."

Mike McCurley wished to dip again into the bouillabaisse of hypothetical questions, to modify the flavor of Dr. Murray's answers.

McCurley's first morsel: ". . . Has something to do with the offering of a car and its effect upon the choice of parents, and you mentioned something about it would depend, perhaps, on the environment we came from.

"The question to you is: In the choice of environment or parents, if you will, would your decision on that topic be influenced by the quality of the home which he went to and the quality of the home he left?"

DR. MURRAY: "I think both."

MCCURLEY: "If, assuming for a moment that the car was a motivating factor, would you be influenced by the fact that some years later, the boy still shared the same opinion, rather than an infatuation with the car, we have a period of a year, would that influence your opinion?"

DR. MURRAY: "As to why he made the move?"

MCCURLEY: "Yes, sir."

DR. MURRAY: "Yes, I think so."

MCCURLEY: ". . . The question of Jimmy's embarrassment. Assume the fact that this boy had seen pictures of his mother and her lover with her made up as a man and the other made up as a woman; assume further in your hypothetical that the boy had been taken or had evidently been taken to a gay bar; assume further that there was testimony concerning the facts that the boy had observed two homosexual men necking at a party—now, would that change your opinion?"

DR. MURRAY: "It might, yes."

MCCURLEY: "There was a hypothetical [question] concerning the effect on Richard, the younger boy, and his being moved from one home to the other. Would your opinion perhaps be different based on the quality of the home he was moved to?"

DR. MURRAY: "No."

MCCURLEY: "You have given an opinion here based on certain facts that you say that there is no reason to move that child from a lesbian family unit. . . . My question is this: Would your opinion about that be changed by the following facts, which I ask you to assume: Number One, that the child would be moved to a good home of two parents, male and female; and assume, further, that there was testimony by an independent court appointed social worker that found the lesbian family unit unacceptable without the issue of homosexuality—would your opinion be different?"

DR. MURRAY: "Yes."

Richard's court-appointed attorney, Barton Bernstein, questioned Dr. Murray. "Doctor, can you suggest to us any problem that might arise other than what you've stated by virtue of this child continuing to live in the home of his mother?"

DR. MURRAY: "One could think of the problem of permanency of the relationship. Of course, the same kind of impermanency has existed with heterosexual families; but, in the past, homosexual relationships have been thought or reputed to be less stable than heterosexual relationships. So, again, we have . . ."

BERNSTEIN: "Is that the current data, Doctor?"

DR. MURRAY: "I say that that is rumor rather than data."

BERNSTEIN: "I'd like to concern ourselves with data."

DR. MURRAY: "If we're dealing with data, we can't substantiate that kind of accusation. But, certainly homosexual relationships are of very many different kinds and homosexual families, where two people decide to live with one another, are presumably, just as permanent as where two heterosexual people decide to live with one another.

"The same degree of permanence or impermanence exists. There are other kinds of homosexual relationships, which are dependent upon transient and brief kinds of relationships, and so, that kind of activity, which is a different kind of relationship than the one we're dealing with here, might, as it were, move, or might, by contamination, as it were, infer that all homosexual relationships are transient.

"And so, when I'm talking about problems, I think that the court might be confused about clumping all homosexual relationships under the one hat . . ."

BERNSTEIN: "I don't think that that's a problem.

"What I'd like to direct your attention to is that if there are any other possible problems that Richard might face, the transient possibility of a homosexual marriage, as you're suggesting, is a rumor, but not necessarily fact."

DR. MURRAY: "Not fact, no. We find that heterosexuals are not any more stable than the homosexuals."

Dr. Murray was excused. Frank Stenger told the court, "The Respondent rests." The testimony was concluded. After a long lunch hour the court would reconvene, the judge would read the charge to the jury, final arguments of counsel would be delivered, and the jury would begin deliberations.

Mary Jo and Ann were drained but relieved; it was over. No more questions, arguments, probes, innuendoes; having to face Jimmy on the stand rejecting their life style; hearing ugly accusations about Judie Ann's legitimacy; enduring predatorial thrusts into what used to be their privacy. The prerogatives were down to yes or no; Richard stays or goes. Momentous, indeed, but simple, ever so simple; yes or no. Live or die. But free of torture. Or so it seemed to Mary Jo and Ann over lunch.

Mike McCurley was flitting from witness to reporter offering little verbal palliatives: "We're still friends, aren't we? This isn't really a gay rights cause." He was puzzled at the antipathy shown him by some of the feminists. "Why, my law firm was among the first to do women's rights cases, even before it was popular." Second thoughts? Hardly. Mike was ambitious, driven by an unconcealed win power; with only one gear or speed and that was forward. To him, there were few subtleties.

There was a tradition in Texas law-politics that went beyond the borders of "situation ethics," and the only things that are an anathema to it were: tentativeness, losing and recognizing that you have *one*, implacable enemy. The embodiment of that tradition was buried along the Pedernales River, not far from Johnson City. Its heirs were everywhere, even in so humble a place as a Dallas domestic relations court.

When the court reconvened, Judge Oswin Chrisman read a carefully worded charge to the jury: "You are instructed that not every change in conditions justifies the modification of the former decree of divorce awarding the managing conservatorship [custody] of the minor child. Such changed conditions must be such as affects the welfare and best interests of the child and be of such nature that to leave the managing conservatorship of the child as previously adjudicated would be injurious to the welfare of the child and require that such managing conservatorship be changed.

"There is a special issue in this case," Judge Chrisman continued in an orotund voice. "Do you find from a preponderance of the evidence that since April 16, 1971, the date of the former judgment granting managing conservatorship of Richard Calvin Risher to Mary Jo Risher, there has occurred such a material and substantial change of conditions that the best interest of said minor child requires a change of managing conservatorship to Douglas L. Risher, Jr.?

"ANSWER: 'Yes' or 'No'."

By mutual agreement, the summations to the jury would be

limited to thirty minutes. The attorney ad litem, Barton Bernstein, would not make any statement or recommendation, at his own choosing.

Frank Stenger stood directly in front of the jury and began a measured, soft and obviously deeply felt plea: ". . . We have proven that Mary Jo is a loving, capable, competent, almost model mother to Richard. She has never let her homosexuality interfere with her ability to take care of or love Richard. Leaving Richard in her home would in no way be harmful. Not only would it not be harmful, but is in the best interest of the child to leave him there.

"Removing him would be harmful, destructive, cause damage and hate. She loves that boy, has taken care of him, provided him a respectable, wonderful, appropriate environment.

"In no way has she let homosexuality interfere. She has taken care of his special needs. Perhaps she is even overcompensating. They love each other; form a family unit, and she provides everything for him to be a stable and productive human being."

Frank reviewed the testimony—Mary Jo's, Ann's, Jimmy's, friends', psychologists'—and how it, for the most part, attested to the suitability of his client as a mother. His long musings evoked strong emotion around the courtroom.

Ann Foreman sat erect on the edge of the spectator bench. There was a trace of moisture on her cheeks mixing with the light face powder. Her eyes, signals of pent-up distress, alternated between Frank, the jury, and Mary Jo.

Jimmy Risher's lower lip was quivering; his face was pale. He glanced around the courtroom in fitful searches.

Delaine Risher held her waning half-smile while her eyes shifted constantly toward her husband.

Doug Risher faced straight ahead, his back to the gallery. He didn't look at Stenger. Motionless.

Mary Jo gripped the arms of her chair, her fingers were mauve from the force. She dabbed a handkerchief to her eyes.

Judge Chrisman looked glum; his chin rested on his chest; his eyes were partially drooped, no longer amiable.

The jury was rapt, paying close attention to every word (to

every aspect of this trial), and still no readable sign of emotion, No smiles, no grimaces, no yawns, no nods. Nothing. A consummate deadpan.

Stenger was winding up his narrative: "Don't punish her because she is a homosexual. More importantly, don't punish Richard because his mother is a homosexual." He slipped into his chair and fingered the edges of his legal pad.

Mike McCurley began his summation halfway across the courtroom and then tracked inward, working his way toward the jury with every new point. Finally, he ended up directly in front of them.

"I am sorry the gay movement has taken this as a cause case, because it is not. There have been hot issues, hot moments. What this case is *not* about is important. It is not about rights of homosexuals, not about the rights of Mary Jo. This case is about the most important thing in the world, custody of little Richard. His destiny is literally laying in your hands today."

McCurley, sensing something about the jury, began a panoramic review of the testimony. It was, naturally, from his perspective, but he conceded points in his summary that he never let stand unchallenged in the examination. He understood the jury; its anatomy of decision-making. He could allow certain liberties now, be gracious.

For thirty minutes Mike conducted a monologue; a curious verbal give-and-take with himself. He tacitly admitted: Yes, his client did drink. Yes, he was arrested. Learned his lesson, though. Doug did, when single, have intercourse with various women. Possibly, he made one pregnant. Yes, he did put some money for an abortion. Maybe Mary Jo and Ann did only show "slight" affection for each other in front of Jimmy. Yes, Jimmy was embarrassed by his mother's homosexuality. Maybe the car was superimportant to Jimmy, but something had to be at home for him to put a car above his mother.

"You've heard it said gay is okay, gay is no problem, no sweat . . . I don't condemn homosexuality; a person's sexual preference is his own business; but when we are talking about a lesbian family unit, that's uncharted waters."

McCurley concluded: "You've heard the court's witnesses say the woman's judgment was bad. They didn't comment on her life style; her judgment was bad. If there is a problem of removal of the child, better do it now.

"Take two things with you into the jury room. Take all the evidence . . . take your common sense, your judgment. Leave out here the interests of Doug, Mary Jo, the gay liberation movement. Consider the best interest of little Richard; don't make him the guinea pig of somebody's social experiment."

Judge Chrisman leaned forward in his chair and addressed the jury: "Ladies and gentlemen of the jury, you have heard the opening statements of counsel, you have heard the evidence, you have heard the court's charge and you have heard the arguments of counsel.

"The issue is now yours to decide. You may retire to the jury room and follow the instructions of the court and notify us when you have reached a verdict."

It was 3:30 P.M. Monday, December 22. Jury selection, testimony and summations had taken five days.

Mary Jo, Frank and Aglaia walked into the hall. "We've done the best we could," Mary Jo told everyone; then she started to cry. A group of the women accompanied Mary Jo to the restroom.

Once inside, Mary Jo broke down. She grasped her mother and sobbed, "He won't let any of us rest. He'll always be after me." Mary Davidson held up her dispirited daughter and tried to comfort her. "I know, Mary Jo, but one day he'll have to answer for what he's doing."

The emotional letdown at the end of the trial was contagious. Most of the women in the restroom were weeping; Charlotte Taft, Leah Sherman, Dolores Dyer, Mary Davidson.

Mary Jo's words reverberated off the tile walls. "It's so humiliating and degrading. He's always known he can't hurt me as a person, unless he uses those boys. When is it going to stop?"

In about fifteen minutes the women emerged to face a horde of cameramen and television lights.

Waiting was never well accomplished. It was the penalty for

beings who are forever wanting something. Chain-smoking, chain-chatter, chain-staring, chain-pacing; waiting. The initial rage was gone, at least sublimated. Fear, omnipresent, was numbed into a vague uneasiness. People waiting for a timed, specific destiny were curiously detached. Say this, think that. Feel this, show that. Nothing was natural, everything appeared natural. Everyone drifted in a private swirl of indiscriminate emotional fog. Mass neuron misfire. Waiting.

Aglaia: "All we can do now is wait." Frank: "I guess we'll have to wait and see." Charlotte: "We've done all we can do." Barton Bernstein: "If you lose remember this, there is only one reason, and that is because of your homosexuality. . . . You definitely showed that you were a good mother. Now, you'll just have to wait it out."

People may have been talking to Mary Jo, but the conversation was floating around her head, she didn't assimilate what they said. She was lost in her own waiting, her thoughts. *The women on that jury. They're from another generation. Five years ago I was that way. The feelings I held about people. It was on their faces, I could see it. You could sense it. Never, never were those women for me. Am I going to lose? My God, I can't lose; what am I going to tell Richard? Will they come in with the verdict today? Will I have to go home and tell him he has to go or that he can stay?*

How will the jury weigh what Jimmy said? He came into the courtroom as a saint. Frank and Aglaia changed that. The jury should be weighing that, weighing everything. I bet they aren't weighing anything. Nothing.

Word was passed around: "They're through for the day." People scrambled into the courtroom to hear Judge Chrisman confirm: "The jury has concluded deliberations for the day and will return tomorrow at 8:25."

On the way home Mary Jo, Ann and Mrs. Davidson talked about the length of time the jury was deliberating. "It could be a good sign," Mary Jo said. "It might mean that some of them are for us," Ann suggested. "They could sway the others." Mrs. Davidson nodded agreement. Not one of them truly believed that.

The next morning Mary Jo and Ann were solemn, uncertain. Mary Jo postponed dressing as late as she could. She didn't want to hear the verdict; that she knew would come sometime that day. "I think I could have gone forever without knowing yes or no," she recalled. "Ann would reach over and take my hand and squeeze it to give me what strength she could. We picked up Mother and rode to the court in silence."

The second day of waiting was like the first; only the reality of what had passed and is about to come was a little further removed. Maybe the jury was deadlocked. Why not?

Two and a half hours had elapsed when Bailiff Taylor scurried about repeating over and over, "There is a verdict."

Within moments, cigarette butts were stumped out, purses and brief cases gathered up, shutter speeds on cameras were checked, and the courtroom was filled; a single mass of hyperventilation.

Judge Chrisman: "Good morning. Ladies and gentlemen of the jury, have you reached a verdict?"

The foreman, Tony Liscio, stood. He was a six-foot-four-inch real estate man with a high forehead, moderately long hair and a bushy, limp mustache. He was huge; a former lineman for the Dallas Cowboys football team.

Liscio read the special issue: "Do you find from a preponderance of the evidence that since April 16, 1971, the date of the former judgement granting managing conservatorship of Richard Calvin Risher to Mary Jo Risher there has occurred such a material and substantial change of conditions that the best interest of said minor child requires a change of managing conservatorship to Douglas L. Risher, Jr.? And your answer . . . YES."

"Oh," Mary Jo cried. She began to weep.

JUDGE CHRISMAN: "Was the verdict unanimous?"

Mary Jo was slowly sinking down in her chair.

LISCIO: "No, it was not."

She had folded at the waist, laying her head on Frank Stenger's shoulder. Deep, wrenching howls.

JUDGE CHRISMAN: "What was the vote?"

Frank held Mary Jo's head.

LISCIO: "Ten to two."

JUDGE CHRISMAN: "Let's poll the jury."

Mary Jo continued to sob and her body trembled uncontrollably.

JUDGE CHRISMAN: "The polling is complete. I want to thank you ladies and gentlemen . . . You've had a rather heavy dose of the kinds of human problems that come before this court . . ."

Mary Jo was . . .

"As a Judge, I know how you have agonized with this verdict . . ."

Doug Risher and Mike McCurley were beaming, still patting each other on the back, as a group of Mary Jo's supporters, led by her mother, rushed to hold her. Ann was standing in the gallery, frozen. Finally she burst through the gate separating the spectators from the court area and ran to Mary Jo. She wiped Mary Jo's eyes with a tissue.

Photographers and TV cameramen swept into the court, jostling and pushing to get a ten-second film clip of a broken-down lesbian mother who had lost her child. Ann tried to cover Mary Jo's face. "Please God, can't you not do this now?" A lone television cameraman responded, "I'm sorry, Ann, it has to be done now. I'm sorry, it has to be done."

Doug, Delaine and Jimmy moved toward the elevators in the glare of the quartz lights.

"Very happy, very happy," intoned Doug in a faint voice.

"Happy, very happy," whispered Jimmy.

Delaine smiled.

Inside the courtroom, Mary Jo was helped to her feet. She staggered a few paces toward the door and was met by another bank of flashes and lights. Someone said, "Let's get her out of this." The entourage went into the jury anteroom. Mary Jo almost had to be carried.

Once inside, with the doors locked, Mary Jo jerked away from the people holding her, pushed a chair out of the way, pounded the wall and wailed, "Oh goddamn that Jimmy Risher, that traitor, he caused all of this. The very one I loved the most put me through all this. He lost me Richard. Oh God, oh God." Mary Jo couldn't raise her arms again to strike the wall; she crumbled into a chair lamenting. "Oh God. Richard, Richard!"

The bailiff, Frank Taylor, knocked on the door. Ann opened it a foot. "Is there anything I can do?" Frank asked. Ann yelled, "It hurts, you know, goddamnit it hurts. She's got a right to be upset."

It would be forty-five minutes before Mary Jo could leave. When she emerged from the anteroom, the television lights swarmed her. She didn't say a word; no one asked a question. None were needed; they looked at her face.

The jury foreman, Tony Liscio, emerged from the judge's chambers. He was one of the two men on the jury who voted to let Mary Jo keep Richard. "I personally felt there had been a change, but not substantial enough.

". . . We tried to keep the homosexual out as best we could . . . But the way the life style was displayed in the home meant a big part, so it did play a part. Most jurors felt Jimmy's testimony played a big part; one stated he felt it was a plea to get his brother out of that particular home. . . . I felt she had a good home. I felt we were taking him out of a good home just to put him in a better one. . . . Not having a man there all the time had an effect on the decision. No one seemed to be on the fence."

By now several of Mary Jo's close friends had joined the cluster of reporters around Liscio. "It was a life style of a lesbian that most jurors felt affected the trial," Liscio continued. He stayed to answer questions for another half hour.

The courtroom was empty except for Charlotte Taft, who sat in the jury box. Her face was tear-streaked, her hands clutched wads of soggy tissues. A look of cutting pathos and bewilderment swept her face as she said, "Did you ask the foreman the one question that matters now; who's going to tell Richard?"

PART III

AFTERMATH

It would be late afternoon before Jan concluded work at the preschool day care center. Richard and Judie Ann spent most of Monday helping Jan amuse and care for the children. Judie Ann, especially, knew that this would be the day the jury would decide if Richard would stay or leave, to live with his father. Every few hours she would confront Jan: "Have you heard anything yet?"

During the lunch hour, Jan heard. A radio bulletin shattered her stubborn optimism: "Self-admitted lesbian mother loses her child. Minutes ago, a Dallas domestic relations court jury voted to remove the nine-year-old son of Mary Jo Risher . . ."

It was all Jan could do to hide her emotions. Judie Ann persisted in her questioning and stared during her stepmother's bumptious hesitations. Judie couldn't figure out if the verdict had been against them or if Jan was overcome by the tension of waiting. Jan would only say, "There's nothing yet, Judie, we'll just have to wait and hope for the best." Jan was determined that Judie Ann and Richard would learn of the news from their mothers, if she could hold up until evening.

Mary Jo was left alone at her mother's house. Ann had taken Mrs. Davidson to the grocery store and bank. Mary Jo changed into a robe and called her sister Pat.

"It's just awful, Mary Jo. I can't believe it's happened. How could they have voted against you?" Pat had heard the verdict on a local radio newscast. She did her best to comfort her sister, if that meant only being there, a voice, an ear, for Mary Jo to utilize.

The needs of grief are slight; a word or two of consolation, tears, rage; most of all, a presence, a sounding board that reflects back to the sufferer her own verbalizations. We work through our grief essentially alone. The people around us are simply tools to preserve our dignity; to literally keep us from talking to ourselves. The catharsis of words is ultimately a soliloquy.

Pat vowed never to talk to Jimmy again. To her, he was the centerpiece of Mary Jo's undoing. Her distributive blame went even further: "Let's not leave out Carol Jean. She was the one who encouraged Jimmy to talk with his father."

Mary Jo knew that Carol Jean had several long talks with Jimmy prior to Doug instigating the custody suit. Since her sister had been negative toward her lesbianism and failed to rally to her cause, it was all the more plausible to Mary Jo that Carol was a culprit.

Thoughts of retribution spurred Mary Jo on; it was easier to channel her frustration into revenge than to accept the magnitude of her loss. She telephoned Carol Jean.

Mary Jo's brother-in-law Dwight answered the phone; Carol Jean was out. "I don't know if you heard the verdict, Dwight."

"No, I haven't," Dwight responded.

"I lost."

"Mary Jo, I'm sorry to hear that."

"Thank you, Dwight. There's one thing I'd like you to relay to my sister. I just found out a little while ago that one of the instigators was Carol Jean."

Dwight sounded surprised. "I don't think so, Mary Jo."

"Well, Pat told me that Carol Jean had encouraged Jimmy to go to his father with the information that I was a lesbian."

"I still don't think so." Dwight was irritated but kept his temper. Mary Jo was convinced. "As far as I am concerned it's true. Just give her this message. I don't ever want to see her again. I'll come over here to Mother's whenever Carol Jean isn't here. As far as I am concerned, Carol Jean and I have nothing left. And as much as I love Jennifer Ann, I feel that since I can't be a mother to my own child, I don't want to be godmother to Jennifer Ann."

Dwight made an attempt to dissuade Mary Jo, but he couldn't break through her cold finality.

Late afternoon, Mary Jo and Ann drove up to their house in Garland, fully expecting to find reporters and television cameras. The only persons waiting for them were Joline and Neila. They already knew.

Jan arrived with the children. Richard yelled a quick greeting to everyone and bounded up the stairs to his room. Judie Ann lingered in the foyer. "Mommy, I want to know now. Tell me the truth. Jan was real upset all day and I know it, I know it. We've lost Richard, haven't we?"

Ann looked around desperately. She had no choice; it was now. "Yes, honey, but Richard doesn't know it yet." Judie Ann collapsed into a tiny heap, on the floor. Ann knelt down. "Judie Ann, we're going to fight to get him back." Judie tugged at her mother, crying plaintively. Ann picked her up and carried her into the bedroom. Judie clung to Ann. She cried for Neila and her daddy. Neila carried Judie around the house for an hour, until Mike arrived.

Richard, who had heard the commotion, came down the steps. Mary Jo shepherded her son into the bedroom and shut the door. She smoothed his hair around his head, held his shoulders firmly, and spoke in a quiet, deliberate voice. "Rich, darling, you've got to go and live with your daddy for a while." Richard struggled against her hold. "Why?" He cried in pathetic, hoarse wails. Mary Jo held him tightly. After a minute he broke away and pulled off his glasses. He rubbed his eyes violently. His body trembled; he almost fell down. "Why didn't you let me tell them? I wish you'd let me go to the court and tell them." His outburst was so intense he strangled on his words. He lunged against his mother. Tears were steaming his glasses; his chest heaved; his mouth opened to gasp air, but no sound came out. Mary Jo rocked her boy back and forth. "We'll get you back," she whispered, "we'll get you back." Richard moaned, "Uh-huh."

"I love you, Richard," Mary Jo repeated in litany. He questioned, "When do I have to go?" Mary Jo didn't know, but she had to tell him something. "It'll take a while, darling. It won't be right away." Richard was soothed enough to ask Mary Jo about the arrangements. "How long will I have to stay, Mamma?" Mary Jo stammered, "I'll try . . . I'll try as hard as I can to . . . to get you back."

Ann opened the door. She sat next to Richard and Mary Jo on the bed. Glances between the two women told her that Mary Jo needed help. "Richard," Ann began, "there were twelve people that didn't understand what the deal was. The attorneys confused them and they couldn't make a good decision. They weren't with us all the time and they couldn't know how happy we were."

Richard nodded. "They didn't know." The emotional buffeting of the custody ordeal had generated a survival instinct in the boy that was surfacing. Adults would sadly misconstrue it as bravery, for Richard appeared to marshal a stoic self-control, compress his lips, and act "normal." Richard wasn't acting; he wasn't mature, beyond his years. He was coping, the only way he could, by blotting the trauma out of his mind, walling it off from his consciousness and greening the area surrounding the wall with fantasy. He was just going for a "visit" to his dad's. A "temporary" thing, like the usual week-long sojourn during the Christmas holidays.

It was Richard who first left the bedroom and went to the living room to sit beside Neila and Judie Ann.

It was Richard, with the frailest hold on his quixotic destiny, who got up off the sofa, ambled toward the door, and went outside, explaining dutifully, "I guess maybe I'd better tell the kids."

Dolores Dyer telephoned. She asked Mary Jo how she was doing and whether she had told Richard. After a reply, Dolores couldn't postpone her news any longer: "I have to tell you now, when Richard leaves on December twenty-sixth for his visitation, he will not come back to you."

Mary Jo dropped the receiver on the kitchen counter, banged at it with her fist, and reeled into the living room shouting, "They promised they wouldn't take him right away. They lied. They lied. They're taking him away. Two days. Two days is all I have." She stumbled into the bedroom.

Ann watched helplessly. She picked up the receiver. "I guess you heard?" Dolores was utterly dejected. "I did everything I could. I told the court that time was needed. They shouldn't yank him away like that. Oh, Ann, I feel awful. It should have been a gradual thing. He won't have any time to adjust. I feel terrible." Ann vaguely thanked Dolores and hung up the phone.

Within thirty minutes Aglaia Mauzy telephoned. Her sense of timing, acute in the courtroom, was deficient outside. She wanted to explain to Mary Jo when Richard would have to leave. Curiously, Mary Jo listened with solicitude while Ann ranted in the background. It was like only one of the women could afford such displays at a time.

Mike Foreman's arrival stemmed Ann's shouting. Her anger subsided when she saw Judie Ann jump into her father's arms for security.

As the evening wore on and Mike, Jan, Neila and Joline drifted home, Ann was busy plotting. She had fashioned an escape; Mary Jo would take Richard and run to another state while she remained behind to bear the brunt. Later, when Doug gave up his search and the court was powerless to intercede, Ann and Judie Ann would join Mary Jo and Richard. Ann's planning went as far as telephoning a few of her friends in Austin and some other lesbian couples she corresponded with out of state. That was Ann's equivalent to Mary Jo's telephone call to Carol Jean. The escape scenario was never taken seriously by Mary Jo, but she knew the value its formulation held for Ann.

The gruesome pattern had taken shape, each day more odious than the last: Mary Jo and Ann on the stand, Doug and Jimmy testifying, the day of the verdict and telling the children, and now, Christmas Eve, and shopping for Richard.

Mary Jo wandered through the stores; a specter of Dickensian dread. Every time she picked up a toy or touched a shirt she gulped, cried, and grew faint. Ann couldn't stand it; she walked away, then returned, afraid Mary Jo would break down completely in the middle of a crowded department store.

Finally, the one hundred dollars that Mike and Jan had given them was used up. The women and children headed home to wrap the presents. Neila and Joline dropped over and brought a copy of the evening paper that contained pictures of all the principals in the trial.

Mary Jo and Ann read the story, folded the paper, and tossed it on the coffee table. Richard and Judie Ann were curious. Richard crumpled up the photograph of his father and punched it violently. No one stirred until Neila nervously turned on the radio. "Let's have some Christmas carols."

Hours before dawn, Richard and Judie were banging on the bedroom door. "Get up, get up, see what Santa brought us." The kids piled onto their mothers' bed, hugging, chatting, exuberant. "Come on, get up."

Richard and Judie Ann had already made a scouting foray into the living room and what they spotted tantalized them into a frenzy. They tugged on ribbons, ripped away wrapping paper, shook boxes, and all the while squealing with delight. "Look, Mommy. Look, look, look at this."

The guests for Christmas dinner were Mary Jo's mother, father, and stepmother and Ann's father. Throughout the day people telephoned to wish them "Merry Christmas." There were several requests for interviews.

Mary Jo and Ann were being pressed by every form of the communications media; radio, television, newspapers, magazines, documentarians, scandal sheets, pulp book authors and newsletters. They were concerned about the way the story was being handled; whom to talk with and, more importantly, whom to avoid. That evening Charlotte Taft and Susan Caudill, from the PBS television station, visited to talk about the media problem. They brought the children an enormous Mexican *piñata* full of candies and small toys.

Shortly before ten the next morning, the photographer from *People* magazine arrived. The editors wanted pictures of Richard with Mary Jo before two o'clock, the hour that Doug would pick up Richard.

Instead of being shy, as Mary Jo had anticipated, Richard was fascinated by the man who would take dozens of shots of his every move. "You wanna take a picture of me eatin' my grandma's pumpkin pie?" Richard was a natural. "How about me drinkin' a glass of milk?" Richard didn't stop talking. During the group poses he was telling the photographer about his school: "We can really get those girls and kiss them all. We chase them to the fence. If we can just herd them into the fence area, we've got it made. They don't have anyplace to go." The photographer grinned. "That's sure one way to get a kiss, Richard."

By noon, the photographer was gone, and Mary Jo helped Richard prepare his belongings. Judie Ann, who was slated for a visit with her father, left the house and stood outside to wait; she couldn't bear watching Richard pack his clothes.

Mary Jo, Richard and Ann drove to Mrs. Davidson's. The transfer of Richard would take place there. Mary Jo had timed their arrival so that she would have a few minutes alone with Richard.

He climbed up into Mary Jo's lap. "Richard, you be a good boy." He smiled coyly. "How long do you think I have to stay out there?" "I can't tell you, darling, but I know now I'm going to work as hard and as fast as I can to get you back. You do believe that, don't you?" Richard threw his arms around Mary Jo's neck. "Yes, Mamma." Mary Jo hugged and kissed Richard. "I'll always love you." She was fighting back her tears, trying not to break down in front of her son. Richard whined. "When can I see you again, Mamma?" Mary Jo held Richard's head in her hands. "Very soon, darling. Don't cry, sweetheart. Just go out there like you were visiting. Okay? Be sure and keep your grades up in school."

Mary Jo didn't know what else to say. She patted and squeezed her boy for several minutes.

Ann called Richard over to the sofa. She kissed him and told him that they would get him back. Doug's car drove up in front of the house.

Mary Jo and Ann went into a bedroom where they could see the front of the house. Doug walked to the door. Immediately, Mrs. Davidson and Richard went to the car. Mrs. Davidson spoke to Jimmy, who was hunched down in the back seat, out of view. In two minutes it was over; Richard was gone.

*　*　*

When she returned to work at Gaston Episcopal Hospital, Mary Jo was surprised at her reception; it was almost as if she had been away for an uneventful vacation. When she walked onto the floor, several nurses said, "Hi, Mary Jo," but nothing else.

Unless they had been out of the city for the past two weeks, there was no way they could have avoided the sight or sound of the lesbian mother futilely fighting for her son. The trial was a daily headliner in the papers and on television.

The surface tranquillity of Gaston puzzled Mary Jo. They knew. Of course they knew. She had been telephoned by a friend who informed her that one nurse had openly threatened to quit if Mary Jo came back to the hospital after the trial. That couldn't have escaped everyone's notice. Yet, they were silent; they disregarded her.

Mary Jo would learn, months later, that there had been an emergency staff meeting at the hospital. Supervisors were instructed to warn their employees to withhold any comments.

Mary Jo's return to work was not without a disquieting incident. In her message box was a tersely worded memo ordering her to remove her name plate and not to pin it on her uniform until further notice. That notice to put her name plate back on would never come. The other slight that Mary Jo detected had to do with nursing assignments. While she remained on the same floor, she gradually realized that she never saw the area where traditionally the wealthier patients were billeted.

She was quite prepared for friction. Mary Jo could function indefinitely in a vacuum, without social intercourse with the other nurses. She would do her work and take her breaks, alone, if necessary. It wouldn't be ideal, but she had to earn a living and nursing was all she knew. All she ever wanted to know. And therein was the crux of the problem; the nightmare that she couldn't have foreseen until she was alone with her first patient.

Throughout her years of nursing, Mary Jo's every moment in the hospital was wrapped up in her patients. She met their needs physically, mentally and spiritually. She was never aloof. She talked with them, held them, comforted them; shared their pain and fears, became enmeshed in their families and jobs; remembered their anniversaries and birthdays, kept track of them and often, too often for her sanity, mourned their deaths. She was a part of all those she served.

Alone, with a critically ill woman, her first day back at nursing, something had changed. Something radical. Mary Jo was gliding through the motions, without feeling. Her effusive humanity was exorcised by a pulsating fear. "There was this helpless woman staring at me. Did she recognize me. Would she think my gestures were immoral? Bathing her, a catheterization; would these routine things send her screaming to the administrators that she was being handled by a lesbian woman?"

Each new patient awakened a larger terror. Mary Jo, who had handily dismissed Mike McCurley's assertions of the stigmatizing aspects of the homosexual life, was suffering a gripping paranoia. She shunted any friendly conversation with the patients. She dismissed inquiries into her personal life with a brusqueness that jolted the pit of her stomach. She had lost her precious spark of dedication. She was distant; never again able to administer to her ill charges with any measure of commitment.

As the weeks passed, Mary Jo went from the slithering fear of withdrawal to a consuming hatred. She hated nursing; to her clouded reasoning, it epitomized society's relegation of the homosexual to a subhuman status. Of course she was giving in, letting herself be manipulated by insidious fear.

Her resistance was minimal; her self-esteem was in flux; her son was gone; her life was adrift. She would hang onto nursing until the summer, not because of the money, although she was thousands of dollars in debt; not to show anyone the gutsiness of an alienated lesbian, the hell with their evil little minds; rather, because she had no place to go every morning. It was that simple. The steadfastness of routine; getting up, dressing in white, driving to a building, standing up all day, bandaging, inoculating, cleaning, wiping, reading charts—a routine. An anchor. Comfort in the mindlessness of a splendid rut.

Ann balked at returning to the bank. It meant leaving Mary Jo's side for the first time in two weeks. Rumors were circulating at the bank and she was convinced she would be fired the moment she stepped in the door. No firing squad greeted her; in fact, no one greeted her at all. Cold silence. Ann hovered at her desk; she didn't dare venture out into the bank, as was her custom. She took her breaks alone, went to lunch by herself. Her only contact was with her boss, who was very formal. One former male friend turned the other way when she walked by. She heard him mutter, "Sick, sick."

It was Ann's second day on the job when the dam of silence trickled its first leak. A woman cautiously cornered Ann and volunteered, "It was awful what the jury did. I'm so sorry you lost."

The latter part of her first week back, a man she knew only by sight approached her in the lunchroom. "It's a great thing, what you and Mary Jo have done. My lover and I think you are very brave. Most gay people wouldn't have the guts to do what you did."

One of the saddest results of the trial was the effect it had on the gay people, both at Ann's office and Mary Jo's hospital. The silent communion that homosexuals shared in the "straight" world vanished. With one or two exceptions, the people that Ann and Mary Jo knew were gay steered away from them on the job. Not just an extra caution; xenophobic avoidance. The risks of identification, the old "fellow traveler" syndrome, was overpowering. The comradeship, in whatever degree it existed before, was aborted dramatically. Mary Jo and Ann were notorious lesbians, walking evidence of the humiliating fate that awaited others if exposed.

Ann's delicate position affected her every action at the bank. She never went to the restroom when she knew it was occupied. If someone came in, she left immediately. She purposely stayed out of closed rooms with another woman. She never leaned over another woman's desk or sat too close. She never went to lunch with the boss again. All this to stifle gossip. Ann was terrified, any step would be a misstep, any gesture would be a lurid overture, any naturalness would be a sexual advance.

To counter the rejection, Ann created a private world within the bank. A nest within the thorn bush. She stayed on the telephone hour after hour, talking law, publicity, psychology, child care or money with friends, reporters, or anyone who had the liberty to while away an hour. At first, her life on the telephone aggravated her supervisors; after all, there was work to be done.

Gradually, as her responsibilities were chipped away, she was permitted to phone away. It seemed, at times, that her new duties were to maintain community relations with friends of Mary Jo Risher.

This "freedom," carried to a logical conclusion, meant that Ann and the bank had mutually agreed. Her career had evaporated and the remaining object was to find a graceful way for her to bow out.

In March, Ann was called to jury duty at the Dallas County Courthouse. She was given time off with pay. Ann had already hinted to the bank that she would seek a leave of absence and the jury call appeared an ideal time.

The leave was a euphemism, a substitute for the inevitable firing or quitting that would have occurred. There was no clearcut discrimination against Ann. Her role was as great as the bank's in the gradual elimination of her job responsibilities.

* * *

The first half of January didn't offer any respite from the numbing realities that Mary Jo had to face. She was morally committed to continue the legal fight to get the decision reversed, and the projected cost was a minimum of $5,000. The attorneys had to be paid on a regular and current basis. Their law practice was new, and Mary Jo's case had taken up all their time for the past month.

Obtaining a transcript of the trial, essential to the appellate process, called for an immediate $2,250 for the court reporter. That sum was arranged by the newly formed organization, *Friends of Mary Jo Risher.*

Friends was a diverse collection of Dallas activists of unquestioned loyalty and energy, devised to assure justice for Mary Jo and extend the doctrine of homosexual rights in general.

While *Friends* managed to salvage an impossible financial situation and offer Mary Jo and Ann a sustaining emotional buttress, its strategy posed a scary dilemma.

In order to raise the thousands of dollars needed, a mammoth publicity campaign was generated with Mary Jo and Ann as the center. Publicity surrounding the trial was widespread, going international through the wire services and the radio networks of Canada, Britain and Australia. Accounts were carried in every major American newspaper and *Time* and *People* magazines did stories with photographs.

Basically, however, it was a one-time affair. Mary Jo and Ann assumed that like most of yesterday's headlines in media fueled by immediacy and novelty they would quickly drop from favor.

Now, if they accepted the well-intentioned manipulation set forth by their supporters, the publicity would be sustained. They would sit under the television lights for months, see their pictures in newspapers for months, have to answer questions about their sexuality for months, defend their rights to a private life for months, be recognized and pointed at for months.

Publicity meant awareness. Awareness fostered sympathy. And that provided money. The ordeal to regain Richard grew more complex.

Mary Jo was a reluctant symbol. Why should she represent the plight of all lesbian mothers? What attributes of her personality entitled her to receive adulation and money from an idol-susceptible public? Where had her "dues" as a leader in the "cause" been paid; she was forced into court against her will.

These were nagging and legitimate questions that haunted Mary Jo from the start of her nebulous public career. The best answer came in a speech she delivered to a regional conference of the National Organization for Women in Denver, Colorado:

"If all this has been thrust upon me and made me a symbol of gay rights; of women's rights, so be it. I may have been reluctant, but I do accept it. Not for any cause, even though the cause is worthy. Not because my going public can help advance gay rights, but God knows any step forward is desperately needed. Not because the feminist movement needs me, even though I am a woman who has put her rights on the line and lost. But simply because I am a fit mother, who deeply loves her son and wants him back. And my son was taken away, solely because our laws and this society have labeled me unfit, evil, subhuman because of my God-given sexuality."

The decision to go public, to court the mass media, was made. For Mary Jo, at this point, survival was her highest obligation. The current of militancy was too swift, the image of Richard being led to his father's car too vivid, to ever reconsider, to temper her methods. She would, she thought, sublimate all else and with unflinching zeal work toward one goal: getting back her son.

The toll this venture was to take on herself, Ann, and the family had to be ignored (if it was ever clearly imagined). Mary Jo believed the scar tissue from the custody fight would shield her from other onslaughts. To doubt was to lose momentum, and crusades were won on momentum, not the justness of the cause.

*   *   *

They arrived in New York a day before the appearances on the syndicated television show "Consenting Adults" and the NBC network program "Tomorrow" with Tom Snyder. Armed with a dozen index cards containing the salient legal and psychological points, prepared by two of the *Friends*, Mary Jo and Ann checked into the Essex House.

Their intention was to relax, gather their thoughts, and practice reciting some of the more complex issues outlined on their index cards. They never had a chance to fully unpack. Local feminists, reporters, writers, gay activists, and assorted cause groupies pounded their door and rang their phone twenty hours a day.

With this cataract introduction to the big time, Mary Jo and Ann missed dinner. Their first day in New York ended with an 11 P.M. radio talk show aimed at lesbians.

Back in their hotel room, accompanied by a *soi-disant* "freelance television producer" who had latched onto them at the radio station, they watched Tom Snyder on his "Tomorrow" show.

That night Mr. Snyder appeared testy as he explored his guest's theories. He used his considerable skills as an inquisitor to unravel his guest's logic and composure.

The victim was not used to the pitfalls and verbal tumblings of what passed for top-flight television talk shows. Mary Jo and Ann sympathized. "Hell, I'm not going on that man's show," Ann vowed. "He'll make a fool of us," Mary Jo warned. "But, we're here, everyone is expecting to see us, what can we do?" Ann answered half jokingly, "Get sick."

The next afternoon, decked out in smart, expensive pant suits, purchased by a *Friend*, Mary Jo and Ann arrived at Metromedia for the taping of the syndicated program "Consenting Adults." Charlotte Taft, who had postponed a family visit in Connecticut to be with Mary Jo and Ann, accompanied them to the studio.

Several hours of waiting in the wings, watching the taping on monitors, did nothing to reassure the women. When their turn came, their voices were constricted with tension. They had no idea of what questions to expect.

The interviewer was a psychologist and author, Sonya Friedman, who was gracious, intelligent and perceptive. Just before the camera lights came on she advised her guests, "Just forget everything you see around you. Pretend we are sitting in your living room back home and we are old friends. Just talk to me calmly and naturally and I know you'll do splendid." They did. A triumph for the power of suggestion.

The lights hadn't cooled on "Consenting Adults" when Mary Jo, Ann and Charlotte stormed the exit, slid into the seats of the NBC limo and were threaded through the traffic to Rockefeller Plaza.

Mary Jo and Ann, by now "old hands," were made up by a technician and led through a hall toward the studio. In a waiting room sat Tom Snyder, getting his powder dusting. "You must be Mary Jo Risher and Ann Foreman." He knew their names, no cue cards or anything. Tom was relaxed and friendly, nothing like the overpowering interviewer they had seen the night before. "I got a call from my brother who lives in Dallas," Snyder said. "He told me, 'Tom, you've got a couple of women from Dallas on your show tonight and I want you to treat them right.'"

Mary Jo and Ann laughed. They might survive, after all. The program covered the history of the custody battle, the trial, and the grounds for the appeal. Mary Jo and Ann looked magnificent, and after a few stiff minutes became loose and informal. Snyder served up his questions in an apologetic, sugar-coated fashion. He was well aware of the touchy nature of the topic and handled his chore with sensitivity and aplomb.

Throughout the program Mary Jo delivered the points outlined on the index cards. The words were hers; she had studied the concepts, assimilated them, and offered them in a spontaneous narrative that was uniquely her own. She was a quick study and her grasp of concepts was genuine. "Because of labels of mental illness and the hostile public attitude, based upon poor information, people who are happy, talented, productive and homosexual are still unwilling to admit their preference."

Ann was equally impressive. "Mary Jo's sexual preference, in the privacy of her bedroom, was allowed to be the only issue in a court of law. Under the Fourteenth Amendment to the Constitution she was denied equal protection with you."

Ann and Mary Jo watched the playback of the "Tomorrow" show in their hotel room. There was an innocent, child-like fascination in watching yourself on television; akin to hearing your voice for the first time on a tape recorder or seeing a snapshot taken in an unguarded moment. So that was me; I really looked that way; how strange I talked; but not really that bad, in fact I sounded intelligent, even witty; look how people responded to me, they took me seriously, respected me; huh.

There were phone calls from family and *Friends* in Dallas. "Marvelous . . . moving . . . you looked beautiful . . . it sounded fine . . . people can identify with you . . . you're going to be TV stars, no, I mean it . . . you should be proud . . . what a boost to the cause . . ." There were sweet dreams in one room of the Essex House that night.

Self-esteem has to be the most unstable element in the anatomical hodgepodge of human personality. Its rapid loss can dehabilitate a body as thoroughly as a virulent microbe. A massive infusion of pride can precipitate such euphoria that lacking perspective, it becomes addictive, the controlling force of the personality. Like all addictions its feeding and care take precedence over everything else.

There were pride pushers on every corner, ready with a fix. The New York *Times*, NBC's News and Information Service, *MS.* magazine, CBS, the National Gay Task Force, *Newsweek*, and a host of lesser corrupters. They were just doing their job; they were there to serve the immutable law of supply and demand. There was no way they could notice the vulnerability of Mary Jo Risher.

She needed the publicity; they needed the story, the fairest of exchanges. The problem, the complication, was the masking of the pain. The loss of self-esteem was a symptom of a festering psyche. Mary Jo couldn't face the loss of Richard, couldn't come to terms with the grief. She wished to postpone the acceptance, suspend time, freeze her emotions.

It was not that she gloried in the attention and status for its own sake; a junkie grows to hate the needle; she had to have the narcotic of pride to obliterate the agony of acceptance.

By the time the women landed in Detroit for a taping of the syndicated "Lou Gordon Show," Ann was feeling the creeping sensation that she was along for the ride. Mary Jo's "we" had become "me." "Our" story was transformed into "my" story. Ann, of course, did her share of the talking, but Mary Jo was beginning to need larger and larger doses of self-importance to dull her pain.

It was during the twenty-four hours in Detroit that Mary Jo encountered the irony of the publicity blitz. That particular weekend was Richard's first visitation and she had to settle for a long telephone call to her son, who was staying with Mrs. Davidson. It was hard for Mary Jo to determine whether the boy understood why his mother was out of town and couldn't see him.

The final day of the trip was a whirlwind romp through Chicago. From the hotel near O'Hare Airport to the halls of WGN television studios for a live one-hour guest slot on the "Phil Donahue" show Mary Jo and Ann were literally on the run. The schedule was so tight that they were led by a galloping Phil Donahue from the make-up room down a hall and into the studio for a breathless opening to the program.

Although his program was shown in over sixty major cities,

Phil appeared unaffected by his prominence. His eager humor, quizzical mind and innate sense of fair play allowed him the uncommon latitude of dealing with the most controversial topics and guests in a manner palatable to his legion of daytime viewers. The Donahue program presented Mary Jo and Ann with the best opportunity to display their personalities and generated more mail than all the other appearances combined.

After a working lunch, with a Chicago magazine writer and a news conference at the hotel, Mary Jo and Ann flew back to Dallas. They were met at the airport by several *Friends* and Judie Ann.

Returning home to Dallas wasn't quite the letdown Mary Jo anticipated. The high adventure of the three-city tour was relived endlessly for relatives and friends; and three benefits were scheduled in gay clubs in Dallas.

February was the first month that Mary Jo paid child support to Doug. Judge Chrisman had set the amount at $95 a month. Mary Jo netted slightly over $450 a month from her job. Her attorneys had sought a smaller amount, more in line with what Doug had paid in proportion to his earnings. They also pushed for the child support money to be placed into a trust fund for Richard's college education. That was rejected by Doug.

The court ordered that all Richard's clothes, toys, and other property be surrendered, along with items that Jimmy claimed. This included beds, a desk, bookcases, televisions, and shotguns.

The terms of the visitation allowed Mary Jo to see Richard every other week from 8 P.M. on Friday until 6 P.M. on Sunday. She also was given three weeks in the summer and every other holiday and birthday; including a week during the Christmas season.

Almost from the beginning there were infractions of the visitation agreement. Richard was withheld from several visits, and Mary Jo and Doug disagreed under what circumstances a visit could be canceled.

The animosity of the telephone exchanges became too much, and Ann and Delaine were pressed into handling the telephone contact needed to co-ordinate the visitations.

When Richard did visit, Mary Jo was beside herself with joy; she would sweep up the boy, hug and kiss him, and shadow his every move. She didn't want to go anywhere, to share Richard with anyone. It was stressful for her if Richard left the room or wandered out to play with his old chums. Every nuance of his behavior caught her attention: why was he so quiet, his laugh had changed, he acted a little nervous, his appetite was different, he couldn't take kidding anymore. His physical appearance obsessed Mary Jo: his hair was cut shorter, he had an infected fingernail, his nose was running, he coughed too much, he wanted to sleep more.

She focused on Richard with laser intensity. Every moment at home had to be perfect, every exchange, activity, conversation just so. Richard was engulfed with the fierce love of a mother who had to compact two weeks of care, sharing and attention into forty-six hours.

Richard, who reveled in the love, wanted to reciprocate. He talked about his new school, a rabbit in the backyard, his new friends, his new bike. The message was excruciating for Mary Jo. Richard's life was going on, with trials and bad moments, periods of altercations and adjustments, but going on—largely without her.

She was an interlude, a grand homecoming, deeply loved, sorely missed, an adored mother, but a part, not a whole. Forty-six hours with her; 290 hours away.

Mary Jo sat watching Richard giggle and joke with Judie Ann. Her face was soft, her lips smiled in gentle longing. Suddenly with no sound or movement tears sprinkled from her eyes.

Ann treaded lightly around Mary Jo's fixation. When her responses toward Richard didn't measure up to Mary Jo's expectations, she was snippishly reprimanded. Even Judie Ann was questioned about why she didn't play more with Richard, why she dared to argue with him. Ann and her daughter didn't care any less for Richard; they looked forward to his visits; it was a matter of Mary Jo caring more.

The halcyon days before the custody matter seemed distant; not just a few months behind them, but light years away. Family life, at best, was a fleeting, stolen moment away from phone calls, speeches, meetings, fund raisers and strategy sessions. Ann, Judie, and Mary Jo moved through outings and dinners with a maundering deference to the past. They hadn't surrendered all hope for a private life; they certainly deemed it worthwhile, but they had watched it atrophy and almost forgot how it was lived.

The emotional gyrations were acute. "One minute everything settled down and Mary Jo and I could talk again about each other; the next minute we were fighting over some minor thing that neither one of us really cared about," Ann ruefully recalled. "Nothing would please Mary Jo, except speaking before some group, hearing how great she was, or getting some contribution. It was impossible to adjust to her wild swings of emotion. Everything Judie Ann and I would say was wrong. Mary Jo and I were drifting apart, somehow, and there was nothing that would stop it."

Mary Jo's beef against Ann, the list of specifics, could just as easily applied to herself: "She didn't really share my loss. Her child hadn't been yanked away. She didn't understand what it was like to be without Richard for weeks at a time, and then not even know for sure until the last minute if you were going to get to see him during the regular visitation time. She expected me to just snap back like that [she snapped her fingers]. She tried to force Judie Ann on me and have us do things together like we did before Richard was taken away. I couldn't bring myself to act like nothing had changed."

Ann sensed the rebuke without analyzing the cause, and this aggravated the rift. Their love for each other, the last and most significant bulwark against disintegration, was under stress. "If she didn't care enough for me to see what I was going through, maybe it was over," Mary Jo postulated. "Of course she had stood by me during the trial, when she could have said, 'It's getting to be too much and I've got Judie Ann to think about and maybe we better call it off.' But I knew there were limits to anyone's endurance. It was entirely possible that Ann couldn't go on, keep fighting."

Ann's hackles were up over the same reason. "I had stood by

her, when anyone else would have split. It was because of me, the work I did researching the trial, getting support from NOW and the gay community, that made Mary Jo's case possible in the first place. Now, I resented her constantly questioning my commitment. I couldn't have the same outlook that she did; I couldn't live my life every minute of the day waiting for revenge on Doug. I couldn't just stop living, until Richard came back, no matter how much I loved Mary Jo. I had a daughter who needed me, needed both of us, more than ever.

"It was one thing to go over the trial three or four times a week, when we were speaking in the community or out of town, and it was another thing to endlessly relive it in our living room. There just didn't seem to be room for anything else in Mary Jo's life. Not me, not Judie Ann. I honestly felt that Mary Jo could go on forever, living that damn trial. It was a living hell. The affection between us, well, it was strained at best. She seemed to shut me out."

Left alone with the interloper of Mary Jo's loss, the two women might have been able to finesse the breakdown in communications in short order. It was extraneous events, involving their families, that precluded stabilization.

Mary Jo's father underwent major surgery and the doctor's prognosis was pessimistic. He suspected cancer of the colon. While Mr. Davidson was in the hospital, Carol Jean stayed with him. She asked Mary Jo to baby-sit with her children. This one gesture, born of desperation, began the process of reconciling the sisters.

Several days and a second operation relieved the crisis. Mr. Davidson was all right; his doctor's initial fear was unfounded. The enervating experience drew the family together. Carol Jean telephoned Mary Jo to thank her for taking care of the children, and this led to personal contact.

The personality conflict over Mary Jo's life style was further alleviated when Carol Jean became critically ill within weeks of Mr. Davidson's hospital stay. She faced her sixth major surgery in under two years. "I think Carol really believed she was going to die this time," her husband Dwight remembered. "She didn't say it, in so many words, but she began to put her life in order and even had consultations with a minister. I think the seriousness of her illness, the intestinal blockage, persuaded her, more than anything else, to make up with Mary Jo."

Mary Jo was cautious about accepting Carol's change of heart. She loved Carol and knew that Carol loved her, but trust was another matter. It would be some time before Mary Jo's reservations vanished.

Carol Jean's chronic medical problems, depressing under normal circumstances, deepened Mary Jo's nihilism. Nothing was going right in her life; all of her doubts about personal redemption galvanized into a spindly melancholy. Her frustrations, once bursting out in peevish episodes with Ann and Judie, were internalized. Days at a time she would sit in silence, watching television or reading the hundreds of letters deluging the post office box.

The letters became a stage-center substitute for her own life. Many were supportive with homiletic little phrases: "Hang in there, you'll win in the end . . . your bravery is impressive . . . you're a wonderful example for others . . . God bless you." There were plentiful examples of hatred. Most of these were from mean little souls who claimed an exclusive pipeline to their narrow, pathological god. Typical of the hubris was a gloating diatribe that began: "Dear Things."

When letters of that ilk first popped up, Mary Jo and Ann hooted with laughter and passed them around to friends. A good laugh was a good laugh. At some point such shtik ceased to be funny for everyone. How many times do you have to see a Charlie Chaplin fall on his butt before you stop snickering? Once the comedic effect of the hate mail subsided for Ann, she tossed the letter away as soon as she gleaned the first irrational thought. Mary Jo took the venom more seriously. She lingered over the wild accusations, actually struggled with the poisonous logic hoping to persuade the writers of such tripe that they were wrong.

Ann was laboring under a similar compulsion to answer some of the inquiries. She, however, was interested in the pleas for help. Dozens of the letters were autobiographical missives, swelling with the exile and misfortune of gay people, either struggling to come out or hiding in stark terror from persecution.

The writers were naïvely looking to Mary Jo and Ann to offer them the magic word, the mythical key to unlock their mental prisons. Ann was eager to assume the role of adviser or surrogate parent to every semiliterate urchin who had the price of a stamp and a sharp pencil. "I could relate to their problems. They all were so desperate. I guess they were looking to us because they didn't have anyplace else to go. Mary Jo thought I was nuts to answer them. There was a danger that I would do more harm than good. And I couldn't offer them the same kind of advice that a psychologist or counselor might be able to, but I felt we owed them something. Our public image was that of superwomen; lesbians, who knew what it was all about, who could thumb their noses at the world, when in reality we were just as messed up as they were."

It was Ann's insistence on providing analysis by mail that soured Mary Jo on all the letters. She put them in folders and locked them in a desk. "Hell, I was being smothered by my own problems and couldn't begin to deal with anyone else's," Mary Jo remarked in retrospect. "At the time I resented additional demands on me. I know it sounds hard, but I was sick of everyone pressuring me, demanding answers that I didn't have. I was hostile toward Ann. Here she was worrying over these strangers and she didn't extend the same concern to me.

"Today, when we get mail, I can suggest organizations and counseling and may even give practical advice based upon my experiences. But when Ann was headlong into answering every letter, I was in much worse shape than the people who were writing us."

The letter phase was barely over when disaster struck Ann's side of the family. Judie Ann's great-grandmother was diagnosed as terminally ill with inoperable cancer. That was bad enough in itself, but it reopened dark memories for Ann that she had shunted away. Her mother had died of cancer. Mrs. Davis, a lovely and kind woman, was worshiped by her daughter, and her death left a deep void. Cancer was again to decimate Ann's family.

Simultaneously Ann's father, Moughon Davis, failed to revive his faltering gasoline station business. He lost money for months and was forced to plow his meager social security checks into the register in order to keep the utilities connected. All of his savings, minus the money he loaned Mary Jo, were gone. His pumps were dry. He hadn't paid for the last consignment of gas and the oil company demanded cash in advance before they would ship him another tank truck of gas. He needed close to five thousand dollars to stay open. Gone were the days when an independent operator could call upon thirty years of association with a giant corporation for extra consideration and a period of grace.

Ann visited her dad's deserted station daily for over two weeks, to convince him of the futility of waiting for the oil company to come through. He sat in the empty station all day and watched the cars roll past. Mr. Davis couldn't fathom that after all the years of business dealings, all the years of plenty, the oil company would ruthlessly shut him off without a second thought.

Moughon was in his seventies, nearly deaf, spry, but fragile and proud. He was unused to his word meaning nothing in matters of business. He had spent his life without contracts and the petty restrictions of bank financing. His handshake was his bond. It was a defeat of immeasurable dimensions for him to give up, lock the doors of his station, and play at being content watching the dreary world of daytime television while the weeds overran his yard.

Ann was guilt-ridden over her father. "I kept thinking: If I had more time to spend on his books, more time away from Mary Jo's troubles so that I could have hired some good help, maybe he could have made it. If we had been able to pay him back the money he loaned us, it could have made a difference. He didn't know what to do with himself; he had always worked."

Right at the time of Mr. Davis' business failure, Neila confided in Ann and Mary Jo that she and Joline were breaking up. Their spats had escalated during the trial; Joline had become convinced that her ex-husband was about to move against her, even though he lived in another state and was financially unable to start a suit. Both had a brief fling at affairs, then reconciled. It was different this time; they had given up. Neila and Joline parted and moved away.

Seeing their best friends' relationship crack had a jolting and profound effect on Mary Jo and Ann. Their lives were too intertwined, their strengths and weaknesses too similar, their triumphs and defeats too closely shared, not to feel an oracular warning. It could happen to them.

Mary Jo and Ann didn't waste any time. They worked, with a gritty determination, to rebuild their floundering lives. With the help of Dolores Dyer, they were spurred to talk candidly about the private devils that were pillaging their store of respect and love for each other. They learned the techniques of fighting fairly; not to use an honest disagreement to bandy about reckless accusations and frustrations.

Gradually, through what Dr. Dyer called "an amazing ability to integrate psychological tools into everyday living," Mary Jo and Ann separated the gist of their love relationship from the horrible financial privations they were enduring.

The whole dynamic of their interactions shifted toward recovery. Ann, who was dangerously close to living her life vicariously through her mate, reasserted her independence. "I was no longer dragging myself around feeling that I had to exist as another Mary Jo Risher. Ann Foreman had value and worth. And the most amazing part was the way Mary Jo responded. She liked it better than I did."

The months of lying around the house, paralyzed by depression, were over. Ann was energized. She grappled with the bills, set up payment schedules, compiled and figured the long overdue income taxes, and sketched out plans for the painting business that she and Mary Jo hoped to establish. For months they had talked with house painters and interior decorators. Now they were free to turn a hobby into a new vocation.

Mary Jo's transformation was an audacious implosion of self-evaluation. Her utter denial of reality was overturned. Her flossy stupor was dissipated as rapidly as the summer sun burned away fog on the Texas plain. Mary Jo coasted into a genuine self-confidence that had been nurturing below the surface during the long months of dueling a hostile public. She could face the loss of Richard, admit the awful possibility that she might never get him back, without being overwhelmed. "I would never give up the fight to get him back until my last dollar was gone and the highest court had said no. I couldn't stop. I owed it to Richard and myself. But I knew I could lose, and if I did, I would have to develop another kind of relationship with my son. I didn't relish that, but I could do it. No matter what the outcome in the courts, I won't lose him completely. They can only take him away physically. If I have to, I'll adjust to it.

"I won't let other people control me. I won't give them that power. I want to live for myself for a change. I can live, can survive, even with the pain. My life hasn't stopped; it goes on with Ann. I want Richard back more than anything in the world, but there are other reasons to keep on going, to live. I am beginning to find those reasons and with Ann at my side, I'll find more."

Mary Jo's brave words were put to the test the same month she uttered them. The semblance of stability returning to their lives was slammed against the most severe barrier concocted since the trial.

Mrs. Davidson telephoned Mary Jo with startling news: "Jimmy's getting married. It's true, Mary Jo, he's getting married and no member of our family has been invited." Mrs. Davidson was indignant. "That's a fine how-ya-do."

Mary Jo felt the hammer blow of rejection. "Could he really be doing this; getting married before he graduates from high school? Would he really get married without asking me, or any member of the family?"

As Jimmy's wedding day approached, May 14, Mary Jo became pensive. "Should I just show up at the church? I don't even know the name of the girl he's going to marry. What was the girl's family thinking? They must know about Jimmy's mother. He's just eighteen by less than a week. So young."

Mary Jo and Ann held several sit-down discussions about the

pending nuptials. Mary Jo dismissed the idea of walking in on the wedding or reception as an amusing flight of fancy. Her only problem was whether to officially recognize the wedding by sending a present, not having received an invitation.

Ann was firm: "Mary Jo should just ignore him the way he did her. She'd given Jimmy all the chances in the world. Why should she always be the one to crawl? He had excluded her. He knew how important a son's wedding was to his mother. It had to be the cruelest thing he had ever done."

Mary Jo suppressed any mean-spirited reaction. She wanted to illustrate her love to Jimmy, despite all else. "He couldn't accept me for what I was, it's true. He rejected me one more time and it hurt. But it was a time to consider Jimmy. I wanted him to know that I didn't begrudge him his happiness, even if I wasn't a part of it. He had to know that I loved him, will always love him, and had a place in my life for him if he ever wanted to return to it." Mary Jo sent a bottle of champagne and a note of congratulations to the newlyweds' hotel suite.

❋　❋　❋

At the end of May an in-depth article was carried in the Dallas *Morning News* about Ann's and Mary Jo's life several months after the trial. The piece was an innocent bit of fluff primarily testifying to the fact that the world hadn't swallowed the two lesbians alive. There was one paragraph that suggested, in Mary Jo's best public relations manner, that she had not encountered any problems returning to work. The impression left by the quote was that the hospital staff supported Mary Jo, not her life style necessarily, but her as a professional.

Several nurses at the hospital went wild. THEY didn't support Mary Jo. THEY thought it was awful. THEY know God was against homosexuality. Unlike the week she returned to work, this new "affront" to the collective morality of the hospital did not go unnoticed. This time the administration got in on the act. After two lengthy discussions Mary Jo tendered her resignation. She had been waiting for Ann to get the painting business underway, but this degrading flare-up moved her timetable ahead.

Mary Jo walked away from Gaston Hospital, free in all respects.

Being broke, sometimes only a point of view away from bank-ruptcy, was not pleasant, yet Mary Jo and Ann took it in stride. They cashed in insurance policies, collected profit-sharing money from their former jobs, made liberal use of a packet of credit cards, and borrowed. They scaled down expenses where possible and paid the creditors with the most insistent threats when possi-ble. Managing with drastically reduced incomes, persevering under thousands of dollars of debts, working side by side to build a neophyte house-painting and decorating business and leaning heavily on one another for love and support were the new order at the Foreman-Risher home.

There was reason for optimism, hard, tangible facts to savor and anticipate. Richard was coming for a three-week summer-time visit; the appeal was being prepared for the winter; a col-lege, Georgia State, in Atlanta, had invited them to speak before a general convocation and for a substantial fee. This was the be-ginning of public appearances not directly linked to the feminist or gay world. There were reasons to live for tomorrow, where before there had only been faith.

* * *

When Mary Jo and Ann were seated near the lectern at Geor-gia State University, in Atlanta, they experienced a strange surge of gastric juices. The hall was packed with indifferent faces. Most of these people were only mildly aware of the case and cer-tainly couldn't be classified as supporters.

This was Mary Jo's and Ann's first opportunity to address a nongay and nonfeminist audience. Both women knew that if so-ciety were going to change its myopic view of homosexuals and the courts were going to accord gays full constitutional rights, millions of people, just like those in the audience, would have to be persuaded. Mary Jo and Ann had prepared extensively for this moment. Their speeches were carefully worded to illustrate the implications the case had on the civil liberties of all citizens, not just gay parents.

Mary Jo saw clearly the link between the denial of her constitutional guarantees and the ever-present danger of the erosion of liberty for all elements of society. She felt that the Bill of Rights had to include everyone, both the despised and favored, or it was worthless. Now the task was to rekindle this tenet in her audience.

Mary Jo and Ann whispered about modifying their speeches, possibly to tone them down. Their public conference was abruptly interrupted when Ann was introduced. She began:

"It's great to be back in Atlanta. This is our second visit this year and it's becoming our home away from home. We have met many wonderful people here." No one smiled.

"Often when you hear speeches by gay activists they say: 'There's no need to tell you about famous homosexuals; everybody knows there have been many famous people who were gay.' After talking to dozens of groups in several states, I'm not sure that's true. The public is not aware of how diverse and large the gay population has been throughout history. For example, here are just a few gay people that were prominent: Sappho, the ancient poet, Emily Dickinson, Gertrude Stein, Virginia Woolf, Socrates, Aristotle, Alexander the Great, he was quite a general. Alexander conquered the known world in his time. In America, gays are kicked out of the military. Some other famous homosexuals were: Richard the Lion-Hearted of England, Leonardo da Vinci, John Milton, Lord Byron, Hans Christian Andersen, Walt Whitman, Tchaikovsky, André Gide, Oscar Wilde, Marcel Proust, Lawrence of Arabia, W. H. Auden, Tennessee Williams and Dag Hammarskjöld, for many years head of the United Nations. My list is brief, only to illustrate a point.

"When someone talks about these men and women, they don't begin by saying, 'Oh, he's only a queer.' Of course not. These famous people are never categorized because of sexual preference. They are remembered for what they did; who they were as people; what contributions they made to the world. These gays were extremely famous, and in some cases powerful.

"Why should sexual preference, alone, characterize our life? When I ask you about your native son, Jimmy Carter, do you begin by saying he's a heterosexual? Of course not. Do you ever talk about anyone by saying, 'You know, of course, that he's a heterosexual?'

"Gay people demand the right to be judged by what they accomplish; the contributions they make; who they are. We are tired of second- or third-class citizenship because of words. Brand me a homosexual and I am automatically a second-class person in this society. Are you afraid to judge me for what I stand for, as a person?

"Gay people must be defined by their total humanity, rather than solely by their sexual preference. A gay person turns to a person of the same sex for emotional and usually sexual gratification. A person is not gay because he or she occasionally indulges in homosexual activity; for example, curious adults or prison inmates. A gay adult is a person whose responses are almost exclusively directed toward their own sex.

"About the custody case: The first level is the Civil Court of Appeal in Dallas. Written and oral arguments will be heard this fall [1976]. The next step would be the state supreme court and then the federal courts.

"The issues of the appeal range from simple technical errors to major constitutional questions. I am not an attorney, but I will outline the appeal for you. First: The evidence in the case did not show that Mary Jo was an unfit mother. There was no evidence that Richard would be harmed in any way if he lived with us. In fact, there was overwhelming evidence by professionals and lay people that he would benefit and thrive from living in our home. Secondly: The bias of the jury against gay people prevented them from rendering a fair verdict. The jury foreman said they couldn't ignore the fact that we were homosexuals.

"Richard was not allowed on the stand. He couldn't even talk about how much he loved his mother, how he loved me, how he loved my daughter, how he wanted to live with us. By preventing Richard from testifying, the best interests of the child were ignored. It didn't matter what he wanted. It was what the State of Texas wanted. What the law wanted, not that little boy.

"The constitutional issues are complex, but most important. Sexual preference is never discussed as evidence except when it means anything but a man on top of a woman. I don't mean to be crude, but until less than a half century ago, any other sexual position was prohibited by law in many states. We thought the courts got out of the bedroom years ago. They did get out of yours. They are still snooping in mine. They must be fascinated." The audience laughed. Ann took deep breaths, turned to smile at Mary Jo, and continued.

"Mary Jo's sexual preference, in the privacy of her bedroom, was allowed to be the only issue in a court of law. Under the Fourteenth Amendment to the Constitution she was denied equal protection with you.

"There has been a long, disgraceful history of discrimination against gays. The court's decision in taking away Mary Jo's son has punished her life style, stopped her from living as she chooses. This denied her due process. Since it was not proven, in any way, that she was an unfit mother, her homosexuality per se was the deciding factor. This condemns gays, as a class, and violates their due process.

"Another constitutional issue is the right to privacy. You have it; we don't. While the state and the court have a right to question parental activities which might adversely affect a child, when there is no conduct that is harmful, the court has no right to question sexual orientation.

"The Supreme Court has found that private relationships are equal or perhaps greater than all the other amendments to the Constitution. The basis for privacy is in the First, Fourth, Fifth, Ninth, and Fourteenth Amendments.

"Mary Jo lost her First Amendment rights in the court. Her gay life style was the key to the decision; thus she was denied freedom of association.

"When gay people form a household, live as a family, they are in effect publicly advocating acceptance of an alternate life style and that advocacy deserves constitutional protection.

"Another First Amendment violation has to do with the so-called Establishment clause of the First Amendment, where no laws are allowed concerning religion. Most laws against homosexuality, among consenting adults, grew out of Jewish-Christian beliefs and teachings. Religion is free to teach what it wants. It is not free to have religious beliefs written into law. Sin is sin, if you believe that way. But sin is not crime in all cases. Not under our constitution.

"Another area of the appeal is the Texas law about custody. It's called the Family Code. The law is vague about what makes up a proper home. It talks about raising children in a religious home. Throughout the trial we were asked about being good Christians. Mary Jo and I are both religious, but I learned back in high-school civics that the state was forbidden from making laws concerning religion.

"The State of Texas says: You must raise your children in a religious home or you can lose your children. Is that constitutional?

"Those are the basic legal issues. The outcome of this case is very important. It involves gay rights, women's rights, but in a larger sense it involves everyone. The right of privacy, the right to associate with whom you choose, the right to be yourself, the right to raise children as you wish, the right to equal protection under the law and the right to due process. In short, the rights of a minority, a gay minority, the forgotten minority."

Ann gathered up her notes and waited. The audience started to clap, then there was a loud rumble of applause and shouts. Twenty or thirty people stood up. She had struck a responsive chord. She beamed, nodded her appreciation, and walked to her chair.

Mary Jo stood at the lectern and allowed the clapping to subside. "A writer in Dallas said I was a reluctant symbol. I don't know about the symbol part, but I know I am reluctant. I didn't imagine the nationwide publicity caused by the trial where I lost custody of my son. I didn't welcome the entire country learning of my sexual preference. I have never been overjoyed that my personal finances have been ruined by the tens of thousands of dollars needed to keep up the fight. I will never get used to the glare of publicity that has eliminated all my privacy and the privacy of my partner, Ann Foreman, and her little girl, Judie Ann.

"Yes, I am a lesbian. I live with, love, and make love to another woman. I am not proud of my sexuality, any more than you are proud of yours. Sexuality is the most natural thing in the human experience, one of our most lasting and important endowments. I don't take pride in being part of a natural process. Nor am I ashamed. I have self-worth. I know who and what I am. I am a whole, complete and unique person. I feel, think, share, suffer, learn and love, the exact same way you do. The one thing that makes me a minority, that puts me in a special category, is what I do in my bedroom with another human being that I love and share my total existence with. For this private moment, a few minutes of my life, I am labeled, denied equal treatment, punished by law and even put in jail. Yes, in most states I can be sent to jail for being a natural creature of God and exercising God's great gift of human sexuality."

Mary Jo reviewed how the case developed and the conduct of the trial. She sifted the evidence and why the jury made its decision against her.

"I can't blame that jury for accepting the narrow-minded, hysterical approach used by my ex-husband's attorney. That jury was a product of our society. The myths surrounding homosexuality are deeply ingrained in our minds; even homosexuals are stung by all the misinformation and stupidity.

"The most prevalent myth is that all homosexuals are sick, mentally ill. In 1975 the American Psychiatric Association dropped homosexuality from its list of illnesses. The American Psychological Association supported that position.

"Furthermore, they said that being gay does not imply any impairment in judgment and stability. These two large and prestigious associations called for mental health professionals to take the lead in removing the stigma of mental illness associated with homosexuality. These groups deplored all public and private discrimination against homosexuals. They passed a resolution supporting the rights of homosexual parents to have custody of their children, if they were otherwise good parents.

"A second, unfortunate, myth is the idea that homosexuals are deviates and mainly concerned with sex. There is where the mass media has done a great disservice to the truth. Most public information about homosexuals comes from newspapers or TV accounts about people who have violated the law or in some other way have been brought to the public's attention. An example would be a child molester. Incidentally, any law enforcement agency will tell you that child molesting is primarily a crime committed by heterosexuals. In any event, such events make sensational, cheap copy that fuels the myth.

"Another problem has been that most research on homosexuals has used as subjects persons who are in mental institutions or in therapy. Just think what would have happened to the black civil rights movement if our opinions were based upon knowledge obtained from black mental patients.

"Just like every other social, economic, and racial group, we have gays that are emotionally ill. Actually the percentage of mentally ill gay people is slightly less than mentally ill heterosexuals. That is amazing, by itself. What society has done to us, as a group, would be enough to put anyone in a mental ward.

"Because of these labels of mental illness and a hostile public attitude, based upon poor information, people who are happy, talented, productive and gay are still unwilling to admit their homosexuality. You have friends, dear friends that you respect and care about that are gay, and you don't know it. There is some public figure that you vote for and trust that is gay and you don't know about it. We are everywhere, at all levels of society. And I think that if the public truly understood this, attitudes would change.

"Fears and myths about gay people are the main reasons that jury took my son away. They were afraid that the children would become homosexuals if they grew up in a home where homosexuals reside. It didn't occur to them that nearly every homosexual alive came from heterosexual parents.

"No one knows the exact reason why people are gay. As a matter of fact, science can't tell us why people are heterosexual. There has been little research on healthy, functioning homosexuals; there has been even less research on gay parents.

"Two psychologists and a psychiatrist said my son was normal, age appropriate and had a firm male sex identity; and he loved me dearly.

"The court-appointed psychologist, who recommended that my ex-husband get custody, based his opinion on what he called my poor judgment. Do you know what bad judgment I exercised? First, I permitted Richard to wear a jean suit that belonged to Ann's daughter, Judie Ann. Never mind that children share unisex clothes. Never mind that the doctor complimented Richard on the outfit, never mind that the damn zipper was in front. I should have known better because I was a lesbian and should be extra careful about such things. That's what he said in court. The second example of bad judgment that I was guilty of and for which this doctor would take away my son, involved a T-shirt. Richard had a YWCA T-shirt. Never mind that Richard took gymnastics at the YWCA along with hundreds of other boys. Never mind that we all wear T-shirts with various slogans on them. Never mind that Richard was proud of his T-shirt and loved to attend gym at the YWCA. Never mind that Richard's sexual identity is secure. Never mind all that. That T-shirt showed my bad judgment. I ask: Whose judgment is poor?"

The audience laughed and applauded. Mary Jo left her text and ad-libbed the following: "You know, while we're on the trial, there were some other things that bothered me as a mother and a woman. The jury foreman, who by the way voted for me, had some startling things to say about the jury deliberations. He said, in public, that the two women on the jury and several of the men were worried that there wasn't a man, a male role model, in the home. That scared me, when I thought about it. What about all the millions of divorced parents—men and women—should they lose custody of their children because of some impractical theory? If they worried about sex role models, what about friends, relatives, teachers and TV? What about single parents and single people who want to adopt children. Can we afford to let that attitude go unchallenged?"

Someone in the hall shouted, "No." There was general applause. Mary Jo returned to her prepared remarks.

"During the trial, they asked Ann and me if we would give up our homosexuality. They didn't know who we were. It's important for children that parents have their own identities, an acceptance of themselves. Modern psychology says it is important that the strongest bonds be between the two adults, so that they can get their needs met. Then, they will have something to offer and give a child.

"There were strong undertones in the trial that suggested two women were not capable of giving children all they needed to thrive as individuals and live normal, productive lives. That is bias against women.

"We heard throughout the trial about the best interest of the child. It was all for his best interest, as if I had not always had that foremost in my mind. It seemed to me that continuing Richard's relationships in his well-known surroundings and environment was essential for his normal development. I had been the parent to whom Richard looked to meet his daily physical needs; the person he looked to for care; the person who protected him, who loved him on a day-to-day basis. I did that for all of his nine years.

"Taking him away from the person he always looked to as a primary parent will harm his development. He will be less able to cope with problems because he has lost the main person he turned to for help and emotional support. Richard, from his child's point of view, will see this as a major desertion and he will have emotional scars that will make it difficult for him to trust others.

"The jury said, take him away; it's for his own best interest. But Richard's good feelings about himself and his own identity have been formed on the love and care he has received from me over the years. Saying that his mother is bad will be saying there is something wrong with him and it will make him feel bad about himself.

"I want to close my talk by sharing with you the toughest question I have to face. It's not the money. I have faith that hard work and the support I've been getting will allow us to go on.

It's not the question of whether we will eventually win, maybe years from now. The toughest question I face is asked every two weeks when Richard comes home for a two-day visitation. The first thing he says is, 'Mommy, when can I come home?' "

EPILOGUE

More than a year after a Dallas Domestic Relations Court jury transferred custody of her son, Richard, to his father, Mary Jo Risher suffered another setback in her struggle to keep her boy. The Fifth Civil Court of Appeals in Dallas, on a legal technicality, dismissed the appeal for "want of jurisdiction."

The next step in the appeals process is the Texas Supreme Court. If the State Supreme Court issues a negative decision and refuses to order the Civil Court of Appeals to consider the merits of the case, Ms. Risher's attorneys plan to take the case directly to the federal courts system.

The National Organization for Women (NOW) continues its

support of Mary Jo in the form of providing an *amicus curiae* brief for the appeal. NOW has obtained the services of noted constitutional attorney Neil Cogan of Southern Methodist University Law School.

Already the lengthy and complex appeals process has taken more time and cost more money than the original custody suit, but Mary Jo Risher and her partner, Ann Foreman, are undaunted. "Whatever the costs and however long it takes, we will continue," Mary Jo said. "I promised my son I would never stop, never give up until I had exhausted every avenue to get him back. I owe it to Richard, to our love for each other."